D1400476

Colonial America
A History in Documents

Colonial America
A History in Documents

Edward G. Gray

OXFORD
UNIVERSITY PRESS

For Sophie

UNIVERSITY PRESS

Oxford New York

Auckland   Bangkok   Buenos Aires   Cape Town   Chennai
Dar es Salaam   Delhi   Hong Kong   Istanbul   Karachi   Kolkata
Kuala Lumpur   Madrid   Melbourne   Mexico City   Mumbai Nairobi
São Paulo   Shanghai   Singapore   Taipei   Tokyo   Toronto

Copyright © 2003 by Edward G. Gray

Design: Sandy Kaufman
Layout: Loraine Machlin
Picture Research: Lisa Barnett

Published by Oxford University Press, Inc.
198 Madison Avenue, New York, New York 10016
www.oup.com

Library of Congress Cataloging-in-Publication Data
Gray, Edward G.
Colonial America : a history in documents / Edward G. Gray.
p. cm. — (Pages from history)
Includes bibliographical references and index.
ISBN 0-19-513747-7 (alk. paper)
1. United States—History—Colonial period, ca.
1600–1775—Sources—Juvenile literature. [1. United States—History—
Colonial period, ca. 1600-1775–Sources.] I. Title. II. Series.
E187 .G73 2002
973.2—dc21
2002004285

Printed in the United States of America on acid-free paper

General Editors

Sarah Deutsch
Associate Professor of History
University of Arizona

Carol K. Karlsen
Professor of History
University of Michigan

Robert G. Moeller
Professor of History
University of California, Irvine

Jeffrey N. Wasserstrom
Associate Professor of History
Indiana University

Board of Advisors

Steven Goldberg
Social Studies Supervisor
New Rochelle, N.Y., Public Schools

John Pyne
Social Studies Supervisor
West Milford, N.J., Public Schools

Cover: *The active harbor of Charleston, South
Carolina, in 1740.*

Frontispiece: *This scene of a New England
wedding was embroidered in 1756.*

Title page: *A colonial family painted in 1750.*

Contents

What Is a Document?

To the historian, a document is, quite simply, any sort of historical evidence. It is a primary source, the raw material of history. A document may be more than the expected government paperwork, such as a treaty or passport. It is also a letter, diary, will, grocery list, newspaper article, recipe, memoir, oral history, school yearbook, map, chart, architectural plan, poster, musical score, play script, novel, political cartoon, painting, photograph—even an object.

Using primary sources allows us not just to read *about* history, but to read history itself. It allows us to immerse ourselves in the look and feel of an era gone by, to understand its people and their language, whether verbal or visual. And it allows us to take an active, hands-on role in (re)constructing history.

Using primary sources requires us to use our powers of detection to ferret out the relevant facts and to draw conclusions from them; just as Agatha Christie uses the scores in a bridge game to determine the identity of a murderer, the historian uses facts from a variety of sources—some, perhaps, seemingly inconsequential—to build a historical case.

The poet W. H. Auden wrote that history was the study of questions. Primary sources force us to ask questions—and then, by answering them, to construct a narrative or an argument that makes sense to us. Moreover, as we draw on the many sources from "the dust-bin of history," we can endow that narrative with character, personality, and texture—all the elements that make history so endlessly intriguing.

Cartoon
This political cartoon addresses the issue of church and state. It illustrates the Supreme Court's role in balancing the demands of the First Amendment of the Constitution and the desires of the religious population.

Illustration
Illustrations from children's books, such as this alphabet from the New England Primer, tell us how children were educated, and also what the religious and moral values of the time were.

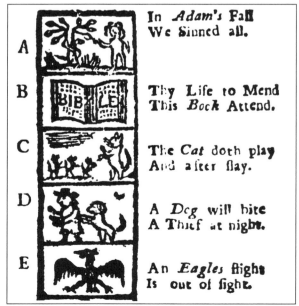

A — In *Adam's* Fall
We Sinned all.

B — Thy Life to Mend
This *Book* Attend.

C — The *Cat* doth play
And after flay.

D — A *Dog* will bite
A Thief at night.

E — An *Eagles* flight
Is out of fight.

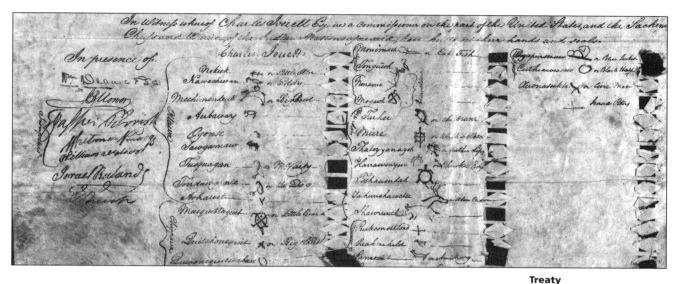

Treaty

A government document such as this 1805 treaty can reveal not only the details of government policy, but information about the people who signed it. Here, the Indians' names were written in English transliteration by U.S. officials; the Indians added pictographs to the right of their names.

Map

A 1788 British map of India shows the region prior to British colonization, an indication of the kingdoms and provinces whose ethnic divisions would resurface later in India's history.

Literature

The first written version of the Old English epic Beowulf, from the late 10th century, is physical evidence of the transition from oral to written history. Charred by fire, it is also a physical record of the wear and tear of history.

How to Read a Document

There are many ways to approach the history of colonial America. One might simply read some of the many books about the period written in our own times. One might also go directly to the sources themselves and read what historians read: primary source material, or documents written by people who lived during that peculiar period in our history. Primary sources give the reader an opportunity to become his or her own historian, to engage with some of the very same documents that professional historians use when piecing together the stories of the early American past.

Such documents might include handwritten letters or diary entries, or printed material such as sermons, political pamphlets, almanacs, government documents, or newspapers. These are fairly conventional sources. It is not difficult, for instance, to extract information from the page excerpted here from the May 3, 1733, edition of Benjamin Franklin's *Pennsylvania Gazette.*

Other kinds of documents are, at first glance, somewhat less revealing. Perhaps the most important of these are material artifacts: furniture, Indian ceremonial objects, weapons, clothing, tools, houses, and other things acquired by the peoples of colonial America. Careful study of such things, however, can reveal much about how the peoples of early America organized their households, how they treated personal property, and how possessions defined families, as they were passed from one generation to the next. Combined with more familiar sorts of written or printed documents, such artifacts allow us to assemble a more complete and vivid picture of life in colonial America.

Source
By the middle of the 18th century, every colonial city had at least one regularly printed newspaper. Next to word of mouth, these cheap periodicals became the primary source of news and information for colonists. Perhaps the most influential colonial newspaper—the source of this advertisement—was Benjamin Franklin's *Pennsylvania Gazette,* first printed in December 1728. It set the standard for colonial newspapers with its combination of political and social commentary, news, advertising, and amusing anecdote.

Fine Print
As the central source of information in the colonies, newspapers came to serve a crucial role in the business affairs of colonists. In a series of finely printed columns, the newspapers ran announcements and advertisements such as these. The first advertisement annoucemences an exchange of paper currency and the second offers a slave woman and her two children for sale. A newspaper's fine print provides significant information about the colonial economy—including the types of "goods" for sale, the price of goods, methods of payment, and details about the "goods" themselves.

Material Culture
Historians often use the phrase "material culture" when referring to the things of everyday life. Objects such as this chest reveal what the colonists purchased, what they made, what they traded, what they sold, and what they used to help them live and work. These material goods also provide information about colonial manufacturing and craftsmanship.

Status
Much as in our own day, things in colonial America had the power to confer status on their owners. They, as much as education or ways of personal conduct, distinguished prominent colonists from ordinary ones. Something so simple as this small chest made in 1679 for Thomas Hart of Lynnfield, Massachusetts, would have been affordable only for well-to-do New Englanders.

Style
The fine carving that gives Hart's chest its distinct style also distinguishes it as an object of particular value. Hart's initials and the date the chest was made are carved in the decorative center star. Only a person of means could afford to pay for such stylish embellishments as these that transformed an ordinary chest into a desirable work of craftsmanship.

THESE are to desire all Persons, who are possess'd of any of the said Bills, to bring them to the General Loan-Office, where they may have them exchanged for New Ones.

N.B. The Currency of the said Bills being expired, they will not be received in Payment; but all Persons bringing them to the said Office, may have them exchanged as above.

THERE is to be sold a very likely Negro Woman aged about Thirty Years who has lived in this City, from her Childhood, and can wash and iron very well, cook Victuals, sew, spin on the Linen Wheel, milk Cows, and do all Sorts of House-work very well. She has a Boy of about Two Years old, which is to go with her. The Price as reasonable as you can agree.

And also another very likely Boy aged about Six Years, who is Son of the abovesaid Woman. He will be sold with his Mother, or by himself, as the Buyer pleases. Enquire of the Printer.

To be Sold,

A VERY good Plantation, containing about 300 Acres, late Nathanael Walton's, deceas'd, together with a good large Brick House, a large Barn, with

Introduction

"No event has been so interesting to mankind in general, and to the inhabitants of Europe in particular, as the discovery of the New World."

—Abbé Raynal, *A Philosophical and Political History of the Settlements and Trade of the Europeans in the East and West Indies, 1777*

The prominent placement of three English monarchs— Elizabeth I, James I, and Charles I—at the top of this frontispiece to Captain John Smith's history of England's early colonial ventures might give the impression that they were closely involved with the goings-on in their new American colonies. In fact, they had little real involvement. Only after the Powhatan rebellion of 1622, when the death and mayhem in Virginia became uncontrollable, did Charles I intervene.

The colonial era of U.S. history is a paradoxical era. It is part of the history of the United States, and yet it precedes the existence of the United States. It is the longest period of U.S. history, spanning nearly two centuries, and arguably much less well understood than the antebellum period, the Gilded Age, the Great Depression, and all the other periods that it preceded. It is an era with many qualities we associate with our own times, such as large movements of peoples, ethnic diversity, contentious politics, international economic relations, religious pluralism, and social conflict.

And yet, it is also perhaps the most distant and foreign period of U.S. history. It was an era when ordinary people believed things many of us would find astonishing—they believed in magic and evil spirits; they explained the seasons and the weather in terms of astrological signs; they blamed themselves for random events like hurricanes, solar eclipses, fires, and crop failure; and perhaps most curious of all, they had very little sense of their own place in history.

Unlike virtually every generation of Americans after them, members of the several colonial generations did not think they were remaking their world or living through the dawn of some kind of new era. Instead, they generally believed that little had changed and little would change in their lifetimes. Even those many English men and women who came to America because they had grown weary of the corrupt ways of the Old World did not envision in America a wholly new, modern world. Rather, they envisioned a colonial world that restored the morality and order of times past; that is, they envisioned a return to an earlier, better age. To the extent that these people believed the world did change, they generally believed it would do so because of forces that were beyond the comprehension and control of ordinary people—forces that, at the very least, were initiated by a select number of powerful men, and, at the very most, were unleashed by God Himself.

What could be further from our way of viewing the world today? For us, the world is a place of constant and dramatic change, a place where each day yields wholly new phenomena and inventions. We are constantly being told about "revolutions" in our midst—revolutions in medicine, in information technology, in transportation, in finance, in the organization of the family and the workplace. All of these revolutions, we have come to believe, will change our world in ways we can only begin to grasp.

Revolutionary change is thus a way of life for us. For colonial Americans, nothing could have been further from the case. Indeed, even the word "revolution" had different connotations for most of the colonial era from those familiar to us. Far from signifying sudden, irreversible historical change, revolution meant something akin to the movements of the planets. They revolve around each other; a full revolution involves a return to an original position. To speak of a "revolution" in 17th- or early 18th-century America was thus to speak of a return—a return to earlier conditions. It was not to speak of an irrevocable break with the past.

Although most colonial Americans had little sense that they were part of a revolutionary age, the reality was very, very different. Ordinary people in the colonial era did initiate change—vast and far-reaching change. And whether they knew it or not, they participated in the creation of a new kind of society. Indeed, one would be hard pressed to identify a period of U.S. history in which change was as dramatic and singular as that which overtook the peoples of colonial America.

In this book, we will explore some of these changes and consider some of the ways they reshaped life in colonial America. But before doing that, we should consider exactly what is meant by "colonial America."

What Is "Colonial America"?

The phrase "colonial America" is, in some sense, misleading. It suggests the existence of a single geopolitical entity in the New World, perhaps having a single, unified history. In fact, no such entity ever existed. For most of the 16th, 17th, and 18th centuries America was a battleground for European nations competing for control of lands and precious materials. Spain, Portugal, Holland, France, Russia, and England all found themselves engaging in this battle, and all claimed territories in the New World. The complexity of this imperial contest was particularly evident in North America—perhaps more so than anywhere else in the Americas except the Caribbean. Colonial America was thus in some sense

"There are no colonies of which the progress has been more rapid than that of the English in North America."
—Scottish economist Adam Smith in *The Wealth of Nations* (1776)

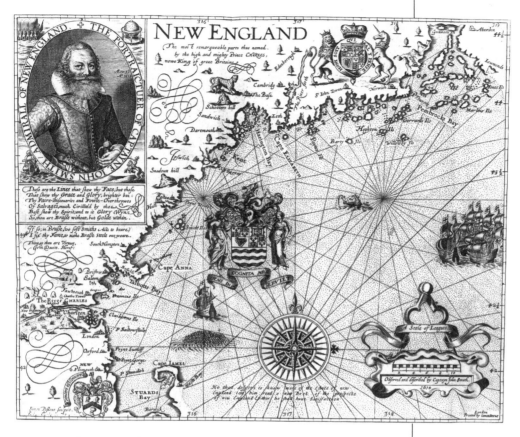

In 1605, two groups of English merchants—one from London, the other from the port cities of Bristol, Exeter, and Plymouth—petitioned King James I for permission to establish two colonies in North America. The petition was accepted and in 1606 the London and Plymouth Companies came into being. The former was granted exclusive control over Virginia and the latter exclusive control over New England. This 1614 map charts the early settlement of New England.

not a single geographic or political entity, but a variety of entities created by a series of European powers, all seeking to exploit the resources of the New World.

For the purposes of this volume, though, colonial America refers to only some of those entities—colonies established and maintained by England and a greater Britain on mainland North America before the end of the Seven Years War in 1763. Those colonies, which eventually numbered 13 in all and which historians have come to call "British North America," constituted a part of Britain's overseas empire, and in the view of some scholars a rather unimportant part at that. Relative to Britain's other possessions, particularly the island colonies of the Caribbean, the mainland colonies produced only modest wealth and elicited equally modest attention from the government. But, it was in part their relative insignificance that allowed the mainland colonies to develop in unique ways—ways that made them fertile ground for the sorts of ideas and social tensions that gave rise to what at the time of its creation was a most curious and novel entity: the United States.

"A colony is to the mother-country as a member [limb] to the body, deriving its action and its strength from the general principle of vitality; receiving from the body, and communicating to it, all the benefits and evils of health and disease; liable in dangerous maladies to sharp [medical] applications, of which the body however must partake the pain; and exposed, if incurably tainted, to amputation, by which the body likewise will be mutilated."

—English lexicographer Samuel Johnson in "Tyrrany no Tyrrany; An Answer to the Resolutions and Address of the American Congress" (1775)

Why Study Colonial America?

There are many reasons to study colonial America. Perhaps the most obvious is simply that it tells us much about the origins of the United States. It tells us about what sorts of people inhabited North America, what these people did, what they believed, and how they organized their families, their businesses, their governments, and their churches. And it allows us to see how these people's actions may have influenced subsequent developments, particularly the earthshaking revolution that swept British North America in the 1770s and 1780s.

Although there can be little doubt that Britain's American colonies gave rise to the United States, the fact remains that before the 1770s, virtually no colonist envisioned such an independent nation. How could they? Almost everything they did bound them to England (and later Great Britain) and a larger Atlantic world. Nearly all their commerce was made possible by Britain's control of Atlantic trade routes; their politics were to varying degrees shaped by British government appointees and ideas originating in tumultuous British provincial politics; their religious life was disproportionately shaped by ministers sent from Britain or trained in British theology.

Much of the labor that made the colonies economically viable came directly from Britain or was supplied by British slave traders. And those colonists who could afford to do so worked almost without end to disassociate themselves from the cultural and social backwater in which they lived. Their ultimate aim was to become like their countrymen who circulated in cosmopolitan England: learned, sociable beings with friends in the highest places.

One of the great riddles of early U.S. history is this state of affairs: British North America was oriented in almost every way toward Great Britain, the mother country. And yet it broke away from Great Britain and became a wholly new kind of nation, a nation that came to bear little resemblance to its colonial predecessor, let alone to Great Britain itself. How was this

The extent to which colonists identified with Great Britain is illustrated by the British flags on a trade card used by the colonial merchant Joseph Webb to advertise his wares.

possible? To answer this question, we must begin by looking at colonial America.

This sort of riddle suggests another justification for studying colonial America. Doing so provides an opportunity for learning about people who lived in a world very different from our own. That world, as one historian has memorably described it, is "The World We Have Lost." It is a world where ordinary people believed things and did things that are almost inconceivable in our own day. And like anthropologists who uncover alien and foreign cultures, so students of colonial America must struggle to reconstruct thoughts, attitudes, and experiences sharply different from their own. It is a kind of struggle generally not required of students exploring other periods of U.S. history. But it is, nonetheless, an essential and rewarding struggle for anyone seeking a full understanding of the history of this country.

"Europe set its glory, its power, and its salvation in far-off, precarious, and useless possessions, purchased at great expense, exploited at great expense, maintained at great expense."

—Pierre Joseph André Roubaud, in *Histoire ge'ne'rale de l'Asie, de l'Afrique et du l'Amerique* (General history of Asia, Africa, and America, 1770–1775)

Chapter One

England Expands

England's interest in the New World arose in fits and starts through the course of the 16th and early 17th centuries. As a relatively poor and weak nation, a nation divided by political faction and the great Reformation struggle between Protestants and Catholics, the small island nation had neither the will nor the resources to entertain ambitious plans to colonize the Americas. But by the last quarter of the 16th century, global politics, and particularly religious tensions throughout Europe, compelled the English monarch, Queen Elizabeth I, to consider establishing colonial settlements in America.

What is striking is not so much that England eventually had designs on America, but rather that although it took nearly a century for those designs to be realized, they nonetheless rested on a profound ignorance of the New World. Perhaps the most acute expression of this was the fact that English promoters of colonization entertained often-sincere hopes that all the Americas were like Mexico and Peru— regions in which the Spaniards had found large, valuable reserves of gold and silver. Nothing could have been further from the truth. As we will see, the first English colonists, expecting to find such precious materials near coastal Virginia, were sorely disappointed.

None of this is meant to suggest that the English were stupid or naïve. Knowledge moved slowly in the 16th century. Books and atlases were scarce; literacy was common but far from universal in England, and much navigational and geographic knowledge was enshrouded in obscure ancient texts written in Latin or Greek. The great explorer Christopher Columbus himself depended on the works of Claudius Ptolemy, the second-century astronomer and geographer from Alexandria, and other ancient geographers, few of whom had ever ventured beyond the rim of the Mediterranean Sea.

As this Belgian map suggests, less than one hundred years after Columbus landed in the New World, little of America's Atlantic Coast remained unexplored.

"[The true seamen will take] charge of the Ship upon them, . . . hoyst forth of the quiet port into the ruffe and boisterous Ocean, where they shall behold many hideous mountains of high threatening billowes, and raging waves, tempestuous gusts, with hayle, raine, and thunder, Shifts of winds, and counter Seas, . . . being deprived of Sun, Moone and Starres for long season, . . . I doe not allow any to be a good Sea-man that hath not . . . in his youth bin bouth taught and inured to all labours; for to keepe a warme Cabbin and lye in sheets is the most ignoble part of a Sea-man; but to endure and suffer, as a hard Cabbin, cold and salt Meate, broken sleepes, mould[y] bread, dead beere, wet Cloathes, want of fire, all these are within board."

—Luke Foxe, in *The Voyages of Captain Luke Foxe of Hull* (1635)

Exploratory expeditions were the best source of accurate geographical information, but they were costly and extremely hazardous. So difficult were such journeys, especially when this involved crossing the Atlantic, it is a wonder they ever succeeded at all. Sailors on the open oceans could expect their months aboard the "wooden world" of the sailing ship to be downright wretched. Ships were crowded, wet, and cold places; food was always scarce, and what food there was was often spoiled. Fresh water was even scarcer. Indeed, it constituted a virtual liquid gold in the vast desert that was the Atlantic Ocean. Shipboard diseases such as scurvy, caused by a vitamin C deficiency, were commonplace, and visits to foreign ports often exposed crews to yellow fever, malaria, typhus, dysentery, and other diseases.

As if these perils did not make long-range voyages miserable enough, seamen faced the constant threat of storms—storms that at best tossed wooden sailing vessels around like toy boats, and at worst, smashed them to splinters. Beyond this, navigation, especially in unfamiliar waters, was still partly a guessing game. To take just one example: 16th-century navigational charts (maps of the seas mariners use to keep themselves in safe waters) were crude even for European coastal areas, and for the Americas, they hardly existed at all. And then there were the pirates to consider. By the end of the 16th century, piracy had become an ordinary part of life in the Atlantic. Cruising coastal waters of Europe, Africa, and the Americas, these seaborne criminals harassed, intimidated, robbed, and often killed sailors.

So, although English interest in America had been germinating for more than three-quarters of a century before any Englishmen actually settled there, the information that inspired that interest was minimal. Beyond this, much of that information came from men who had an interest in encouraging England to explore and colonize America—men who were the 16th-century equivalent of our modern-day real-estate promoters. These individuals saw in the New World the potential for immense profits, and believed that if they could convince both the monarch and ambitious Englishmen that the Americas were worth settling, they could realize those profits. They were, in a sense, propagandists for colonization, with little incentive to depict the New World accurately.

When trying to understand England's earliest interest in America, we are thus left to study ill-informed and often deliberately misleading documents. Nevertheless, these documents are worth examining in some detail. When read carefully, they reveal

some of the different reasons for English interest in the New World. But they also explain some of the mistakes made by early colonists—mistakes that often had catastrophic results. England's earliest American colonial ventures were immensely costly in both money and lives. And those costs owed much to the scarcity of valid information about what English men and women would find when they came to America. To be fair, however, they also owed something to the rising ambitions and expectations of an English nation, a nation that by 1600 had experienced a revolution in its self-image. Englishmen were beginning to see themselves as a people with a special kind of character, a kind of character that would allow them to rule the seas and build a vast intercontinental empire.

England and Europe Look West

Fifteenth-century Italy was a breeding ground for ambitious, adventuresome, and learned navigators, of whom Columbus is only the most famous—or perhaps just the luckiest.

"If we consider the many millions [in gold and silver] which are dayly brought out of Peru into Spaine, . . . we finde that by the abundant treasure of that countrey the Spanish king vexeth all the princes of Europe, and is become, in a few yeeres, from a poore king of Castile, the greatest monarch of this part of the world, and likely every day to increase, if other princes forslow the good occasions offered, and suffer him to adde this empire to the rest, which by farre exceedeth all the rest: if his golde now indanger us, hee will then be unresistable."

—Sir Walter Raleigh on the Spanish conquest of Peru, from *The Discovery of Guiana* (1595)

The Venetian-born seafarer John Cabot traveled to Seville and Lisbon before finding in Bristol, England, support for his plans to sail west to Asia.

Another was a man by the name of Giovanni Caboto, better known as John Cabot. Like Columbus, Cabot believed that Asia could be reached by sailing west, across the Atlantic, and he set about trying to convince wealthy merchants and monarchs of this fact. In pursuit of his goal, Cabot made his way to the maritime city of Bristol, England, and there acquired the support of some local merchants, and eventually the English king, Henry VII. With this sponsorship, Cabot was able to undertake a series of exploratory ventures in the mid-1490s, one of which appears to have brought him to the coast of Nova Scotia or Cape Breton, in what is now Canada. Cabot thought he had discovered northern Asia, the homeland of Genghis Khan, but aside from enormous stocks of fish, his voyages yielded little, and in 1498, he died at sea, still believing that he had found a way to the rich trading centers of Asia. For the next decade, Cabot's sons continued to pursue their father's Asian dream, but with little real success.

Nevertheless, the king's initial interest in Cabot's theories are plain. He clearly knew that if Cabot was right, and if England could find an easy westerly way to Asia, the nation would prosper and rise to greatness in much the way Portugal, another small, obscure nation, was doing at the time. To this end, he issued Cabot a "patent," a legal agreement that granted Cabot and his associates a series of privileges, including control of any territories or nations they might discover. In return, the king expected, among other things, a sizable portion of any income generated by these exploits.

Be it known and made manifest that we have given and granted as by these presents we give and grant, for us and our heirs, to our well-beloved John Cabot, citizen of Venice, and to Lewis, Sebastian and Sancio, sons of the said John, and to the heirs and deputies of them, and of any one of them, full and free authority, faculty and power to sail to all parts, regions and coasts of the eastern, western and northern sea, under our banners, flags and ensigns, with five ships or vessels of whatsoever burden and quality they may be, and with so many and with such mariners and men as they may wish to take with them in the said ships, at their own proper costs and charges, to find, discover and investigate whatsoever islands, countries, regions or provinces of heathens and infidels, in whatsoever part of the world placed, which before this time were unknown to all Christians. We have also granted to them and to any of them, and to the heirs and deputies of them and any one of them, and have given licence to set up our afore-said banners and ensigns in any town, city, castle, island or main-land whatsoever, newly found by them. And that the beforemen-tioned John and his sons or their heirs and deputies may conquer, occupy and possess whatsoever such towns, castles, cities and islands by them thus discovered that they may be able to conquer, occupy and possess, as our vassals and governors lieutenants and deputies therein, acquiring for us the dominion, title and jurisdic-tion of the same towns, castles, cities, islands and mainlands so discovered: in such a way nevertheless that of all the fruits, prof-its, emoluments, commodities, gains and revenues accruing from this voyage, the said John and sons and their heirs and deputies shall be bounden and under obligation for every their voyage, as often as they shall arrive at our port of Bristol, at which they are bound and holden only to arrive, all necessary charges and expens-es incurred by them having been deducted, to pay us, either in goods or money, the fifth part of the whole capital gained, we giv-ing and granting to them and to their heirs and deputies, that they shall be free and exempt from all payment of customs on all and singular the goods and merchandise that they may bring back with them from those places thus newly discovered. . . .

In witness whereof, etc. Witness ourself at Westminster on the fifth day of March. By the King himself, etc.

Although the English Crown's interest in the New World faded in the immediate aftermath of the Cabot journeys, a constant flow of literature concerning the Americas inspired some of England's most learned authors and philosophers. One such figure was the lawyer, intellectual, and statesman Sir Thomas More. In 1516, he wrote his best-known work, _Utopia_, which describes the fictitious travels of Raphael Hythlodaye, who stumbles upon the Isle of Utopia on a voy-age to America. Utopia was a kind of ideal society, a society lacking in much of the selfishness, greed, and corruption More saw as threatening his own Christian world. In the pas-sage below, More describes the Utopians' beliefs about inter-national treaties, a subject that was particularly germane at the time. The year before he completed _Utopia,_ More had been appointed by King Henry VIII to negotiate a commercial treaty with the Dutch. Frustrations in this endeavor no doubt led More to contemplate a world in which such formal agree-ments were not used. That world, as described in _Utopia,_ bore a striking resemblance to contemporary idealized

depictions of Native American societies, societies that most European observers believed lacked the legal and political institutions that made such formalities necessary. So similar was More's depiction of Utopia to popular images of Native American societies that some of his readers actually accepted it as fact. Some even proposed an expedition of Christian missionaries to the pagan island.

Treaties which all other nations so often conclude among themselves . . . [the Utopians] never make with any nation. "What is the use of a treaty," they ask, "as though nature of herself did not sufficiently bind one man to another? If a person does not regard nature, do you suppose he will care anything about words?"

They are led to this opinion chiefly because in those parts of the world treaties and alliances between kings are not observed with much good faith. In Europe, however, and especially in those parts where the faith and religion of Christ prevails, the majesty of treaties is everywhere holy and inviolable, partly through the justice and goodness of kings, partly through the reverence and fear of the Sovereign [Popes]. Just as the latter themselves undertake nothing which they do not most conscientiously perform, so they command all other rulers to abide by their promises in every way and compel the recalcitrant by pastoral censure and severe reproof. Popes are perfectly right, of course, in thinking it a most disgraceful thing that those who are specially called the faithful should not faithfully adhere to their commitments.

But in that new world, which is almost as far removed from ours by the equator as their life and character are different from ours, there is no trust in treaties. The more numerous and holy the ceremonies with which a treaty is struck the more quickly it is broken. They find some defect in the wording, which sometimes they cunningly devise of set purpose, so that they can never be held by such strong bonds as not somehow to escape from them and break both the treaty and their faith. If this cunning, nay fraud and deceit, were found to have occurred in the contracts of private persons, the treaty-makers with great disdain would exclaim against it as sacrilegious and meriting the gallows—though the very same men plume themselves on being the authors of such advice when given to kings. . . .

This behavior, as I said, of rulers there who keep their treaties so badly is, I suppose, the reason why the Utopians make none; if they lived here, they would perhaps change their minds.

Nevertheless, they believe that, though treaties are faithfully observed, it is a pity that the custom of making them at all had grown up. The result . . . is men's persuasion that they are born one another's adversaries and enemies and that they are right in aiming at one another's destruction except insofar as treaties prevent it. What is more, even when treaties are made, friendship does not grow up but the license of freebooting continues to the extent that, for lack of skill in drawing up the treaty, no sufficient precaution to prevent this activity has been included in the articles. But the Utopians, on the contrary, think that nobody who has done you no harm should be accounted an enemy, that the fellowship created by nature takes the place of a treaty, and that men are better and more firmly joined together by good will than by pacts, by spirit than by words.

If More's *Utopia* seems partly inspired by images of a simpler, less legalistic New World, other works were inspired by something very different. Perhaps the most notorious of these was a book by the Spanish priest Bartolomé De Las

The first edition of Thomas More's Utopia *included this image of the island of Utopia alongside the alphabet of the Utopians. Written in that alphabet and translated into Latin is a poem describing the Utopians' earnest desire to share their philosophical discoveries with the wider world.*

Casas entitled *The Devastation of the Indies*. First published in Seville in 1552, the work was a scathing indictment of Spanish treatment of the native peoples of the Americas. Las Casas's brief polemic found a ready readership among English Protestants hostile to Spain and the other Catholic powers of Europe, then unified in the Holy Roman Empire. For such readers, the book reinforced the so-called "Black Legend," a sort of 16th-century smear campaign launched by Protestant propagandists that depicted Spanish conquerors of America as cruel satanic beasts.

In his book, Las Casas describes the Spanish conquest of what is now Mexico. Perhaps the most powerful element of this story, and the host of similar episodes Las Casas recounts, was the depiction of local peoples as charitable and trusting, qualities that made them ripe for Christian conversion. Not discussed by Las Casas were the native peoples who allied themselves with the Spanish conquistadors in order to be liberated from the yoke of Aztec dominance. Similarly, Las Casas says little about the diseases Europeans brought with them, diseases that caused the deaths of far more Indians than any direct Spanish action.

Thus, from the beginning of their discovery of New Spain, that is to say, from the eighteenth of April in the year one thousand five hundred and eighteen until the year thirty, a period of twelve whole years, there were continual massacres and outrages committed by the bloody hands and swords of the Spaniards against the Indians living on the four hundred and fifty leagues of land surrounding the city of Mexico, which comprised four or five great kingdoms as large as and more felicitous than Spain. Those lands were all more densely populated than Toledo or Seville and Valladolid and Zaragoza all combined, along with Barcelona. Never has there been such a population as in these cities which God saw fit to place in that vast expanse of land having a circumference of more than a thousand leagues. The Spaniards have killed more Indians here in twelve years by the sword, by fire, and enslavement than anywhere else in the Indies. They have killed young and old, men, women, and children, some four million souls during what they call the Conquests, which were the violent invasions of cruel tyrants that should be condemned not only by the law of God but by all the laws of man. . . . And this does not take into account those Indians who have died from ill treatment or were killed under tyrannical servitude.

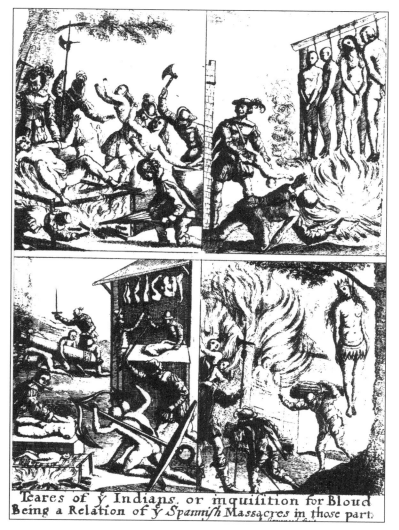

Teares of y Indians, or inquisition for Bloud
Being a Relation of y Spannish Massacres in those part.

In particulars, no tongue would suffice, nor word nor human efforts, to narrate the frightful deeds committed simultaneously by the Spaniards in regions far distant from each other, those notorious hellions, enemies of humankind. And some of their deeds committed in the Indies, in their quality and circumstances, truly they could not, even with much time and diligence and writing, could not be explained. I will narrate, along with protests and sworn statements by eyewitnesses, only some portions of the story, for I could not hope to explain a thousandth part.

Among other massacres there was the one in a big city of more than thirty thousand inhabitants, which is called Cholula. . . . the Spaniards agreed to carry out a massacre, or as they called it a punitive attack, in order to sow terror and apprehension, and to make a display of their power in every corner of that land. . . .

Cacique

An Indian chief

With this aim, therefore, they sent a summons to all the caciques and nobles of the city and in the localities subject to it, and also the head chieftain, and as they arrived to speak with the Spanish captain they were taken prisoner, so unexpectedly that none could flee and warn the others. The Spaniards had asked for five or six thousand Indians to carry their cargo. When all the chiefs had come, they and their burden-bearers were herded into the patios of the houses. . . . [The burden-bearers] were all made to squat down on their haunches like tame sheep.

When they were all placed close together they were bound and tied. At the closed doorways armed guards took turns to see that none escaped. Then, at a command, all the Spaniards drew their swords or pikes and while their chiefs looked on, helpless, all those tame sheep were butchered, cut to pieces. At the end of two or three days some survivors came out from under the corpses, wounded but still alive, and they went, weeping, to the Spaniards, imploring mercy, which was denied. The Spaniards had no compassion but drove them back and cut them down. Then the Spaniards had the chiefs, a total of more than a hundred, who were already shackled, burned at the stakes that had been driven into the ground.

Through the 16th century, English merchants could only watch with envy as the Portuguese and Spanish enriched themselves through a burgeoning trade in Asia. But so long as familiar Asian trade routes were controlled by these powers, there was little chance of England ever savoring this economic bounty. The only viable alternative still seemed to be that imagined by John Cabot: a "Northwest Passage," or sea route, through polar ice flows that linked the North Atlantic to the Pacific.

Cathay

A medieval name for China

A promoter of colonization in Ireland as well as America, the statesman Sir Humphrey Gilbert had also long been committed to the idea of a Northwest Passage. In 1566 he wrote *A discourse of a discoverie for a new passage to Cataia [Cathay]*, a carefully assembled compilation of various ancient and modern authorities whose writings suggested the existence of a northern passage around North America. The following selection from the *Discourse* provides a vivid example of the nature of geographical research in the middle of the 16th century. Expeditions were justified not so much by evidence or firsthand experience, but by theories and ideas with little grounding in factual reality. Indeed,

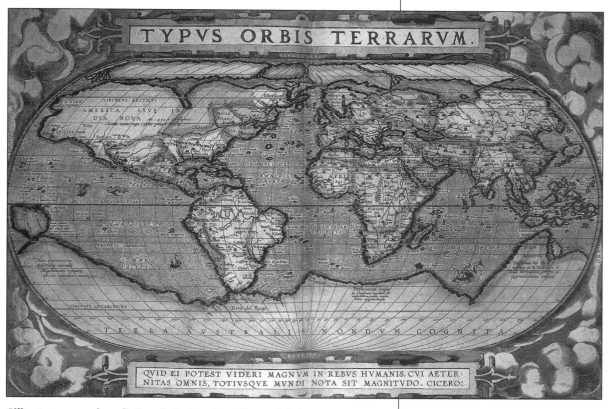

TYPVS ORBIS TERRARVM.

QVID EI POTEST VIDERI MAGNVM IN REBVS HVMANIS, CVI AETER-
NITAS OMNIS, TOTIVSQVE MVNDI NOTA SIT MAGNITVDO. CICERO:

Gilbert even employs fictional stories about the mythic lost continent of Atlantis to support his claims.

When I gave my self to the studie of Geographie, after I had perused and diligently scanned the descriptions of Europe, Asia, and Afrike, and conferred them with the Mappes and Globes both Antique and Moderne: I came in fine to the fourth part of the worlde, commonly called America, which by al descriptions I founde to be an Islande environed round about with the Sea, having on the southside of it . . . the strayte of Magellan, on the West side Mare de sur [or Pacific Ocean] . . . On the East part our Weste Ocean [or the Atlantic], and on the Northside the sea that severeth it from [Greenland through which] the passage lyeth, which I take now in hande to discover. . . .

So that in these our dayes there can no other mayne or Islande bee founde, or judged to be parcell of this Atlantis, then those Westerne Islandes, which beare now the name of America: countervailing thereby the name of Atlantis, in the knowledge of our age.

Then, if when no part of the said Atlantis was oppressed by water, and earthquake, the coastes rounde about the same were

Sir Humphrey Gilbert's hopes of finding a northerly route to Asia were no doubt encouraged by the cartographers of his day, many of whom produced maps suggesting the existence of a Northwest Passage. One of the most influential cartographers was Abraham Ortelius, maker of this 1598 world map.

In tribute to Queen Elizabeth, who was known as the "Virgin Queen," Sir Walter Raleigh named England's recently claimed American territory "Virginia."

navigable: a far greater hope now remaineth of the same by the Northwest, seeing the most parte of it was, since that time, swalowed up with water, which coulde not utterly take away the olde deepes and chanels, but rather, be an occasion of the inlarging of the olde, and also an inforcing of a great many new: why then should we nowe doubte of our Northwest passage and navigation from Englande to India . . . seeing that Atlantis, now called America, was ever knowen to be an Islande, and in those days navigable round about, which by accesse of more water coulde not be diminished. . . .

Wherefore I am of opinion that America by the Northwest, wilbe founde favorable to this our enterprise, and am the rather imboldened to beleeve the same, for that I finde it not onely confirmed by Plato, Aristotle, and other auncient Philosophers: but also by al the best moderne Geographers . . . Al which learned men and painful travellers have affirmed, with one consent and voice, that America was an Iland: and yt there lyeth a great Sea betweene it, Cataia, and Grondland [Greenland], by the which any man of our countrey, that wil give the attempt, may with smal danger passe to Cataia, the Moluccae [Indonesia], India, and al other places in ye East, in much shorter time, then either the Spaniard, or Portingale doth, or may do, from the neerest part of any of their countries with Europe.

India

During the colonial era this term was also used to refer to Asia in general.

Portingale

A term for Portuguese used in the 16th and 17th centuries

The Push for Colonies

Richard Hakluyt was a tireless researcher and archivist who devoted himself to the collection and publication of virtually every document relevant to English overseas exploration produced before 1600. But Hakluyt was much more than a mere compiler. He was also a skilled writer who used his talents to promote English expansion. Perhaps the best expression of this was his *Discourse of Western Planting*, which he wrote in 1584. The purpose of the document was to persuade Queen Elizabeth I to provide direct state support for a settlement or "plantation" of some of her subjects in the newly claimed territory of Virginia. Although Hakluyt's plea was ultimately unpersuasive, it contains some of the more authoritative and pointed justifications for English overseas colonies. In the selection below, Hakluyt stresses what to the queen would have been one of the more appealing benefits of a North American plantation: productive employment for

growing numbers of petty criminals and landless poor. Hakluyt's claim that such unwanted Englishmen might be productively employed in American gold mines, silk works, vineyards, and other lucrative enterprises was typical of the hopeful tone of such promotional tracts. But it was also an unfortunate inducement to the sad lot of English migrants whose hopes for quick riches were usually dashed in early colonial America.

Yea many thousandes of idle persons are within this Realme [of England], which havinge no way to be sett on worke be either mutinous and seeke alteration in the state, or at leaste very burdensome to the common wealthe, and often fall to pilferinge and thevinge and other lewdnes, whereby all the prisons of the lande are daily pestred and stuffed full of them, where either they pitifully pyne awaye, or els at lengthe are miserably hanged . . . whereas yf this voyadge were put in execution, these pety theves mighte be condempned for certen yeres in the westerne partes, especially in Newfounde Lande in sawinge and fellinge of tymber for mastes of shippes and . . . boordes, in burninge of the firres and pine trees to make pitche tarr rosen and sope asshes, in beatinge and workinge of hempe for cordage: and in the more sowtherne partes in settinge them to worke in mynes of golde, silver, copper, leade and yron, in dragginge for perles and currall [coral], in plantinge of suger canes as the Portingales have done in Madera, in mayneteynaunce and increasinge of silke wormes for silke and in dressinge the same: in gatheringe of cotten whereof there is plentie, in tillinge of the soile there for graine, in dressinge of vines whereof there is great aboundaunce for wyne, olyves whereof the soile is capable for oyle, trees for oranges, lymons, almondes, figges, and other frutes all which are founde to growe there already . . . in dressinge of raw hides of divers kindes of beastes, in makinge and gatheringe of salte . . . in killinge the whale, seale, porpose . . . for trayne oile, in fisshinge, saltinge, and dryenge of linge, codde, salmon, heringe, in makinge and gatheringe of hony, wax, turpentine, in hewinge and shapinge of stone . . . in making of caske, oares, and all other manner of staves; in buildinge of fortes, townes, churches; in powderringe and barrellinge of fishe, fowles, and fleshe, which will be notable provision for sea and lande. . . . Besides this, such as by any kind of infirmitie cannot passe the seas thither, and now are chardgeable to the Realme at home, by this voyadge shalbe made profitable members by employinge them in England in makinge of a thousande

An England in Miniature

For most Americans, the word plantation describes the agricultural enterprises that dotted the landscape of the American South during the half-century before the Civil War. It evokes images of African slaves working in cotton or tobacco fields, and elegant Victorian mansions housing wealthy, refined Southern white women and men. But the term has not always been used in this way. When 16th-century English writers wrote of the settlement of the English in foreign lands, they often referred to "plantations," or places where English people settled, bringing the seeds of their culture and religion, with the expectation that those seeds would yield fruit in the form of an England in miniature. Implied in such thinking was the idea that any preexisting ways of life—of Native Americans, for instance—would be quickly and easily supplanted by that of the English.

In addition to founding the Roanoke colony, Sir Walter Raleigh led an expedition to South America in search of El Dorado, a mythic city of gold. But like so many pipe dreams of the colonial era, that quest yielded little more than hardship.

The Ultimate Renaissance Man

It took a man like Sir Walter Raleigh to finally establish an English colony in the New World. He was, in the truest sense of the phrase, a "Renaissance man." Indeed, there was little in Elizabethan England that a man could do that the dashing, fearless Raleigh did not do. He was at various points in his career a soldier of fortune, a sea captain, an explorer, a colonizer, a poet, a political essayist, a historian, a confidant of Queen Elizabeth, a businessman, a landlord, a scientist, a philosopher, a privateer, and a knight. Raleigh was also embroiled in the mysterious, conspiratorial politics of the Elizabethan era, and, as in the case of his friend the playwright Christopher Marlowe, this involvement eventually cost him his life. On October 29, 1618, Sir Walter Raleigh was executed by the state for treason.

triflinge thinges, which will be very goodd marchandize for those Contries where wee shall have moste ample vente thereof. And seinge the savages of the graunde Baye and all alonge the mightie Ryver that ronneth upp to Canada . . . are greately delighted with any cappe or garment made of course wollen clothe, their Contrie beinge colde and sharpe in the winter, yt is manifeste wee shall finde greate [demand for] our clothes . . . whereby all occupacions belonginge to clothinge and knittinge shalbe . . . sett [to] worke, as cappers, knitters, clothiers, wollmen, carders, spynners, weavers, fullers, sheremen, dyers, drapers, hatters and such like, whereby many decayed townes may be repaired: In somme this enterprice will mynister matter for all sortes and states of men to worke upon: namely all severall kindes of artificers, husbandmen, seamen, marchauntes, souldiers, capitaines, phisitions, lawyers, devines, Cosmographers, hidrographers, Astronomers, historiographers, yea olde folkes, lame persons, women, and younge children by many meanes which hereby shall still be mynistred unto them, shalbe kepte from idlenes, and be made able by their owne honest and easie labour to finde themselves withoute surchardginge others.

The first full-fledged English attempt to establish a colony in America occurred in the spring of 1585, when the adventurer and statesman Sir Walter Raleigh sent seven ships, carrying 100 colonists to Roanoke Island, on the outer banks of present-day North Carolina. Raleigh undertook this venture primarily to establish a safe haven for English sailing vessels engaged in government sponsored piracy, or "privateering," against Spanish treasure ships in the mid-Atlantic. By the fall of 1585, more than 100 Englishmen (no women came) were living in a fort at Roanoke. Suffering from a lack of supplies, the surviving Roanoke colonists abandoned the colony the following spring. But Raleigh and his associates were not deterred. By the end of the summer, they had installed more colonists at Roanoke, but most of these also perished or left the colony.

Finally, in 1587, Raleigh sent a third group of colonists that was to have the makings of a more lasting settlement. In addition to the usual soldiers of fortune, the group included 17 women and 11 children—115 people in all. The fate of these people is one of the more tragic chapters in the history of colonial North America. A massive Spanish assault on England in 1588 delayed supply ships Raleigh planned to send to

the colony. This assault by the so-called Spanish Armada—the huge sailing fleet sent by King Philip II of Spain to conquer England—culminated in an utterly unexpected English victory, a triumph the likes of which England had not known for centuries. But for the Roanoke colonists, it was too little, too late. Stranded in an alien land, with inadequate supplies and hostile Indian neighbors, they vanished without a trace. The next English ship to reach them arrived some three years after the colonists had initially settled the island. Part of what the sailors on that ship found is described in the excerpt below by the ship's captain, John White. One clue the colonists had left about their fate were the letters CRO carved on a tree. This suggested that the more than 100 English men, women, and children living on Roanoke Island had fled to the island of Croatoan, near Cape Hatteras, but White and his men were never able to confirm this. And to this day, historians cannot say for certain what befell the colonists of Roanoke.

The 15 of August towards Evening we came to an anker at Hatorask . . . three leagues from the shore. At our first comming to anker on this shore we saw a great smoke rise in the Ile

O, wonder!
How many goodly
* creatures are there here!*
How beauteous mankind
* is! O brave new world,*
That has such people in 't!
  —William Shakespeare,
    The Tempest (1611)

Protestants throughout Europe joined England in celebrating the defeat of the Spanish Armada. This silver medal commemorating the event was produced in Holland.

Perhaps as an incentive for enduring the hardships that awaited them, Sir Walter Raleigh and his associates granted leaders of the Roanoke colony these coats of arms, much like an English aristocrat would have had.

Raonoake neere the place where I left our Colony in the yeere 1587, which smoake put us in good hope that some of the Colony were there expecting my returne out of England.

The 16 and next morning our 2 boates went a shore, & Captaine Cooke & Captain Spicer & their company with me, with intent to passe to the place at Raonoak where our countreymen were left. At our putting from the ship we commanded our Master gunner to make readie 2 Minions and a Falkon [small cannon] well loden, and to shoot them off with reasonable space betweene every shot, to the ende that their reportes might bee heard to the place where wee hoped to finde some of our people. This was accordingly performed, & our twoe boats put off unto the shore, in the Admirals boat we sounded all the way and found from our shippe untill we came within a mile of the shore nine, eight, and seven fadome: but before we were halfe way betweene our ships and the shore we saw another great smoke to the Southwest of Kindrikers mountes: we therefore thought good to goe to that second smoke first: but it was much further from the harbour where we landed, then we supposed it to be, so that we were very sore tired before wee came to the smoke. But that which grieved us more was that when we came to the smoke, we found no man nor signe that any had bene there lately, nor yet any fresh water in all this way to drinke. Being thus wearied with this journey we returned to the harbour where we left our boates. . . .

Our boates and all things fitted againe, we put off from Hatorask, being the number of 19 persons in both boates: . . . we went . . . to the place where I left our Colony in the yeere 1586. In all this way we saw in the sand the print of the Salvages feet of 2 or 3 sorts troaden that night, and as we entred up the sandy banke upon a tree, in the very browe thereof were curiously carved these faire Romane letters CRO: which letters presently we knew to signifie the place, where I should find the planters seated, according to a secret token agreed upon betweene them & me at my last departure from them, which was, that in any wayes they should not faile to write or carve on the trees or posts of the dores the name of the place where they should be seated; for at my comming away they were prepared to remove from Roanoak 50 miles into the maine. Therefore at my departure from them in Anno 1587 I willed them, that if they should happen to be distressed in any of those places, that then they should carve over the letters or name; a Crosse . . . but we found no such signe of distresse. And having well considered of this, we passed toward the place where they were left in sundry houses, but we found the houses taken downe, and the place very strongly enclosed with a high palisado of great trees, . . . From thence wee went along by the water side, towards the poynt of the Creeke to see if we could find any of their botes . . . but we could perceive no signe of them.

The tragedy at Roanoke Island was eclipsed in the English mind by the small nation's astounding naval victory over the Spanish in 1588—a victory, it should be said, greatly aided by foul weather in the North Atlantic. This triumph boosted English spirits, inspired a new sense of national destiny, and severely curtailed Spanish sea power. Taken together, these ingredients fed continued English interest in America, and a growing sense that the New World provided more than simply riches or an outlet for surplus labor. It also provided an arena for England to show its greatness to the wider world. In

Roanoke: The Missing Link?

One of the explanations for the fate of the Roanoke colonists is that they were adopted by local native communities. This view was espoused as early as 1709 by the trader and colonist John Lawson in his book, *A New Voyage to Carolina*: "The *Hatteras Indians*, who either then lived on *Ronoak-*Island, or much frequented it. . . . tell us, that several of their Ancestors were white People, and could talk in a Book [read], as we do; the Truth of which is confirm'd by gray Eyes being found frequently amongst these *Indians*, and no others."

1606, one year before England established its first successful colony, an obscure poet, Michael Drayton, expressed these feelings in his "To the Virginian Voyage." The poem is striking not only for its overtones of nationalism, but also for its depiction of Virginia as some sort of bounteous paradise. Game, wine grapes, fine woods, and fertile soil, Drayton indicated, abounded and were free for the taking. Once again, as we shall see, such depictions were dangerously misleading.

You brave heroique minds,
Worthy your countries name,
   That honour still pursue,
   Goe, and subdue,
Whilst loyt'ring hinds
Lurke here at home, with shame.

Britans, you stay too long,
Quickly aboord bestow you,
   And with a merry gale
   Swell your stretch'd sayle,
With vowes as strong,
As the winds that blow you.

Your course securely steere,
West and by south forth keepe,
   Rocks, lee-shores, nor sholes,
   When Eolus scowles,
You need not feare, So absolute the deepe.

And cheerefully at sea,
Successe you still intice,
   To get the pearle and gold,
   And ours to hold,
Virginia,
Earth's onely paradise.

Where nature hath in store,
Fowle, venison, and fish,
   And the fruitfull'st soyle,
   Without your toyle,
Three havests more,
All greater than you wish.

And the ambitious vine
Crownes with his purple masse,
   The Cedar reaching hie
   To kiss the sky,

Hind

A female deer

Eolus

The god of winds

"I know that I have the body, but of a weak and feeble woman, but I have the heart and Stomach of a King, and of a King of England too, and think foul scorn that . . . any Prince of Europe should dare invade the borders of my Realm, to which rather than any dishonour shall grow by me, I my self will take up arms, I my self will be your General, Judge, and Rewarder . . ."

—Queen Elizabeth in a speech to her army in 1588, the year the English defeated the Spanish Armada

ELIZABETA D. G. ANGLIÆ. FRANCIÆ. HIBERNIÆ. ET VERGINIÆ
REGINA CHRISTIANAE FIDEI VNICVM PROPVGNACVLVM .

Immortalis honos Regum, cui non tulit ætas   *Queis ipsæ tantum superant reliqua omnia regna ,*
  Olla prior, veniens nec feret vlla parem ,   *Quantum tu maior Regibus es reliquis ,*
Sospite quo nunquam terras habitare Britannas   *Viue precor felix tanti in moderamine regni ,*
  Desinet alma Quies , Iustitia atque Fides ,   *Dum tibi Rex Regum cælica regna paret .*

Queen Elizabeth I provided little direct support for England's New World ventures, but in leading the nation in its battle against the Spanish empire, she prepared the way for future undertakings.

The Cypresse, pine
And use-full Sassafras.

To whose, the golden age
Still natures lawes doth give,
    No other cares that tend,
But them to defend
From winters age,
That long there doth not live.

When as the lushious smell
Of that delicious land,
    Above the seas that flowes,
    The cleere wind throwes,
Your hearts to swell
Approaching the deare strand.

In kenning of the shore
(Thanks to God first given,)
    O you the happy'st men,
    Be frolike then,
Let cannons roare,
Frighting the wide heaven.

And in regions farre
Such heroes bring yee foorth,
    As those from whom we came,
    And plant our name,
Under that starre
Not knowne unto our north.

And as there plenty growes
Of lawrell every where,
    Apollo's sacred tree,
    You it may see,
A poets browes
To crowne, that may sing there.

Thy voyages attend,
Industrious Hackluit,
    Whose reading shall inflame
    Men to seeke fame,
And much commend
To after-times thy wit.

Whatever tragedies the English suffered during their various New World enterprises, none compared to those experienced by the native peoples of North America. Thousands of Native Americans died from typhus, measles, smallpox and other European diseases to which they had little resistance. Native peoples who survived the horrific onslaught of disease did so in communities forever changed by the effects of these epidemics. These survivors were nonetheless able to maintain some connection to the worlds of their ancestors, mostly through oral traditions, or accounts and stories passed on from one generation to the next by word of mouth. One such account describes the emotions and thoughts the first sighting of a European sailing vessel elicited in a group of Montagnais Indians in eastern Canada.

When there were no people in this country but Indians, and before any others were known, a young woman had a singular

Prom Lupi.

Portus Regalis, ſiue F.S.Helenæ.

dream. She dreamed that a small island came floating in towards the land, with tall trees on it, and living beings,—among whom was a man dressed in rabbit-skin garments. The next day she related her dream, and sought for an interpretation. It was the custom in those days, when any one had a remarkable dream, to consult the wise men, and especially the magicians and soothsayers. These pondered over the girl's dream, but could make nothing of it. The next day an event occurred that explained all. Getting up in the morning, what should they see but a singular little island, as they supposed, which had drifted near to the land and become stationary there! There were trees on it, and branches to the trees, on which a number of bears, as they supposed, were crawling about. . . . what was their surprise to find that these supposed bears were men, and that some of them were lowering down into the water a very singularly constructed canoe, into which several of them jumped and paddled ashore. Among them was a man dressed in white,—a priest with his white stole on,—who came towards them making signs of friendship, raising his hand towards heaven, and addressing them in an earnest manner, but in a language which they could not understand.

The European idea that America was a land of plenty is expressed in this 16th-century French engraving depicting happy natives, abundant game, and bounteous fruit trees along the coast of Florida. Perhaps most striking of all is the depiction of wine grapes on the vine. Many European colonizers hoped to find in America a climate conducive to wine production, but, in fact, few did.

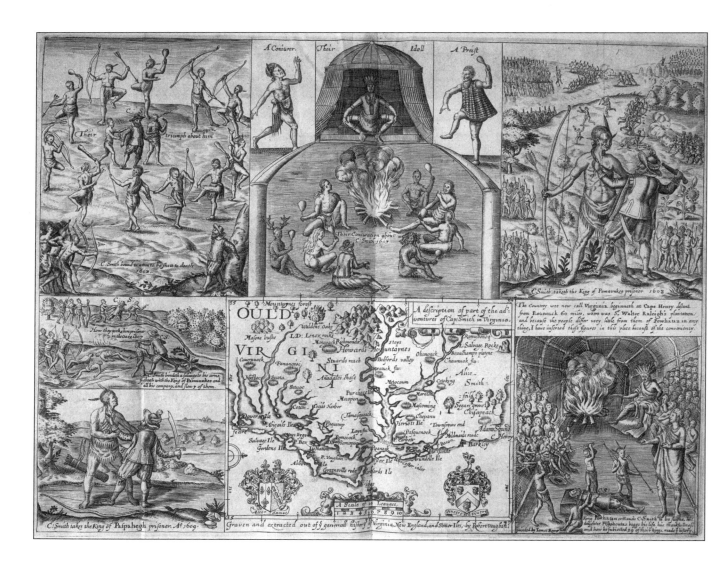

A Coniurer.   Their   Idoll   A Preist

Their   triumph about him

C: Smith bound readie to be shott to death: 1607

Their Conivration about C: Smith. 1607

C: Smith taketh the King of Pamavnkee prisoner 1608

How they take him prisoner in the oaze.

C: Smith bindeth a salvage his arme, fight with the King of Pamavnkee and all his company, and slew 7 of them.

C: Smith takes the King of Paspahegh prisoner. A°. 1609.

OULD
VIRGINIA

Mountaynes forest
Waldens Oake
Masons bushe   LD: Lenox rocks
Monapack Richmonde
Cawrnock   Howards Mountaynes   Ohanoack   Ramuhcong
Pananaac   Stuards reach   Bedfords valley   Salvage Rockes
Nefioc   Scota   Anadales shase   Beaulhamps playne
Setuoe   Kecock fiu: Chawnok fiu:
Purchasis   Mecoum   Alice Smith
Dovers Ile   Neopon   Segars grove
Abigails Ile   Catoking   Chisapeack
Salvage Ile   Layefiu   Townserows end
Gordens Ile   Biquimp   Chepanu   Alldents roade   Adams Sound
Adlohs   P: Vaughan   Pasquenock   P: Corbett   P: Baxton   Barkley
P. Hatton   Rowecock   P: Corbett   P: Barkley
Greenevill rode   Roanak   Gosnolds Ile   Arundells Ile
Afhfors Ile   Herford's Ile

A description of part of the adventures of Cap: Smith in Virginia.

The Country wee now call Virginia, beginneth at Cape Henry distant from Roanock 60 miles, where was S. Walter Raleigh's plantation: and because the people differ very little from them, of Powhatan in any thing, I have inserted these figures in this place because of the convemency.

A Scale of Leagues.
1 2 3 4 5 6 7 8 9 10

Graven and extracted out of ye generall history of Virginia, New England, and Sommer Iles, by Robert Vaughan.

King Powhatan commands C: Smith to be slayne, his daughter Pokahontas beggs his life, he thankfulnes and how he subjected 39 of their kings, reade ye history.

Chapter Two

New Lands, New Lives

These engravings appeared in Captain John Smith's General History of Virginia *published in 1624. They depict Smith's heroics as the leader of the Virginia Colony, and are perhaps a reflection of Smith's lasting concern for his reputation in history.*

Queen Elizabeth I did not live to see England establish a lasting presence in the New World. But her successor, James I, did—a fact which for him proved to be as much a burden as a blessing. For what was true of England in the early 17th century was even more true of its first permanent American colony. If the former endured nearly endless political conflict, the latter experienced that and more.

In 1607, a group of savvy English entrepreneurs organized the Virginia Company, a private business entity that—with carefully negotiated government permission—established a new colony called Jamestown (named after King James I) in the swampy, low-lying terrain along the James River in Virginia. Unlike Raleigh and the other founders of Roanoke, the directors of the Virginia Company founded their colony not so much as an outpost to support English privateers, but rather as a means of extracting precious metals and other valuable commodities from the American countryside. This ambition reflected the directors' more immediate goal: quick and handsome profits for the Company's investors.

This turned out to be a recipe for disaster. Among other things, it meant that the company sent to Virginia people equipped to discover valuable trade goods, but entirely lacking in the skills needed to sustain human life in an alien land. Rather than ordinary artisans and farmers, most of the people who first went to Jamestown were young aristocratic gentlemen or soldiers of fortune, lured by the prospect of easy riches and land ownership. Such men were hardly the types to work for the collective good of a colony. Instead, they worked for personal fortune and glory, searching for valuable treasures or fighting with the Indians.

This selfish spirit added to the colonists' difficulties, particularly the bleak and ever-present prospect of starvation—a problem that at times

"There remained not past sixtie men, women and children, most miserable and poore creatures; and those were preserved for the most part, by roots, herbes, acornes, walnuts, berries, now and then a little fish: . . . Nay, so great was our famine, that a Salvage we slew, and buried, the poorer sort tooke him up againe and eat him, and so did divers one another boyled and stewed with roots and herbs: And one amongst the rest did kill his wife, powdered her, and had eaten part of her before it was knowne, for which hee was executed, as hee well deserved; now whether shee was better roasted, boyled . . . , I know not."

—Captain John Smith, from his *Generall Historie of Virginia*, on the winter of 1609–10 at Jamestown (1624)

became so severe some were allegedly driven to cannibalism. To counter chronic food shortages, colonists obtained food from local Indians, often using trickery and violence, but this only resulted in more death and despair. Cycles of vengeance and retaliation between Native Americans and colonists became a part of everyday life in the colony. The end result was, in a word, death. Of the 120 or so English to settle at Jamestown in 1607, after the first nine months, only 38 survived. The Virginia Company replenished the colony's population yearly, but this did little to counter the overall trend: by 1610, of the 1,200 people the Virginia Company had sent to the colony, half were dead. And this trend continued for the next decade. By 1624, of the 8,000 colonists who had settled in Jamestown, only 1,300 survived.

Desperate, on edge, and often starving, those colonists that did survive found themselves in a state of almost ceaseless turmoil. As food grew scarce and treasure proved even scarcer, people's fuses shortened, and the colony found itself plagued by infighting. Part of the problem was simply that the young gentlemen who settled Virginia were a particularly quarrelsome lot. As sons of privilege, they expected to give orders, not receive them from the colonial council and a series of elected presidents of the colony. Far from the sort of unified front one might expect from a group consisting mostly of soldiers, Jamestown was thus a place of constant bickering, back-stabbing, and treachery.

All these ingredients made for a chaotic and volatile mix, and it is a wonder the colony survived at all. The constant loss of life, the internal strife, the atrocious relations with the Indians, all culminated in a decision by the Crown to take control of the colony. As it turned out, the king was able to do little more than the Virginia Company did to bring peace and stability.

The early history of the second and third successful mainland English colonies—the colony at Plymouth and the Massachusetts Bay Colony—at first glance suggests something totally different from that of Jamestown. If the latter was populated mostly by young, avaricious men and aristocratic soldiers, these colonies were populated by pious families—ordinary English men and women, people of a middling sort, some of whom were skilled artisans, including barrel makers, carpenters, shoe makers, and weavers. The Virginia colonists lived with the specter of death hanging over them, these New England colonists (after initial hardships) were able to establish safe, productive, and self-sustaining communities. If Virginia appeared chaotic and unstable, the New England colonies appeared peaceful and orderly.

Underlying these differences was the important fact that the colonies differed sharply in their initial purposes. If Jamestown was established to generate material riches, the first New England colonies were established to produce spiritual riches (although the New England colonists also expected to find furs, sassafras, and other lucrative commodities). They were intended to be refuges, refuges for persecuted religious minorities in search of a place free of the corruption, the irreligion, and perhaps, above all, the disorder that seemed rife in England.

It is, nevertheless, important to acknowledge that the differing characters of the Virginia and New England colonies only went so far. Not long after it was founded, the Massachusetts Bay Colony also proved to be an intensely contentious kind of place. Bitter and violent theological divisions emerged as colonists wrestled with the divisive question of exactly what kind of society they were creating. Would it be a society of individuals, all living according to their own values? Or would it be a communal society whose individual members sacrificed personal freedom for the sake of some grand, unifying ideal? Such perennial questions produced more than just abstract theological argument. They also led to fierce feuds over land distribution, town governance, and Native American–white diplomacy. The colonial government struggled endlessly to contain all this strife and uphold the colonists' initial vision of an orderly, peaceful commonwealth. But in a sense, these struggles produced only further strife, eventually contributing to a decision by the Crown to do what it had already done in Virginia: take direct control of the colonies.

The unruly world of 17th-century English politics thus echoed through all the colonies, but another aspect of contemporary English history was also evident. The English were becoming an intensely mobile people. In the 16th and 17th centuries, ordinary English men and women in ever-greater numbers were beginning to leave their birthplaces for more promising places in the British Isles and across the Atlantic Ocean. And this trend did not stop when English men and women reached the shores of new lands; it continued for generations, as children of colonists in Virginia, New England, and elsewhere left family homes and migrated inland, forming new frontier settlements.

NOVA BRITANNIA.
OFFRING MOST
Excellent fruites by Planting in
VIRGINIA.

Exciting all such as be well affected
to further the same.

LONDON
Printed for SAMVEL MACHAM, and are to be sold at
his Shop in Pauls Church-yard , at the
Signe of the Bul-head.
1 6 0 9.

The officials of the Virginia Company produced many promotional tracts to encourage settlement of the colony. This title page of Robert Johnson's Nova Britannia *(New England) tempts potential colonists with "excellent fruites."*

The Trials of Settlement

Much of what we know about life in the Jamestown Colony comes from one of the most controversial of all colonists (or

"planters," as they were called), Captain John Smith. A professional soldier, adventurer, explorer, author, and all-
around man on the make, Smith was also remarkably
self-assured—one might even say arrogant. Experience in
battle left him with a combination of physical strength and
calculating political shrewdness, precisely the qualities
needed to lead a group of equally arrogant, if less skilled,
English gentlemen. And, indeed, the young Smith (he was 26
years old when he arrived at Jamestown) is usually credited
with keeping the colony from suffering the same fate as
Roanoke. Between September 1608 and August 1609, he
served as president of the colonial council and imposed a
strict work regimen on the rambunctious colonists.

Smith left Virginia in 1609, and although he made one
final trip to New England in 1614, he spent most of the rest
of his life chronicling his adventures and promoting English

*Few early colonial maps convey the
density and complexity of Native
American settlement on the American
East Coast, but this map by Captain
John Smith is a rare exception.
Drawing on information provided by
Native Americans, it indicates the
numerous kin groups and villages of
the Powhatan Confederacy.*

colonization. In 1612, he published *Proceedings of the Eng-* *lish Colonie in Virginia,* **the most comprehensive contempo-** **rary account of the early years of the Jamestown venture. In** **the passage below, Smith describes the trials of the** **colonists' first months in the New World. War, political** **intrigue, and disease are all part of the story.**

Untill the 13 of May they [the colonists] sought a place to plant in, then the Councell was sworne, Master Wingfeild was chosen Precident, and an oration made, . . . Now falleth every man to worke, the Councell contrive the Fort, the rest cut downe trees to make place to pitch their Tents; some provide clapbord to relade the ships, some make gardens, some nets, etc. The Salvages often visited us kindly. The Precidents overweening jealousie would admit no exercise at armes, or fortification, but the boughs of trees cast together in the forme of a halfe moone by the extraordinary paines and diligence of Captaine Kendall. Newport, with Smith, and 20 others, were sent to discover the head of the river: by divers smal habitations they passed, in 6 daies they arrived at a town called Powhatan, consisting of some 12 houses pleasantly seated on a hill; before it 3 fertil Iles, about it many of their corne-fields. The place is very pleasant, and strong by nature. Of this place the Prince is called Powhatan, and his people Powhatans, to this place the river is navigable; . . . The people in al parts kindly intreated them, til being returned within 20 miles of James towne, they gave just cause of jealousie . . . , but had God not blessed the discoverers otherwise then those at the fort, there had then beene an end of that plantation; for at the fort, where they arrived the next day, they found 17 men hurt, and a boy slaine by the Salvages, and had it not chanced a crosse barre shot from the ships strooke down a bough from a tree amongst them that caused them to retire, our men had all been slaine, being securely all at worke, and their armes in drie fats.

Hereupon the President was contented the Fort should be pal-lisadoed, the ordinance mounted, his men armed and exercised, for many were the assaults, and Ambuscadoes of the Salvages, and our men by their disorderly stragling were often hurt, when the Salvages by the nimblenesse of their heeles well escaped. What toile wee had, with so smal a power to guard our workmen adaies, watch al night, resist our enimies and effect our businesse, to relade the shops, cut downe trees, and prepare the ground to plant our corne, etc. . . . Six weekes being spent in this manner, Captaine Newport . . . was to return with the ships. Now Captaine

Crosse Barre

Lethal kind of cannon shot.

Fats

Casks for storing various provisions.

Pocahontas remained a prominent historical figure throughout the colonial era. This painting from around 1730 suggests that she had acquired special significance for colonial girls. The artist, Mary Woodbury, was a mere 13 years old when she painted the picture.

Family Ties: Powhatan and Pocahontas

Powhatan is known as much for being the head of the powerful Powhatan Confederacy as for being the father of Pocahontas, the young Indian woman often credited with saving Captain John Smith's life. According to popular myth—perpetuated by Smith himself—Pocahontas had fallen in love with Smith and intervened just as her father was about to execute him. In all probability, though, Smith mistook a common initiation ritual for an execution ceremony, and similarly mistook Pocahontas's role in that ceremony for an effort to save his life, which was not actually in jeopardy. Pocahontas is also known for her 1614 marriage to another Englishman, John Rolfe. Hindsight suggests that the marriage was at least partly a calculated act by Rolfe and his associates to relieve tensions between colonists and Indians. If so, it worked, but only temporarily. Relations between Indians and English deteriorated catastrophically in 1622.

Smith, who all this time from their departure from the Canaries was restrained as a prisoner upon the scandalous suggestions of some of the chiefe . . . who fained he intended to usurpe the government, murder the Councell, and make himselfe king, that his confederats were dispearsed in all the three ships, and that divers of his confederats that revealed it, would affirme it, for this he was committed. 13 weekes he remained thus suspected, . . . many untruthes were alleaged against him; but being so apparently disproved begat a generall hatred in the harts of the company against such unjust commanders; many were the mischiefes that daily sprong from their ignorant . . . spirits; but the good doctrine and exhortation of our preacher Master Hunt reconciled them, and caused Captaine Smith to be admitted of the Councell; the next day all received the Communion, the day following the Salvages voluntarily desired peace, and Captaine Newport returned for England with newes. . . .

Being thus left to our fortunes, it fortuned that within tenne daies scarse ten amongst us could either goe, or well stand, such extreame weaknes and sicknes oppressed us. And thereat none need mervaile, if they consider the cause and reason, which was this; whilest our ships staied, our allowance was somewhat bettered, by a daily proportion of bisket which the sailers would pilfer to sell, give or exchange with us, for mony, saxefras, furres, or love. But when they departed, there remained neither taverne, beere-house nor place of relief but the common kettell. Had we beene as free from all sinnes as gluttony, and drunkennes, we might have bin canonized for Saints; But our President would never have bin admitted, for ingrossing to his privat, Otemeale, sacke, oile, aquavitae [spirits], beefe, egs, or what not; but the kettel, that indeede he allowed equally to be distributed, and that was halfe a pinte of wheat and as much barly boyled with water for a man a day, and this . . . contained as many wormes as graines; . . . our drinke was water, our lodgings castles in aire. With this lodging and diet, our extreame toile in bearing and planting pallisadoes, so strained and bruised us, and our continuall labour in the extremity of the heate had so weakened us, as were cause sufficient to have made us as miserable in our native country, or any other place in the world.

The political tumult of 17th-century England was perhaps a reflection of the profoundly complex English political environment. To an extent unfamiliar to monarchs elsewhere in Europe, English kings and queens constantly faced the

difficult problem of identifying exactly where their power ended and where their subjects' power began. In the colonial world, similar uncertainties about government jurisdiction revealed themselves in the many power struggles that plagued early Virginia. Perhaps aware of these problems, the founders of the Plymouth Colony worked to create a political system that would avert such conflicts, and this meant, to begin with, establishing some kind of loyalty to the new colonial government. To achieve this, the leaders of the colony acted while still aboard the *Mayflower*, the ship that took the Pilgrims to America. They brought together many of the male colonists (women were generally excluded from politics by law) to sign a declaration of allegiance to the new colonial government. This document, known as the Mayflower Compact, is a striking expression of the English idea that government should be founded on the consent of the people. But it is also indicative of the acute fears that leaders of the colony had about the potential for political strife, even among this pious band of religious pilgrims.

In The Name of God, Amen.

We whose names are underwritten, the loyal subjects of our dread Sovereign Lord King James, by the grace of God of Great Britain, France, and Ireland King, Defender of the Faith, etc.

Having undertaken, for the glory of God and advancement of the Christian faith and honor of our king and country, a voyage to plant the first colony in the northern parts of Virginia, do by these presents solemnly and mutually in the presence of God and one of another, covenant and combine ourselves together into a civil body politic, for our better ordering and preservation and furtherance of the ends aforesaid; and by virtue hereof to enact, constitute, and frame such just and equal laws, ordinances, acts, constitutions, and offices, from time to time, as shall be thought most meet and convenient for the general good of the colony, unto which we promise all due submission and obedience. In witness whereof we have hereunder subscribed our names at Cape Cod, the 11th of November, in the year of the reign of our Sovereign Lord King James, of England, France, and Ireland the eighteenth, and of Scotland the fifty-fourth. Anno Domini 1620.

The seal of the Massachusetts Bay Company presents a Native American of ambiguous gender saying "Come over and help us." The image is indicative of the company's efforts to portray itself as an organization whose purpose was in part to convert Native Americans to Christianity.

For all their sincere efforts to establish a tranquil and productive colony, the Pilgrims still faced problems similar to those of the Virginia colonists. During their first winter at

The Ravages of Scurvy

During the more than two months it took to sail from England to America, colonists were susceptible to scurvy, a painful and debilitating disease produced by a vitamin C deficiency. The illness produces an excruciating swelling of the gums, which made it almost impossible to consume the tough dried meats and hard biscuits that were a main source of nourishment at sea. Indeed, many fatalities from the disease resulted not from the disease itself, but rather from starvation. It was not until the end of the 18th century that British naval officers began to routinely provide sailors with citrus juices, effectively preventing this ailment.

A Morning Draft

Consistent with 17th-century English habits, thirsty colonists of all ages drank beer, ale, and hard cider. Indeed, English adults and children would regularly drink a "morning draft" of beer or ale. They believed that the latter helped maintain good health while water, in contrast, promoted ill health. In some ways, this perception was not without justification. With no real systems of filtration, drinking water was often quite filthy and unappetizing.

Plymouth, the colonists suffered dreadfully, half of them perishing from illness and starvation. But, unlike the Virginians, the Pilgrims expected to work in the New World, and they expected to live an austere, dutiful existence, an existence consistent with their intense Christian beliefs. And, indeed, after that grim first year, life in Plymouth Colony began to improve. William Bradford, the governor of the colony, described the events of this first year in his history, *Of Plymouth Plantation.* Having served as governor of the colony for most of its first 36 years, Bradford was especially well suited to write such a history.

But that which was most sad and lamentable was, that in two or three months' time half of their company died, especially in January and February, being the depth of winter, and wanting houses and other comforts; being infected with the scurvy and other diseases which this long voyage and their inaccommodate condition had brought upon them. So as there died some times two or three of a day in the foresaid time, that of 100 and odd persons, scarce fifty remained. And of these, in the time of most distress, there was but six or seven sound persons who to their great commendations, be it spoken, spared no pains night nor day, but with abundance of toil and hazard of their own health, fetched them wood, made them fires, dressed them meat, made their beds, washed their loathsome clothes, clothed and unclothed them. In a word, did all the homely and necessary offices for them which dainty and queasy stomachs cannot endure to hear named; and all this willingly and cheerfully, without any grudging in the least, showing herein their true love unto their friends and brethren; a rare example and worthy to be remembered. Two of these seven were Mr. William Brewster, their reverend Elder, and Myles Standish, their Captain and military commander, unto whom myself and many others were much beholden in our low and sick condition. And yet the Lord so upheld these persons as in this general calamity they were not at all infected either with sickness or lameness. And what I have said of these I may say of many others who died in this general visitation, and others yet living; that whilst they had health, yea, or any strength continuing, they were not wanting to any that had need of them. And I doubt not but their recompense is with the Lord.

. . . As this calamity fell among the passengers that were to be left here to plant, and were hasted ashore and made to drink water that the seamen might have the more beer, and one in his sickness desiring but a small can of beer, it was answered that if he were their own father he should have none. The disease began to fall amongst them also, so as almost half of their company died before they went away.

It is difficult to think about the Pilgrims of Plymouth Colony without conjuring images of the first Thanksgiving. As always, such images, so much a part of American national memory, are shrouded in complex layers of truth and fiction. In the case of the first Thanksgiving holiday, there is very little information with which to separate fact from fiction. The only surviving account of the event comes in a letter written by Edward Winslow on December 11, 1621. The letter was published as an addendum to a promotional tract, no doubt to serve as evidence of New England's rich natural bounty, the accounts of which promoters hoped would lure other planters to the Plymouth Colony. In any case, Winslow's account seems credible if for no other reason than that there were many precedents in English society for harvest festivals, or days of thanks for harvests gone well. It is probable that the pious Pilgrims held such celebrations, and the first Thanksgiving was one of them.

In this little time that a few of us have been here, we have built seven dwelling-houses, and four for the use of the plantation, and have made preparation for divers others. We set the last spring some twenty acres of Indian corn, and sowed some six acres of barley and peas, and according to the manner of the Indians we manured our ground with herrings, or rather shads, which we have in great abundance and take with great ease at our doors. Our corn did prove well, and, God be praised, we had a good increase of Indian corn . . .

Our harvest being gotten in, our governor sent four men on fowling, that so we might after a special manner rejoice together after we had gathered the fruit of our labors. They four in one day killed as much fowl as, with a little help besides, served the company almost a week. At which time, amongst other recreations, we exercised our arms, many of the Indians coming amongst us, and among the rest their greatest king, Massasoit, with some ninety men, whom for three days we entertained and feasted. And they went out and killed five deer, which they brought to the plantation and bestowed on our governor, and upon the captain and others. And although it be not always so plentiful as it was at this

VIRGINIA'S God be Thanked,
OR
A SERMON OF THANKSGIVING
FOR THE HAPPIE
succeffe of the affayres in
VIRGINIA this laft
yeare.

Preached by PATRICK COPLAND at Bow-Church in Cheapfide, before the Honorable VIRGINIA COMPANY, on Thurfday, the 18. of April 1622. And now publifhed by the Commandement of the faid honorable COMPANY.

Hereunto are adjoyned fome Epiftles, written firft in Latine (and now Englifhed) in the Eaft Indies by Peter Pope, an Indian youth, borne in the bay of Bengala, who was firft taught and converted by the faid P. C. And after baptized by Mafter Iohn Wood, Dr in Divinitie, in a famous Affembly before the Right Worfhipfull, the Eaft India Company, at S. Denis in Fan-Church ftreete in London, December 22. 1616.

LONDON
Printed by I. D. for William Sheffard and Iohn Bellamie, and are to be fold at his fhop at the two Greyhounds in Corne-hill, neere the Royall Exchange. 1622.

In April 1622 the Reverend Patrick Copland, a Virginia Company stockholder, preached this sermon before the members of the company. The sermon, which celebrated the achievements of the colonists, particularly seven years of peaceful relations with the Powhatan, was perhaps the most badly timed document in colonial history. Unbeknownst to either Copland or his audience, the Powhatan Rebellion had brought that peace to a cruel and bloody end just four weeks before he delivered the sermon.

time with us, yet by the goodness of God, we are so far from want that we often wish you partakers of our plenty.

The Great Migration

For almost a decade after the Pilgrims arrived in Plymouth, only a trickle of English men and women came to New England. But beginning in 1630, hundreds of English families began flooding into the newly established Massachusetts Bay Colony, north of Plymouth. Between 1630 and 1640, more than 13,000 men, women, and children made the Atlantic crossing to New England. Historians have debated the sources of the "Great Migration," as it came to be called, but one factor seems almost indisputable: religion. The vast majority of these migrants were, much like the Pilgrims, members of a dissident religious minority. These "Puritans," as their opponents called them, believed that the Church of England and, in turn, the English nation as a whole, needed spiritual purification. The New World seemed to offer the prospects of starting over, of building a new society from scratch, founded entirely on fundamental Biblical principles and freed from the corrupting influences of the Old World.

The prospects not only of worshipping as they wished, but also of living in the kind of society they had been envisioning for years, stimulated in Puritan migrants a heady sort of anticipation. This sentiment is particularly evident in a letter from the governor of the Massachusetts Bay Colony, John Winthrop, to his wife. The governor wrote this letter as he and several of his sons were about to set sail for New England. Winthrop's letter is also instructive for its personal content. Far from the ascetic, unfeeling Puritans so often depicted in such popular writings as Nathaniel Hawthorne's novel *The Scarlet Letter* (1850), it shows a loving husband and father who cannot conceal his conflicting emotions upon leaving his wife and his country.

April 28, 1629

My faithful and dear Wife,

It pleaseth God, that thou shouldst once again hear from me before our departure, and I hope this shall come safe to thy hands. I know it will be a great refreshing to thee. And blessed be his mercy, that I can write thee so good news, that we are all in very good health, and, having tried our ship's entertainment now more

Indian Corn

Like so many of the products we eat today, maize—or "Indian Corn" as the English called it—originated in the New World. Archaeologists and historians call the area encompassing much of what is now Mexico "Mesoamerica"—or middle America. Beginning in roughly 7000 BC, peoples in this region began cultivating a wild grass known as "teo-centli." Through a process of breeding and cultivation that lasted about 3,000 years, this grass became maize, which was somewhat like the corn we consume today. Over the course of the next few thousand years, trade carried maize across the North American continent where it became a crucial food for dozens of Native American societies.

than a week, we find it agree very well with us. Our boys are well and cheerful, and have no mind of home. They lie both with me, and sleep as soundly in a rug (for we use no sheets here) as ever they did at Groton [in England]; and so I do myself, (I praise God). The wind hath been against us this week and more; but this day it has come fair to the north, so as we are preparing (by God's assistance) to set sail in the morning. We have only four ships ready, and some two or three Hollanders go along with us. The rest of our fleet (being seven ships) will not be ready this sennight. We have spent now two Sabbaths on shipboard very comfortably, (God be praised,) and are daily more and more encouraged to look for the Lord's presence to go along with us. Henry Kingsbury hath a child or two in the Talbot sick of the measles, but like to do well. One of my men had them at Hampton, but he was soon well again. We are, in all our eleven ships, about seven hundred persons, passengers, and two hundred and forty cows, and about sixty horses. The ship, which went from Plimouth, carried about one hundred and forty persons, and the ship, which goes from Bristowe, carrieth about eighty persons. And now (my sweet soul) I must once again take my last farewell of thee in Old England. It goeth very near to my heart to leave thee; but I know to whom I have committed thee, even to him who loves thee much better than any husband can, who hath taken account of the hairs of thy head, and puts all thy tears in his bottle, who can, and (if it be for his glory) will bring us together again with peace and comfort. Oh, how it refresheth my heart, to think, that I shall yet again see thy sweet face in the land of the living!—that lovely countenance, that I have so much delighted in, and beheld with so great content! I have hitherto been so taken up with business, as I could seldom look back to my former happiness; but now, when I shall be at some leisure, I shall not avoid the remembrance of thee, nor the grief for thy absence. Thou hast thy share with me, but I hope the course we have agreed upon will be some ease to us both. Mondays and Fridays, at five of the clock at night, we shall meet in spirit till we meet in person. Yet, if all these hopes should fail, blessed be our God, that we are assured we shall meet one day, if not as husband and wife, yet in a better condition. Let that stay and comfort thy heart. Neither can the sea drown thy husband, nor enemies destroy, nor any adversary deprive thee of thy husband or children. Therefore I will only take thee now and my sweet children in mine arms, and kiss and embrace you all, and so leave you with my God. Farewell, farewell. I bless you all in the name of the Lord Jesus. I salute my daughter Winth. Matt. Nan.

Give Thanks for Turkey

Turkey, that indispensable part of any modern Thanksgiving dinner, may well have been eaten by the Pilgrims during their first Thanksgiving. They would have been familiar with the meaty birds, which had been consumed in England since the mid-16th century and abounded in New England. As the Reverend Francis Higginson explained in his 1630 pamphlet *Short and True Description of the Commodities and Discommodities of that Countrey,* "Here are likewise aboundance of Turkies often killed in the Woods, farre greater then our English Turkies, and exceeding fat, sweet and fleshy, for here they have aboundance of feeding all the yeere long, as Strawberries, in Summer all places are full of them, and all manner of Berries and Fruits."

John Winthrop's career as governor of the Massachusetts Bay Colony reflected the tumultuousness of colonial politics. He was voted out of office on three separate occasions and struggled through a nearly endless parade of political and theological crises.

and the rest, and all my good neighbors and friends. Pray all for us. Farewell. Commend my blessing to my son John. I cannot now write to him; but tell him I have committed thee and thine to him. Labor to draw him yet nearer to God, and he will be the surer staff of comfort to thee. I cannot name the rest of my good friends, but thou canst supply it. I wrote, a week since, to thee and Mr. Leigh, and divers others.

Thine wheresover,

Jo. Winthrop

One of the more striking qualities of the Great Migration is that it was mostly composed not of the poor, the downtrodden, or the wretched, but rather of people with means, people with comfortable levels of wealth, stable livelihoods, families, and homes. It was composed, in other words, of people relatively secure in the world. Why then, would such people pick up and leave this security for the uncertain prospects of life in a new land? Again, religion was the key factor. Puritans believed that what mattered was not life in this world, but rather life in the next world. They believed that one worked hard not to have a more comfortable life but to have a more comfortable afterlife. As the following poem by Puritan minister Thomas Tillam suggests, the constant sense of duty that this thinking entailed tempered whatever sense of excitement and hope Puritans may have felt upon arriving in America.

Upon the first sight of New-England
June 29, 1638

Hayle holy-land wherein our holy lord
Hath planted his most true and holy word
Hayle happye people who have dispossest
Your selves of friends, and meanes, to find some rest
For your poore wearied soules, opprest of late
For Jesus-sake, with Envye, spight, and hate
To yow that blessed promise truly's given
Of sure reward, which you'l receve in heaven
Methinks I heare the Lambe of God thus speake
Come my deare little flocke, who for my sake
Have lefte your Country, dearest friends, and goods
And hazarded your lives o'th raginge floods
Posses this Country; free from all anoye
Heare I'le bee with you, heare you shall Injoye

My sabbaths, sacraments, my minestrye
And ordinances in their puritye
But yet beware of Sathans wylye baites
Hee lurkes amongs yow, Cunningly hee waites
To Catch yow from mee; live not then secure
But fight 'gainst sinne, and let your lives be pure
Prepare to heare your sentence thus expressed
Come yee my servants of my father Blessed

   Thomas Tillam

The Puritans were not the only dissident religious group to seek refuge in North America. Another was a band of English Catholics, individuals who remained loyal not to the Protestant Church of England, but rather to the Roman Catholic Church. Perhaps even more than the Puritans, Catholics in England endured endless harassment and persecution. The idea of some sort of safe New World refuge was thus quite appealing. King Charles I agreed and in 1632, granted a prominent Catholic, George Calvert, the first Lord Baltimore, formal permission to establish the colony of Maryland

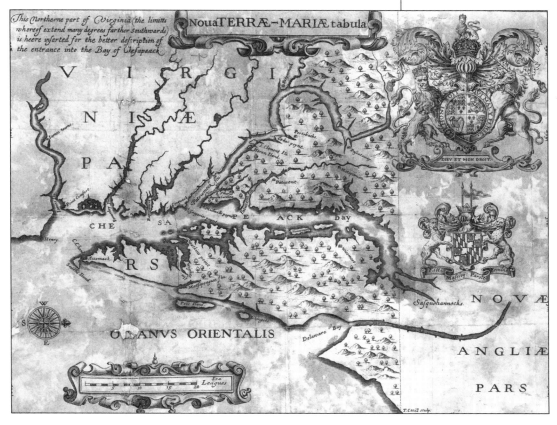

This map of Maryland appeared in the 1635 pamphlet A Relation of Maryland and was the first map of the new colony. Maryland was founded as a refuge for English Catholics.

The Terrifying Rattlesnake

Of all the hazards that colonists faced, few elicited as much dread as the terrifying rattlesnake. In his New England's Prospect *(1634), a work intended to promote settlement in New England, William Wood, who resided in Massachusetts during the early 1630s, could not ignore this American menace, but he did his best to minimize its powers:*

That which is most injurious to the person and life of man is a rattlesnake, which is generally a yard and a half long, as thick in the middle as the small of a man's leg. She hath a yellow belly, her back being spotted with black, russet, yellow, and green colors placed like scales; at her tail is a rattle with which she makes a noise when she is molested or when she seeth any approach near her. Her neck seems to be no thicker than a man's thumb yet can she swallow a squirrel, having a great wide mouth, with teeth as sharp as needles wherewith she biteth such as tread upon her . . . When any man is bitten by any of these creatures, the poison spreads so suddenly through the veins and so runs to the heart that in one hour it causeth death unless he hath the antidote to expell the poison, . . .

This is a most poisonous and dangerous creature, yet nothing so bad as the report goes of him in England. For whereas he is said to kill a man with his breath, and that he can fly, there is no such matter, for he is naturally the most sleepy and unnimble creature that lives, never offering to leap or bite any man if he be not trodden on first.

These letters indicate English currency denominations

l=pound
s=shilling
d=penny or pence

(named for King Charles I's queen, Henrietta Maria) on the northern banks of the Potomac River. Lord Baltimore died before the colony was actually established, but his son, Cecilius Calvert, the second Lord Baltimore, carried out his father's ambitious plan, and although he never actually visited the new colony, he spent his long life managing his family's American interests.

While Maryland was intended to be a refuge for English Catholics, it was also intended to be a profitable venture for its proprietors, the Calvert family. This would have been very difficult had the colony excluded everyone but Catholics. Lord Baltimore thus adopted an unusually tolerant religious doctrine in the colony, insisting that Catholic and Protestant colonists live peacefully together. And when, in 1634, colonists began arriving in Maryland, most of them were in fact Protestants, recruited by the Calverts to cultivate tobacco and other crops on land owned by them and several other prominent Catholic families. Whether Protestant or Catholic, these colonists were immigrants, and like all other immigrants to the new English colonies, they faced the prospect of life in a hostile environment, an environment that would yield the basic human necessities only with hard labor. Short-term survival thus depended on preparation. Aware of this fact, associates of Lord Baltimore produced a pamphlet in 1635 entitled *A Relation of Maryland*, which contained, among other things, the following list of essential provisions. Alongside each item is a price, presumably of value in helping potential colonists estimate the costs of going to America.

A particular of such necessary provisions as every Adventurer must carry, according to the number of his servants: together with an estimate of their prices.

In Victualls.

	l.	s.	d.
For one man, for a yeere,			
Imprimis, eight bushells of meale	2	8	0
Item, two bushells of Oatmeale	0	9	0
Item, one bushell of Pease	0	4	0
Item, one gallon of Oyle	0	3	6
Item, two gallons of Vinegar	0	2	0
Item, one gallon of Aquavite [a liquor]	0	2	6
Item, one bushell of Bay-salt	0	2	0
Item, in Sugar, Spice and Fruit	0	6	8
Summ.	3	17	8

In Apparrell.

For one man,	l.	s.	d.
Item, two Munmoth caps or hats	0	4	0
Item, three falling Bands	0	1	3
Item, three shirts	0	7	6
Item, one Wastcoate	0	2	2
Item, one suite of Canvas	0	7	6
Item, one suite of Frize	0	10	0
Item, one suite of Cloth	0	16	0
Item, one course cloth, or frize coate	0	15	0
Item, three paire of stockings	0	4	0
Item, six paire of shooes	0	13	0
Item, Inkle [broad tape] for garters	0	0	2
Item, one dozen of points [laces]	0	0	3
Summ.	4	0	10

In Bedding.

For two men,	l.	s.	d.
Item, two paire of Canvas sheets	0	16	0
Item, seven ells of Canvas to make a bed and boulster to be fill'd in the country	0	8	0
Item, one Rugg for a bed	0	8	0
Item, five ells of course Canvas to make a bed at Sea, to be fill'd with straw	0	4	0
Item, one course Rugg at Sea	0	6	0
Summ.	2	2	0
whereof one mans part is,	1	1	0

In Armes.

For one man,	l.	s.	d
Item, one musket	1	0	0
Item, 10 pound of Powder	0	11	0
Item, 40 pound of Lead, Bullets, Pistoll and Goose shot, of each sort some.	0	4	0
Item, one sword	0	5	0
Item, one belt	0	1	0
Item, one bandeleere and flaske	0	2	0
Item, in Match	0	2	6
Summ.	2	5	6

In Tooles.

For five persons, and so after the rate for more or lesse.	l.	s.	d
Item, 5 broad Howes, at 2 s. a piece	0	10	0
Item, 5 narrow Howes, at 16 d. a piece	0	6	8
Item, 2 broad Axes, at 3 s. 8 d. a piece	0	7	4

Few textiles remain from the early colonial era. These remarkable examples—a ceremonial shirt and mitts for performing a christening—belonged to Governor William Bradford of Plymouth.

Prospective colonists could expect to spend much of their time in the New World building things—particularly houses and fences—making tools such as this handsaw, vise, compass, and hammer indispensable.

	l.	s.	d.
Item, 5 felling Axes, at 1 s. 6 d. a piece	0	7	6
Item, 2 steele Hand-sawes, at 1 s. 4 d.	0	2	8
Item, Two-handsawes at 5 s.	0	10	0
Item, a Whip-saw set and filed, with boxe, file and wrest	0	10	0
Item, 2 Hammers, at 12 d.	0	2	0
Item, 3 Shovells, at 1 s. 6 d.	0	4	6
Item, 3 Spades, at 1 s. 6 d.	0	4	6
Item, 2 Awgurs, at 6 d.	0	1	0
Item, 6 Chissells at 6 d.	0	3	0
Item, 2 Piercers stocked, at 4 d.	0	0	8
Item, 3 Gimlets, [a tool for boring holes] at 2 d.	0	0	6
Item, 2 Hatchets, at 1 s. 9 d.	0	3	6
Item, 2 Frowes [wedge for splitting logs] to cleave Pales, at 1 s. 6 d.	0	3	0
Item, 2 Hand-bills, at 1 s. 8 d.	0	3	4
Item, one Grindstone	0	4	0
Item, Nailes of all sorts	2	0	0
Item, 2 Pickaxes, at 1 s. 6 d.	0	3	0
Summ.	6	7	2
whereof one mans part is	1	5	8

Houshold Implements.			
For 6 persons, and so after the rate, for more	l.	s.	d.
Item, one Iron pot	0	7	0
Item, one Iron kettle	0	6	0
Item, one large Frying-pan	0	2	6
Item, one Gridiron	0	1	6
Item, two Skillets	0	5	0
Item, one Spit	0	2	0
Item, Platters, Dishes, and spoones of wood	0	4	0
Summ.	1	8	0
whereof one mans part is,	0	4	8

However well prepared early-American immigrants may have been, the immigrant experience was still extremely difficult. For the basic fact of colonial life was that it involved "starting anew" in the fullest sense of the phrase. Arriving colonists had to build houses, clear land for fields and pastures, and form entirely new towns and communities—something few of them had ever done. Land was abundant, but almost everything else was scarce and costly.

Whereas in England, an ordinary farmer could simply walk into town to trade for tools or cloth or nails, early colonists often had to fashion such goods themselves or wait for the next ship from England—a wait that could be months long. And when those ships arrived, the goods they bore were often extremely expensive. With little to show from their own labors and a pressing need for costly imported goods, many colonists thus found themselves fighting to stave off complete poverty.

This fight is given a poignant immediacy in the following letter home from a young Massachusetts colonist, about whom we know nothing other than his last name: Pond.

To my loving father William Pond, at Etherston in Suffolk, give this. Most loving and kind Father and Mother:

My humble duty [be] remembered unto you, trusting in God you are in good health. And, I pray, remember my love unto my brother Joseph and thank him for his kindness that I found at his hand at London, which was not the value of a farthing. I know, loving father, and do confess that I was an undutiful child unto you when I lived with you and by you, for the which I am much sorrowful and grieved for it, trusting in God that He will guide me that I will never offend you so anymore; and I trust in God you will forgive me for it.

[The reason for] my writing this unto you is to let you understand what a country this New England is, where we live. Here are but few Indians; a great part of them died this winter; it was thought it was [because] of the plague. They are a crafty people, and they will cozen and cheat, and they are a subtle people. And whereas we did expect great store of beaver, here is little or none to be had; . . . They are proper men and clean-jointed men, and many of them go naked with a skin about their loins, but now some of them get Englishmen's apparel. And the country is very rocky and hilly, and [there is] some champion ground, and the soil is very flete. And here is some good ground and marsh ground, but here is no Michaelmas. Spring cattle thrive well here, but they give small store of milk. The best cattle for profit is swine, and a good swine is here at five pounds' price. . . . Here are good stores of wild fowl, but they are hard to come by. It is harder to get a shot than it is in old England. And people here are subject to disease, for here have died of the scurvy and of the burning fever nigh two hundred and odd. Besides, as many lyeth lame; and all Sudbury [a newly founded town] men are dead but three, and [some] women and some children; and provisions are here at a wonderful [high]

Michaelmas

The September 29 feast celebrating St. Michael the Archangel.

rate. Wheat meal is 14 shillings a bushel, and peas 10 shillings, and malt 10 shillings, and Einder seed wheat is 15 shillings, and their other wheat is 10 shillings. Butter [is] 12 pence a pound, and cheese is 8 pence a pound, and all kind of spices [are] very dear and [there are] almost none to be got.

. . . loving father, I would entreat you that you would send me a firkin of butter and a hogshead of malt unground, for we drink nothing but water; and a coarse cloth of four pounds price, so it [will] be thick. [As] for the freight, if you of your love will send them I will pay the freight. . . . Here is no cloth to be had to make no apparel; and shoes are at five shillings a pair for me; and that cloth that is worth two shillings [and] eight pence a yard is worth here five shillings. So I pray, father, send me four or five yards of cloth to make us some apparel. And, loving father, though I be far distant from you, yet I pray you remember me as your child. And we do not know how long we may subsist, for we cannot live here without provisions from old England. Therefore, I pray, do not put away your shop stuff, for I think that in the end, if I live, it must be my living. For we do not know how long this plantation will stand, for some of the magnates that did uphold it have turned off their men and have given it over. Besides, God hath taken away the chiefest stud in the land, Mr. Johnson, and the lady Arabella, his wife, which was the chiefest man of estate in the land and one that would have done most good.

Here came over 25 passangers, and there came back again four score and odd persons; and as many more would have come if they had wherewithal to bring them home. For here are many that came over last year, which was worth two hundred pounds before they came out of old England, that between this [time] and Michaelmas will hardly be worth 30 pounds. So here we may live if we have supplies every year from old England; otherwise we cannot subsist. I may, as I will, work hard, set an acre of Einder wheat; . . . , if we set it without fish [a costly fertilizer], they shall have but a poor crop. So, father, I pray, consider of my case; for here will be but a very poor being—no being—without, loving father, your help with provisions from old England. I had thought to have come home in this ship, for my provisions were almost all spent; but [you should know] that I humbly thank you for your great love and kindess in sending me some provisions, or else I should and might have been half famished. But now I will—if it please God that I have my health—I will plant what corn I can; and if provisions be not cheaper between this [time] and Michaelmas, and [assuming] that I do not hear from you what I was best [advised] to do, I purpose to come home at Michaelmas.

My wife remembers her humble duty unto you and to my mother; and my love to my brother Joseph and to Sarah Myler. Thus I leave you to the protection of the Almighty God.

From Watertown in New England, the 15 of March, 1630.

The vast majority of men and women who came to the colonies left no record. We can never know for certain why they came, or how they fared. But there are documents that tell us basic facts about these people. Especially valuable are the passenger lists that ships' captains and ships' owners kept. They tell us exactly who traveled to America and when; they tell us the age of passengers; they often indicate family relations among passengers; sometimes they indicate occupations; and they tell us the proportions of men and women among passengers. Such information is especially valuable for understanding the varying social character of the American colonies. The passenger list from a ship bound for Virginia includes mostly unrelated men and few women. The passenger list from a ship bound for Massachusetts includes entire families and their servants.

Ultimo [last] July, 1635

These underwritten names are to be transported to Virginia, embarked in the *Merchant's Hope,* Hugh Weston, Master, per examination by the minister of Gravesend touching their conformity to the Church discipline of England, and have taken the oaths of allegiance and supremacy:

Edward Towers	26	Charles Rinsden	27
Henry Woodman	22	Jo. Exston	17
Richard Seems	26	Wm. Luck	14
Allin King	19	Jo. Thomas	19
Rowland Sadler	19	Jo. Archer	21
Jo. Phillips	28	Richard Williams	25
Vyncent Whatter	17	Francis Hutton	20
James Whithedd	14	Savill Gascoyne	29
Jonas Watts	21	Rich. Bulfell	29
Peter Loe	22	Rich. Jones	26
Geo. Brocker	17	Tho. Wynes	30
Henry Eeles	26	Humphrey Williams	22
Jo. Dennis	22	Edward Roberts	20
Tho. Swayne	23	Martin Atkinson	32

"From Dane, from Hollander, and Swede, from Wales, and from the north of Tweed our first Supply's came o'er, from france a band of refugees, and from fair Ireland rapparees, came crowding to this Shore a mungrell brood of canting Saints, that filled all Europe with complaints came here to fix their stakes."

—Governor Lewis Morris on immigrants to the colony of New Jersey, in a poem from the 1730s

Although healthier conditions, a different work ethic, and less contentious race relations gave the settlers of Massachusetts longer life expectancies than those in the southern colonies, few lived as long as Anne Pollard. She was the last surviving member of the 1630 migration and this portrait was painted on her 100th birthday.

Edward Atkinson	28	Richard Williams	18
Wm. Edwards	30	Jo. Ballance	19
Nathan Braddock	31	Wm. Baldin	21
Jeffrey Gurrish	23	Wm. Pen	26
Henry Carrell	16	Jo. Gerie	24
Tho. Ryle	24	Henry Baylie	18
Gamaliel White	24	Rich. Anderson	50
Richard Marks	19	Robert Kelum	51
Tho. Clever	16	Richard Fanshaw	22
Jo. Kitchin	16	Tho. Bradford	40
Edmond Edwards	20	Wm. Spencer	16
Lewes Miles	19	Marmaduke Ella	22
Jo. Kennedy	20		
Sam Jackson	24	**WOMEN**	
Daniel Endick	16	Ann Swayne	22
Jo. Chalk	25	Eliz. Cote	22
Jo. Vynall	20	Ann Rice	23
Edward Smith	20	Kat. Wilson	23
Jo. Rowlidge	19	Maudlin Lloyd	24
Wm. Westlie	40	Mabell Busher	14
Jo. Smith	18	Annis Hopkins	24
Jo. Saunders	22	Ann Mason	24
Tho. Bartcherd	16	Bridget Crompe	18
Tho. Dodderidge	19	Mary Hawkes	19
		Ellin Hawkes	18

The people on this list were bound for New England from Weymouth on the southern coast of England.

WEYMOUTH [ENGLAND], THE 20TH OF MARCH, 1635

1. Joseph Hull, of Somerset, a minister, aged 40 years
2. Agnes Hull, his wife, aged 25 years
3. Joan Hull, his daughter, aged 15 years
4. Joseph Hull, his son, aged 13 years
5. Tristram, his son, aged 11 years
6. Elizabeth Hull, his daughter, aged 7 years
7. Temperance, his daughter, aged 9 years
8. Grissell Hull, his daughter, aged 5 years
9. Dorothy Hull, his daughter, aged 3 years
10. Judith French, his servant, aged 20 years
11. John Wood, his servant, aged 20 years
12. Robert Dabyn, his servant, aged 28 years
13. Musachiall Bernard, of Batcombe, clothier

in the county of Somerset, 24 years
14. Mary Bernard, his wife, aged 28 years
15. John Bernard, his son, aged 3 years
16. Nathaniel, his son, aged 1 year
17. Rich. Persons, salter and his servant, 30 years
18. Francis Baber, chandler, aged 36 years
19. Jesope, joyner, aged 22 years
20. Walter Jesop, weaver, aged 21 years
21. Timothy Tabor, in Somerset of Batcombe, tailor, aged 35 years
22. Jane Tabor, his wife, aged 35 years
23. Jane Tabor, his daughter, aged 10 years
24. Anne Tabor, his daughter, aged 8 years
25. Sarah Tabor, his daughter, aged 5 years
26. William Fever, his servant, aged 20 years
27. John Whitmarke, aged 39 years
28. Alice Whitmarke, his wife, aged 35 years
29. James Whitmarke, his son, aged 11 years
30. Jane, his daughter, aged 7 years
31. Onseph Whitmarke, his son, aged 5 years
32. Rich. Whitmarke, his son, aged 2 years
33. William Read, of Batcombe, taylor in Somerset, aged 28 years
34. [name not entered]
35. Susan Read, his wife, aged 29 years
36. Hannah Read, his daughter, aged 3 years
37. Susan Read, his daughter, aged 1 year
38. Rich. Adams, his servant, 29 years
39. Mary, his wife, aged 26 years
40. Mary Cheame, his daughter, aged 1 year
41. Zachary Bickewell, aged 45 years
42. Agnes Bickewell, his wife, aged 27 years
43. John Bickewell, his son, aged 11 years
44. John Kitchin, his servant, 23 years
46. George Allin, aged 24 years
47. Katherine Allin, his wife, aged 30 years
48. George Allin, his son, aged 16 years
49. William Allin, his son, aged 8 years
50. Matthew Allin, his son, aged 6 years
51. Edward Poole, his servant, aged 26 years

Chapter Three

Colonists Confront First Nations

ontrary to what they often said, the English did not find a barren wilderness in North America. Instead, they found a land occupied by native peoples, peoples who farmed and hunted on that land; who fought amongst themselves for possession of that land; who crisscrossed that land—from the lower Mississippi Valley to Nova Scotia, from Florida to the Great Lakes—with an interwoven web of trails; and who organized on that land a vast network of trade that moved goods from one end of the continent to the other.

And the English colonists, as is all too well known, often clashed with these peoples, engaging in some of the bloodiest warfare anywhere in the contemporary Western world. In the early 17th century, when the English presence was small, the dimensions of these battles were small, albeit cruel and violent. Through the course of the 17th and 18th centuries, their scope expanded, as did their devastating effects on Native American and European towns and settlements. Indeed, it is fair to say that for most of the 18th century, western parts of Virginia, Pennsylvania, South and North Carolina, and to a lesser extent Georgia and New York, were plagued by near-constant warfare. This warfare disrupted families, shattered lives, and left thousands dead.

The cause of much of this conflict was land. As colonists transformed forests into pastures and fields, as they allowed their domestic animals to roam freely through the countryside, the hunting grounds upon which Native American communities depended began to disappear. Indians were then forced to move to new hunting grounds, which often were already claimed by other, hostile native groups. Caught between such hostile Indians on the one side and land-hungry

Colonial diplomatic meetings, such as that depicted in this 20th-century rendering, were usually complex, highly ritualized affairs, often involving lengthy orations by Native American spokesmen.

Wampum—small beads made from seashells that were often strung together in elaborate belts—was for eastern native peoples the equivalent of a signature for the English. At diplomatic meetings, Indians presented wampum as a gesture of trust and allegiance. In 1665 native peoples residing in the lower Hudson Valley gave this particular belt to Richard Nicolls, leader of the English conquest of what became New York State.

colonists on the other, and facing dwindling resources, native peoples periodically resorted to war. Although this response produced much suffering among the colonists, over the long run it did little to stem the ceaseless expansion of colonial settlements.

Perhaps the natives would have been better able to counter European intrusions had it not been for one additional factor: disease. As we have seen, European diseases wreaked havoc on the native societies of eastern North America. Before the English had even established permanent settlements, sporadic contact with disease-carrying explorers, fishermen, and mariners had had devastating effects on native societies. Whole communities perished, and many that remained were severely weakened, often little more than collections of refugees from earlier epidemics, scarcely able to feed themselves, let alone defend their lands from aggressive Europeans.

All this might lead us to conclude that Native Americans became merely hapless victims of colonization, that they were simply trampled by more powerful colonists. But this was not the case. After the initial shock waves of disease and war, surviving native peoples began finding ways to adapt to their own "new world." In part, this meant giving up hunting lands; it meant abandoning traditional modes of agriculture; it meant embracing new kinds of commerce; and it meant altering traditional religious practices. But it also meant sustaining formidable political barriers to the growing European presence.

A number of native groups in eastern North America had organized into powerful confederacies, or agglomerations of tribes, the most powerful of which was the great Iroquois Confederacy in what is now upstate New York. Much like the European powers they sought to counter, these confederacies had considerable economic, diplomatic, and military power. And they effectively used that power to gain concessions from European nations. Indeed, over the course of the 18th century, the British government found itself increasingly dependent on Native American allies. Without them, this most powerful of European states would have been unable to resist the American expansion of France, its archrival. This, in turn, created a strange situation: the British Crown was increasingly obliged to protect native peoples from its own land-hungry subjects.

Such developments should not, however, mask the fundamental tragedy of Native American history in the colonial era. As European colonies expanded, native societies shrank. Disease, war, even famine, all took their toll on native peoples. But none of these factors weighs as heavily as the unrelenting European appetite for land. That appetite drew thousands of immigrants to North America, and allowed the European population in North America to double every 25 years during the 18th century. And it was that appetite that gave the vast majority of immigrants a sense that the land was rightfully theirs, and that Native Americans were merely impediments to the proper use of that land.

War

By 1620, Virginia Company officials had begun to recognize that their only hope for financial success lay not in discovering precious metals, gems, or other valuable commodities, but rather in cultivating a potentially lucrative crop: tobacco. As they implemented policies intended to spur tobacco production, company officials stimulated the rapid geographic growth of the Virginia Colony, growth that intruded on local Indian lands—a development that Opechancanough, leader of the powerful Powhatan Confederacy, found increasingly intolerable.

Frustrated by this English onslaught, on the morning of Good Friday, 1622, he led the Powhatan in a violent attack on the colonists, nearly obliterating the Jamestown settlement. Some 350 English men, women, and children were killed; livestock, food stores, and homes were destroyed. In total, one third of the colony's population perished. Opechancanough and his warriors might have killed the entire English population, but a warning delivered to the colonists by a friendly Indian on the morning of the attack saved many lives. Although the attack was a military victory for the Powhatan, it was a huge propaganda victory for some colonial officials.

The cruelty of the 1622 massacre, these officials proclaimed, demonstrated once and for all that the natives lacked all humanity, and therefore English dealings with them no longer had to be constrained by the rule of law or feelings of compassion. Now the colonists could freely drive Native Americans from their lands, enslave them, and otherwise treat them like inferior beings. This view is expressed in

Who Owns the Land?

The English generally believed that Native Americans did not fully exploit the land through farming and pasturage, and therefore had no rightful claim of ownership. As the influential 17th-century philosopher John Locke explained, it was God's intention that what a man "tilled and reaped, laid up and made use of, . . . that was his [property]; whatsoever he enclosed [to make a pasture] . . . was also his. But if either the Grass of his Inclosure rotted on the Ground, or the Fruit of his planting perished without gathering, . . . this part of the earth, . . . was still to be looked on as Waste, and might be the Possession of any other."

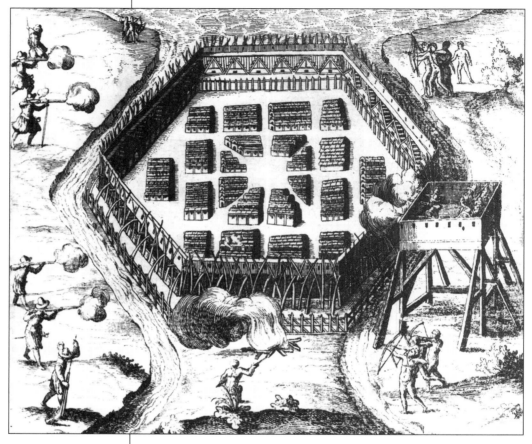

This image depicting an attack by French soldiers and their Indian allies on an Indian village might suggest that Europeans had a monopoly on firearms. In fact, by the end of the 17th century, most eastern native groups also possessed these European weapons.

the records of the Virginia Company by Edward Waterhouse, a Jamestown colonist.

"We perceive and well know you intend to destroy us, that are here to intreat and desire your friendship, and to enjoy our houses and plant our fields, of whose fruit you shall participate: otherwise you will have the worse by our absence; for we can plant any where, . . . and we know you cannot live if you want our harvest, and that reliefe we bring you. If you promise us peace, we will beleeve you; if you proceed in revenge we will abandon the Country."

—The orator Okaning warning Captain John Smith and the Jamestown colonists of their fate if they refuse peace with the Powhatan Indians. John Smith reproduced the speech in his greatest written work, *The Generall Historie of Virginia, New-England, and the Summer Isles . . .* (1624)

Thus haue you seene the particulars of this massacre, . . . wherein treachery and cruelty haue done their worst to vs, or rather to themselues; for whose vnderstanding is so shallow, as not to perceiue that this must needs bee for the good of the Plantation after, and the losse of this blood to make the body more healthfull, as by these reasons may be manifest.

First, Because betraying of innocency neuer rests unpunished:

Secondly, Because our hands which before were tied with gentlenesse and faire vsage, are now set at liberty by the treacherous violence of the Sauages, not vntying the Knot, but cutting it: So that we, who hitherto haue had possession of no more ground then their waste, and our purchase at a valuable consideration to their owne contentment, gained; may now by right of Warre, and law of Nations, inuade the Country, and destroy them who sought to destroy vs: whereby wee shall enioy their cultiuated places, . . . Now their cleared grounds in all their villages . . . shall be inhabited by vs, whereas heretofore the grubbing [clearing] of woods was the greatest labour.

Thirdly, Because those commodities which the Indians enjoyed as much or rather more than we, shall now also be entirely possessed by vs. The Deere and other beasts will be in safety, and infinitly increase, which heretofore . . . were destroied at all times of the yeare, without any difference of Male, Damme, or Young. The like may be said of our owne Swine and Goats, whereof they haue used to kill eight in tenne more than the English haue done. There will be also a great increase of wild Turkies, and other waighty Fowle, for the Indians neuer put difference of destroying the Hen, but kill them whether in season or not, whether in breeding time, or sitting on their egges, or hauing new hatched, it is all one to them: whereby, as also by the orderly vsing of their fishing Weares, no knowne Country in the world will so plentifully abound in victuall.

Fourthly, Because the way of conquering them is much more easie then of ciuilizing them by faire meanes, for they are a rude, barbarous, and naked people, scattered in small companies, which are helps to Victorie, but hinderances to Ciuilitie: Besides that, a conquest may be of many, and at once; but ciuilitiy is in particular, and slow, the effect of long time, and great industry. Moreover, victorie of them may bee gained many waies; by force, by surprize, by famine in burning their Corne, by destroying and burning their Boats, Canoes, and Houses, by breaking their fishing Weares, by assailing them in their huntings, whereby they get the greatest part of their sustenance in Winter, by pursuing and chasing them with our horses, and blood-Hounds to draw after them, and Mastiues [mastiff, a large, powerful breed of dog] to teare them, which take this naked, tanned, deformed Sauages, for no other then wild beasts, and are so fierce and fell vpon them, that they feare them worse then their old Deuill which they worship, supposing them to be a new and worse kinde of Deuils then their owne. By these and sundry other wayes, as by driuing them (when they flye) vpon their enemies, who are round about them, and by animating and abetting their enemies against them, may their ruine or subjection be soone effected. . . .

Fiftly, Because the *Indians*, who before were vsed as friends, may now most iustly be compelled to seruitude and drudgery, and supply the roome of men that labour, whereby euen the meanest of the Plantation may imploy themselues more entirely in their Arts and Occupations, which are more generous, whilest Sauages performe their inferiour workes of digging in mynes, and the like, . . .

A More Compassionate View of the Natives

Waterhouse's view was considerably different from that of early promoters of the Virginia venture. As Robert Gray wrote in *A Good Speed to Virginia* (1609), "it is everie mans dutie to travell both by sea and land, and to venture either with his person or with his purse, to bring the barbarous and savage people [of America] to a civill and Christian kinde of government, under which they may learne how to live holily, justly, and soberly in this world, and to apprehend the meanes to save their soules in the world to come, rather than to destroy them, or utterly to roote them out."

Native peoples employed a wide range of methods for obtaining food and trade goods. Shorebirds provided both—in the form of meat and feathers—to peoples living along the North Atlantic.

Sixtly, This will for euer hereafter make vs more cautelous [cautious] and circumspect, as never to bee deceiued more by any other treacheries, but will serue for a great instruction to all posteritie there, to teach them that *Trust is the mother of Deceipt,* . . . and make them know that kindnesses are misspent vpon rude natures, so long as they continue rude; as also, that Sauages and Pagans are aboue all other for matter of Iustice ever to be suspected. . . .

Lastly, We haue this benefit more to our comfort, because all good men doe now take much more care of vs then before, since the fault is on their sides, not on ours.

Instead of a powerful Native American confederacy, colonists in the Massachusetts Bay area encountered scattered and dissipated Algonquian-speaking peoples. Between 1616 and 1619, epidemics killed 90 percent of the native population of eastern Massachusetts, leaving the remnants vulnerable to attack by more powerful groups to the south and west. Tipping the balance even further in favor of the English, a smallpox epidemic swept through eastern Massachusetts in 1633. In his journal, John Winthrop vividly recounts the devastating

effects of the epidemic. But what is perhaps most striking about Winthrop's account is the apparent desire of dying natives to be embraced by the Englishmen's God.

[December, 1633] 5. John Sagamore died of the smallpox, and almost all his people (above 30 buried by Mr. Maverick of Winesementt in one day). The [English] towns in the [Massachusetts] Bay took away many of the children, but most of them died soon after. James Sagamore of Saugus died also, and most of his folk. John Sagamore desired to be brought among the English (so he was) and promised (if he recovered) to live with the English and serve their God. He left one son which he disposed to Mr. Wilson, the pastor of Boston, to be brought up by him. He gave to the governor a good quantity of wampumpeag [wampum], and to divers others of the English he gave gifts and took order for the payment of his own debts and his men's. He died in a persuasion that he should go to the Englishmen's God. Divers of them in their sickness confessed that the Englishmen's God was a good God and that if they recovered they would serve him.

It wrought much with them that when their own people forsook them yet the English came daily and ministered to them, and yet few (only 2 families) took any infection by it. Among others, Mr. Maverick of Winnissimet is worthy of a perpetual remembrance. Himself, his wife, and servants went daily to them, ministered to their necessities, and buried their dead, and took home many of their children. So did other of the neighbors. . . .

[February, 1634]. . . . Such of the Indians' children as were left were taken by the English, most . . . did die of the pox soon after; 3 only remaining, whereof one which the governor kept was called Knowe God (the Indians' usual answer being, when they were put in mind of God, Me no know God).

English and Dutch settlers who began migrating to Connecticut in the mid-1630s found a situation more like that of Virginia than of Massachusetts. The Pequots dominated a large portion of the region, extending from the Thames River to Rhode Island and across the Long Island Sound to portions of Long Island itself. For colonists in the region, the powerful Pequot presence constituted a serious threat. To counter that threat, authorities from Connecticut, Massachusetts Bay, and the Plymouth Colony elected to combine forces and enlist the help of the Pequots' Narraganset enemies in preparation for full-scale war. In late May 1637, an English force surrounded

Though Native Americans did not initially possess alphabetic writing, by the mid-18th century, many had begun to use it for communication. Catawba Indians wrote this letter to the governor of South Carolina describing a smallpox epidemic that hit the tribe in 1759.

the **Pequot stronghold at Mystic, Connecticut, set fire to some 80 huts housing 8,000 Indians, and killing as many as 700 men, women, and children in a single hour. Over the course of the next year, surviving Pequots were pursued by the English and their Indian allies. Some were enslaved and taken to English colonies in the West Indies; others were forced to join former enemy tribes as slaves; and others were simply killed. By the fall of 1638, the powerful Pequot Nation had been almost entirely dispersed, and English dominance in southeastern Connecticut had been secured.**

In his history of Plymouth Plantation, Governor William Bradford described the genesis of the Pequot conflict and the English attack at Mystic. His account suggests that, like most frontier battles, this one was far from a simple affair of Indians against Europeans. The natives often formed alliances with Europeans, and similarly, Europeans worked endlessly to build alliances with native groups, groups that were in most cases much better equipped than the colonists to fight in the American backcountry. Bradford's account also suggests that the Pequot War was a particularly cruel and bloody war. But in reality, the violence depicted here was all too typical of interracial conflict in colonial America.

"In our first war with the Indians, God pleased to shew us the vanity of our military skill, in managing our arms, after the European mode. Now we are glad to learn the [Indians'] skulking way of war."

—Puritan missionary John Eliot describes the colonists' new way of war in a letter to his patron Robert Boyle (1677)

In the fore part of this year [1637], the Pequots fell openly upon the English at Connecticut, in the lower parts of the river, and slew sundry of them as they were at work in the fields, both men and women, to the great terrour of the rest, and went away in great pride and triumph, with many high threats. . . .

. . . the Pequots . . . sought to make peace with the Narragansetts, and used very pernicious arguments to move them thereunto: as that the English were strangers and began to overspread their country, and would deprive them thereof in time, if they were suffered to grow and increase. And if the Narragansetts did assist the English to subdue them, they did but make way for their own overthrow, for if they were rooted out, the English would soon take occasion to subjugate them. And if they would hearken to them they should not need to fear the strength of the English, for they would not come to open battle with them but fire their houses, kill their cattle, and lie in ambush for them as they went abroad upon their occasions; and all this they might easily do without any or little danger to themselves. The which course being held, they well saw the English could not long subsist but they would either be starved with hunger or be forced to forsake the country. . . . [W]hen they considered how much wrong they had received from the Pequots, and what an opportunity they now had by the help of the English to right themselves; revenge was so sweet unto them as it prevailed above all the rest, so as they resolved to join with the English against [the Pequots], and did. . . .

From Connecticut, who were most sensible of the hurt sustained and the present danger, they set out a party of men, and another party met them from the [Massachusetts] Bay, at Narragansetts', who were to join with them. The Narragansetts were earnest to be gone before the English were well rested and

Captain John Underhill's depiction of the English assault on the Pequot fort at Mystic, Connecticut, in 1637 was widely published. The attack resulted in the deaths of hundreds of Pequots, many of whom were women and children.

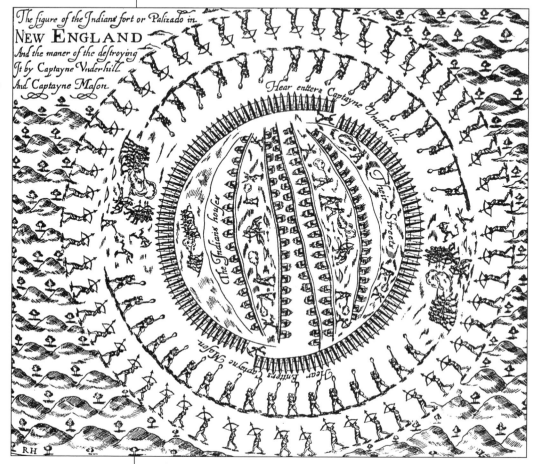

refeshed, especially some of them which came last. It should seem their desire was to come upon the enemy suddenly and undiscovered. There was a bark [small sailing ship] of this place, newly put in there, which was come from Connecticut, who did encourage them to lay hold of the Indians' forwardness, and to show as great forwardness as they, for it would encourage them, and [an] expedition might prove to their great advantage. So they went on, and so ordered their march as the Indians brought them to a fort of the enemy's (in which most of their chief men were) before day. They approached the same with great silence and surrounded it both with English and Indians, that they might not break out; and so assaulted them with great courage, shooting amongst them, and entered the fort with all speed. And those that first entered found sharp resistance from the enemy who both shot at and grappled with them; others ran into their houses and brought out fire and set them on fire, . . . and standing close together, with the wind all was quickly on a flame, and thereby more were burnt to death than was otherwise slain; It burnt their bowstrings and made them unserviceable; those that scaped the fire were slain with the sword, some hewed to pieces, others run through with their rapiers, so as they were quickly dispatched and very few escaped. It was conceived they thus destroyed about 400 at this time. It was a fearful sight to see them thus frying in the fire and the streams of blood quenching the same, and horrible was the stink and scent thereof; but the victory seemed a sweet sacrifice, and they gave the praise thereof to God, who had wrought so wonderfully for them, thus to enclose their enemies in their hands and give them so speedy a victory over so proud and insulting an enemy.

Captured by the Indians

For nearly 50 years after the Pequot War, southern New England was a relatively tranquil place. But the continued influx of English immigrants, the proliferation of a new, native-born Anglo-American population, and the relatively long lifespans of New Englanders meant a significant rise in population. That rise, in turn, meant an ever-expanding appetite for new farmlands. By the 1670s, native groups that had been driven to the far fringes of English settlement in the 1630s began finding themselves living alongside the English. Whatever frustrations these developments entailed for native peoples were aggravated by events surrounding the murder of John Sassamon, a Christian Indian and interpreter. Authorities at Plymouth accused, tried, and executed three Native Americans for the crime, prompting the Wampanoag leader, Metacom (or King Philip as he was known among the English), to initiate a rebellion that swept through southern and central New England. The rebellion has come to be known as King Philip's War, perhaps the cruelest and bloodiest of all colonial wars.

For colonists, one of the more startling aspects of the war was the tendency of enemy Native Americans to capture seemingly innocent white women and children. The experience of these "captives" was never more vividly depicted than in the account of Mary Rowlandson, a minister's wife from Lancaster, Massachusetts, who was held captive for three months. Mary's account is filled with tales of her own suffering, but it also provides glimpses of some of the more ordinary aspects of a captive's life. In the following passage,

"If dogs were trained up to hunt Indians as they do bears, . . . these dogs would be such a terror to them that after a little experience it would prevent their coming, and men would live more safely in their houses and work more safely in the fields and woods."

—1703 letter from the Reverend Solomon Stoddard to Governor Joseph Dudley of Massachusetts explaining how to prevent frontier violence

Mary describes her first night in captivity, and her discovery that captivity meant, among other things, sleeping outside, with little protection from the elements.

Now away we must go with those Barbarous Creatures, with our bodies wounded and bleeding, and our hearts no less than our bodies. About a mile we went that night, up upon a hill within sight of the Town, where they intended to lodge. There was hard by a vacant house (deserted by the English before, for fear of the *Indians*). I asked them whither I might not lodge in the house that night? to which they answered, what will you love *English-men* still? This was the dolefullest night that ever my eyes saw: oh the roaring, and singing and dancing, and yelling of those black creatures in the night, which made the place a lively resemblance of hell! And as miserable was the waste that was there made of Horses, Cattle, Sheep, Swine, Calves, Lambs, Roasting Pigs, and Fowls, (which they had plundered in the Town,) some roasting, some lying and burning, and some boyling, to feed our merciless Enemies; who were joyful enough, though we were disconsolate.

In the next passage, Mary describes the most traumatic event of her captivity: the death of her youngest child, Sarah. Her description of this event reveals much about the natives' way of dealing with death, as well as about Mary's status as a captive—she was not a mere prisoner of war, but rather the servant of an Indian chief and his several wives.

Nine dayes I sat upon my knees, with my babe in my lap, till my flesh was raw again; my child, being even ready to depart this sorrowful world, they bad me carry it out to another Wigwam . . . whither I went with a very heavy heart, and down I sate with the picture of death in my lap. About two hours in the Night, my sweet Babe, like a Lamb, departed this life, . . . In the morning, when they understood that my child was dead, they sent for me home to my Master's Wigwam: (by my Master, in this writing, must be understood Quannopin, who was a Saggamore, and married King Philip's wife's Sister; not that he first took me, but I was sold to him by another *Narhaganset Indian,* who took me when first I came out of the Garrison). I went to take up my dead Child in my arms to carry it with me, but they bid me let it alone; there was no resisting, but go I must and leave it. When I had been a while at my Master's wigwam, I took the first opportunity I could get to go look after my dead child. When I came, I asked them what

Saggamore

A Native American political leader, also known as a sachem

they had done with it. They told me it was upon the hill; then they went and shewed me where it was, where I saw the ground was newly digged, and there they told me they had buried it.

In this final section, Mary describes some of the events leading up to her release from captivity. The passage is particularly interesting for what it says about the predicament of Mary's native captors. Even though King Philip's War began as a rebellion against the English presence, Mary's account suggests that European goods—particularly apparel—retained strong symbolic value among northeastern native peoples. The passage also raises the interesting possibility that Mary developed affection for her captors or they did for her.

On a Sabbath day, the Sun being about an hour high, in the Afternoon, came Mr. John Hoar [a lawyer hired by Mary's husband to secure her release], . . . I begged of [the natives] to let me see the *English-man,* but they would not; . . . When they had talked their fill with him, they suffered me to go to him. We asked each other of our welfare, and how my Husband did, and all my Friends? he told me they were all well, and would be glad to see me. Amongst other things which my Husband sent me, there came a pound of *Tobacco;* which I sold for nine shillings in Money: for many of the *Indians,* for want of *Tobacco,* smoaked *Hemlock,* and *Ground-ivy.* It was a great mistake in any who thought I sent for *Tobacco:* for through the favour of God, that desire was overcome. I now asked them, whether I should go home with Mr. Hoar? they answered No, one and another of them: and it being Night, we lay down with that Answer: in the Morning Mr Hoar invited the *Saggamores* to Dinner; . . . Mr. Hoar called them betime to Dinner; but they ate very little, they being so busie in dressing themselves, and getting ready for their Dance; which was carried on by eight of them, four Men and four Squaws; my Master and Mistress being two. He was dressed in his Holland shirt, with great Laces sewed at the tail of it; he had his silver Buttons, his white Stockings, his Garters were hung round with shillings, and he had Girdles of *Wampom* upon his Head and Shoulders. She had a Kersey [wool] Coat, and covered with Girdles of Wampom from the Loins and upward; her Arms, from her elbows to her Hands, were covered with Bracelets; there were handfuls of Neck-laces about her Neck, and several sorts of Jewels in her Ears. She had fine red Stockings, and white Shoes, her Hair powdered and her face painted Red, that was always before Black; and all the Dancers were after the same manner. There were

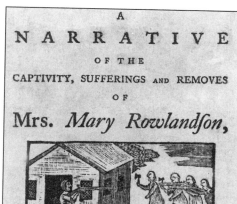

Mary Rowlandson's captivity narrative went through dozens of printings during the colonial era. The title page from this 1773 edition depicts a defiant Mary confronting her captors with a musket.

Tainted beyond Redemption?

Not all Europeans responded to captivity as Mary Rowlandson did. In a May 1753 letter to his English friend Peter Collinson, Benjamin Franklin observed, "[W]hen white persons of either sex have been taken prisoners young by the Indians, and lived a while among them, tho' ransomed by their Friends, and treated with all imaginable tenderness to prevail with them to stay among the English, yet in a Short time they become disgusted with our manner of life, and the care and pains that are necessary to support it, and take the first good Opportunity of escaping again into the Woods, from whence there is no reclaiming them."

two other singing and knocking on a Kettle for their Musick. They kept hopping up and down one after another, with a Kettle of Water in the midst, standing warm upon some Embers, to drink of when they were a-dry. They held on till it was almost night, throwing out Wampom to the standers by. At night I asked them again, if I should go home? . . .

At first they were all against it, except my Husband would come for me; but afterwards they assented to it, and seemed much to rejoyce in it; some asking me to send them some Bread, others some Tobacco, others shaking me by the hand, offering me a Hood and Scarf to ride in; not one moving hand or tongue against it. Thus hath the Lord answered my poor desire, and the many earnest requests of others put up unto God for me. . . . So I took leave of them, and in coming along my heart melted into Tears, more than all the while I was with them, and I was almost swallowed up with the thoughts that ever I should go home again.

Mary Rowlandson's description of her captivity was among the first of what would become one of the most popular literary forms in colonial America: the so-called captivity narrative. For the most part, these stories resembled Mary's: They detailed the sufferings of captives and described the events that brought them back to white society. But by the middle of the 18th century, it was becoming clear to more astute European observers that Native American captives were not simple prisoners of war. The following account of Huron and Iroquois war-making practices, written by French missionary Father Joseph Lafitau and published in 1724, reveals that far from the usual practice of taking prisoners as an alternative to killing the enemy, these native peoples took captives as a way of replenishing valuable human resources. Thus, captives were often adopted as wives, children, servants, and even warriors. Lafitau's account is also instructive for what it suggests about the prominence and influence of female leaders, or "matriarchs," in northeastern native societies.

War is a necessary exercise for the Iroquois and Huron, perhaps also for all the other American Indians for, besides the usual motives which people have in declaring it against troublesome neighbours who offend them or furnish them legitimate causes by giving them just reasons for complaint, it is indispensable to them also because of one of their fundamental laws of being.

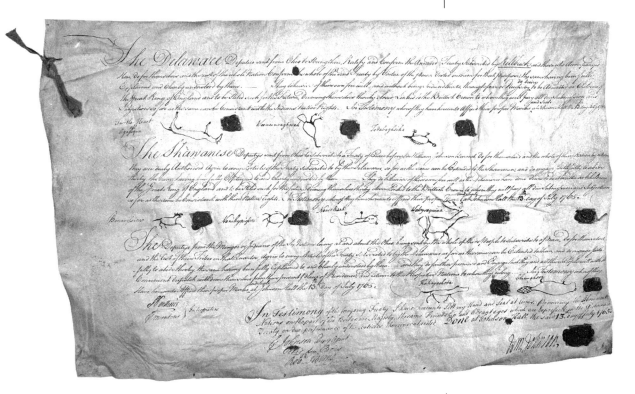

The families . . . are sustained only by the number of those composing them, whether men or women. It is in their number that their main force and chief wealth consist. The loss of a single person is a great one, but one which must necessarily be repaired by replacing the person lacking by one or many others, according to the importance of him who is to be replaced.

It is not up to the members of the household to repair this loss, but to all those men who have marriage links with that house, or their *Athonni*, as they say; and in that fact, resides the advantage of having many men born in it. For these men, although isolated at home and limited to themselves, marry into different lodges. The children born of these different marriages become obliged to their fathers' lodge, to which they are strangers, and contract the obligation of replacing them [those who are lost] so that the matron, who has the principal authority in this household, can force these children to go to war if it seems best to her, or keep them at home if they have undertaken a war displeasing to her.

When, then, this matron judges it time to raise up the tree again, or to lay again on the mat someone of her family whom death has taken away from her, she addresses herself to some one of those who have their *Athonni* [sire] at her home and who she

The small drawings or pictographs on this 1765 treaty between the British and several groups of Native Americans were the signatures of the tribal leaders. The signature at the left of the top row, for example, is of Delware chief Agassqua, or Turtle Heart. These signatures provide graphic evidence of how the diplomacy between Indians and whites came to involve both indigenous and European practices.

believes is most capable of executing her commission. She speaks to him by a wampum belt, explaining her intention of engaging him to form a war party. This is soon done.

Costs of Colonization

Next to disease, nothing took a greater toll on native peoples than alcohol. Fur traders and land speculators knew that natives were vulnerable to the intoxicating effects of drink (usually rum), and took advantage of this during business transactions. The short-term consequences were that drunk natives were often deliberately deceived by greedy Europeans intent on unfair trade and corrupt land sales. The long-term results were more pernicious: native populations found themselves lacking essential ammunition, food, and clothing as more and more resources were used to obtain liquor. The resulting downward spirals of poverty and starvation devastated native communities. Colonial officials enacted various prohibitions against selling liquor to Indians, but these had little real impact. In the following selection from his *Autobiography*, Benjamin Franklin described a scene of native drunkenness, and although he somewhat dramatizes the effects of liquor on the Eastern native population, he nonetheless recognized how damaging they could be.

A Treaty being to be held with the Indians at Carlisle [Pennsylvania], the Governor sent a Message to the House, proposing that they should nominate some of their Members to be join'd with some Members of Council as Commissioners for that purpose. The House nam'd the Speaker (Mr Norris) and my self; and being commission'd we went to Carlisle, and met the Indians accordingly.—As those People are extreamly apt to get drunk, and when so are very quarrelsome & disorderly, we strictly forbad the selling any Liquor to them; and when they complain'd of this Restriction, we told them that if they would continue sober during the Treaty, we would give them Plenty of Rum when Business was over. They promis'd this; and they kept their Promise—because they could get no Liquor—and the Treaty was conducted very orderly, and concluded to mutual Satisfaction. They then claim'd and receiv'd the Rum. This was in the Afternoon. They were near 100 Men, Women & Children, and were lodg'd in temporary Cabins built in the Form of a Square just

INDIAN LETTER.

Extract of a letter from Capt. HENDRICKS, *an Indian Chief, of the Stockbridge nation, to Col.* PICKERING, *one of the Commissioners appointed by the President of the United States, for holding a treaty with the Six Nations, at Canandaigua, in the fall, 1794:*

"THERE is a powerful strong man, that has long made war against all the nations of Indians, and made dreadful havock amongst them. He has also attacked our nation, and cut off almost all our young men and warriors; and many of our old men have been slain by him. This strong man, our enemy, is named RUM! and he is your son, and begat by the white people; and we believe you have power to control him; we therefore, hope you will chain him down, and confine him among yourselves, and never let him again loose among us poor Indians."

✳✳✳✳✳

AN ADDRESS TO DRUNKARDS, CONCERNING THE GREAT SIN OF DRUNKENNESS.

DRUNKENNESS is of that pernicious, destructive, and infatuating nature, that it debases reason, benumbs the senses, confounds the judgment, besots the understanding, overwhelms the mind, steals away the heart, defiles the conscience, and begets a spiritual lethargy. It impairs the health, disorders the body, inflames the blood, infects the breath, intoxicates the brain, deforms the visage, and engenders an unnatural thirst. It is a work of darkness, an annoyance to modesty, a disclosure of secrets, a betrayer of trust, a waster of time, a foe to industry, and a forerunner of want and misery. It wounds men's credit, ruins their reputation, consumes their wealth, violates the rules of temperance, and perverts the order of nature. It is the parent of vice, the author of mischief, and a promoter of rioting, madness and fury. It stirs up vain mirth, foolish jesting, wantonness, gaming and debauchery. It causeth stammering, staggering, vomiting, filthiness, woes, sorrows, wounds, headaches, surfeits, diseases, and untimely deaths. It occasions swearing, cursing, lying, ranting, quarrelling, fighting, bloodshed and murder. It produces cheating, pilfering, robbing, stealing, and too often brings to the gallows. It makes people stupid, idle, sottish, and unfit for business, and renders them contemptible, in the sight of God and all good men. It quenches the Spirit, stifles the conviction of conscience, and plucks up religion by the roots. It causeth forgetfulness of God, provokes him to anger, draws down his judgments, and in the end destroys the soul.

A drunkard is a thief to himself, a slave to his lust, a laughing-stock to the profane, a dishonor to God, an enemy to his own peace, and a disgrace to mankind. He is indisposed to virtue, is worse than the beasts; a traveller to destruction, an abuser of God's mercies, a transgressor of his laws, and at last excluded his kingdom.

A drunkard takes himself from under the protection of heaven, exposes his soul to the merciless tyranny of the world, the flesh and the devil; and unless he repents, and turns at the reproofs of God's Spirit, which smites him in secret for so doing, he must drink of the cup of God's wrath and fiery indignation, without the least respite or intermission, or so much as a drop of water to allay the heat of his scorching tongue.

Drinking to drive away cares, troubles and anxieties of mind is flying to the devil to get rid of, or to be eased of them, who, Pharaoh like, instead of lessening, adds to their weight, and greatly triumphs over such wretches.

Wherefore, as there is no flying from Divine justice, no evading God's righteous laws, nor any bribing the Divine witness in our own bosoms; let every drunkard in particular, and the whole bulk of mankind in general, seriously consider in whose presence they now are, and before whom we must appear in the great and awful day of account, when all our words and deeds, with every secret thing, must come under the notice and inspection of our great and all discerning Judge.

Reader, art thou guilty of the sin of drunkenness? —If so, let the above reflections sink deep into thine heart, and let the things of God, and thine own peace, be duly reverenced and regarded, that so, the Almighty may be gracious to thee, and pour forth of his blessings on thy soul, lest that awfully solemn day of death and judgment overtake thee unprepared.

And as nothing but the Divine law, or grace of God in the heart, can truly reform or enable us effectually to amend our ways; which Divine law and grace of God, do I earnestly recommend the children of men to seek after.

N. COVERLY, Jr. Printer, Milk-Street, Boston.

Alcohol use among Native Americans continued to be a problem after the colonial era despite the efforts of Native American leaders such as the author of this open letter from 1794. Throughout the colonial era, Indian leaders, missionaries, and others urged British government officials to end the rum trade, but their efforts had little effect.

without the Town. In the Evening, hearing a great Noise among them, the Commissionrs. walk'd out to see what was the Matter. We found they had made a great Bonfire in the Middle of the Square. They were all drunk Men and Women, quarrelling and fighting. Their dark-colour'd Bodies, half naked, seen only by the gloomy Light of the Bonfire, running after and beating one another with Firebrands, accompanied by their horrid Yellings, form'd a Scene the most resembling our Ideas of Hell that could well be

"We know our Lands are now become more valuable. The white People think we do not know their Value; but we are sensible that the Land is everlasting, and the few Goods we receive for it are soon worn out and Gone."

—From a speech by the Onondaga leader Canasatego delivered in 1742

imagin'd. . . . The next Day, sensible they had misbehav'd in giving us that Disturbance, they sent three of their old Counsellors to make their Apology. The Orator acknowledg'd the Fault, but laid it upon the Rum; and then endeavour'd to excuse the Rum, by saying, *"The great Spirit who made all things made every thing for some Use, and whatever Use he design'd any thing for, that Use it should always be put to; Now, when he made Rum, he said,* LET THIS BE FOR INDIANS TO GET DRUNK WITH. *And it must be so."*—And indeed if it be the Design of Providence to extirpate these Savages in order to make room for Cultivators of the Earth, it seems not improbable that Rum may be the appointed Means. It has already annihilated all the Tribes who formerly inhabited the Seacoast.

Throughout the colonial period, but particularly after the initial phase of settlement, English authorities struggled to impose some sort of legal order on the exchange of land. This meant, among other things, the creation of formal deeds or titles, signed by Indians and acknowledging the sale of lands to English or other European purchasers. Although they were often fraudulent, these deeds nonetheless contain much information about Native American customs and social patterns. In the one below, an Abenaki called by the English "Jane of Scarborough," sells a tract of land to Andrew and Arthur Alger. Among the more intriguing aspects of this transaction is the fact that the seller was a woman, an indication that Abenaki women, unlike most of their European counterparts, were able to own land.

The 19the of Septembr 1659:

The declaration of Jane the Indean of Scarbrough concerneing Land/

This aforesayd Jane alias uphanum doth declare that her mother namely Naguasqua the wife of Wickwarrawaske Sagamore, & her brother namely ugagoyuskitt & her selfe namely uphannu : coæqually hath sould unto Andrew Alger, & to his brother Arther Alger a Tract of Land, beginning att the Mouth of ye River Called blew Poynt River, where the River doth part, & soe bounded up along with the River Called Oawascoage in Indean, & soe up three scoore poole above the falls, on the one side, & on the other side bounded up along with the Northermost River, that Treaneth by the great hill of Abram Jocelyns & goeth Northward, bounding from the head of ye River South West & soe to the aforesd bounds, namely three scoore pooles, above the Falls; This aforesayd Uphanum doth declare, that her mother & brother & shee hath already in hand received full satisfaction of the aforesayd Algers for the aforesd the Land from the beginning of the world to this day provided on conditions that for tyme to come from yeare to yeare yearly, the aforesd Algers shall peaceably suffer uphannum to plant In Andrew Algers fejld, soe long as uphannu : & her mother Neguasqua doe both live/ & alsoe one busll of corne for acknowledgmt every yeare soe long as they both shall Live/ Uphannu : doth declare that ye bargan was made In the yeare 1651 : unto which shee doth subscribe/

During the 18th century, as the European population of North America expanded, the scramble for native lands intensified. Native peoples living as far west as the Ohio River Valley found themselves engaged in a fierce struggle to preserve independent control of territory—territory that had earlier been secured by treaties signed with the British.

11th mo the 12 Day 1661

Know all men whome this may Concern that I Maurorock, Pawquaa Rackealls Pawwaytahan Mawmatoe Stowinse have bargained sold and Delivered unto John Budd a neck of land bounded by a neck of land he bought of me and other Indians on ye South and with Merremack River on the West and with marked Trees to the north with Twenty mile feeding Ground for Cattle with all the woods Trees Maurodes Meadow [illegible] and have received full Satisfaction in Coats and three score [illegible] to warrant ye sale hereof against all men English Dutch [illegible] and for the faithfull performance hereof I have sett my hand in the presence of Thomas Close and William Jones this day and year above written

Witness Thom: Close
William Jones his mark

The mark of Maurorock
Mawmato his mark
Rawmaqua his mark
Stowinis his marke Prain his [illegible]
razi his mark

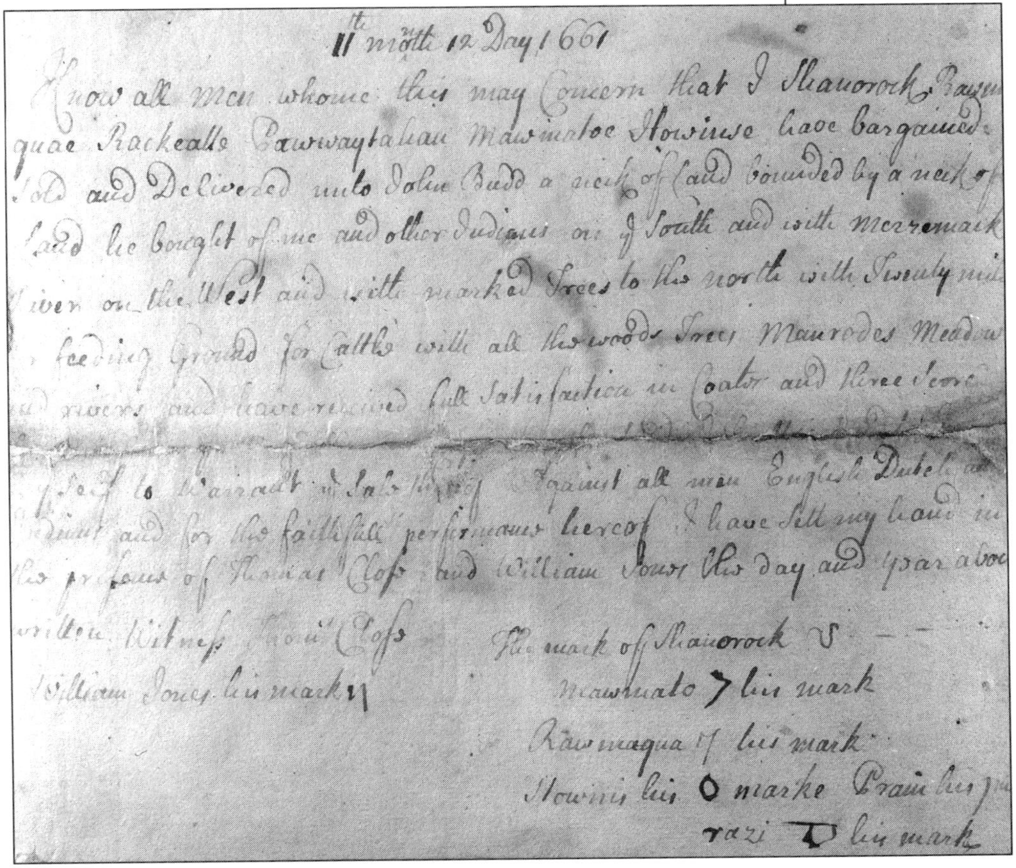

The Native Americans who signed this 1661 land deed used identifying pictographs, or small symbols related to their names, as their "marks."

"The [colonists], who were confined to narrow farms in their native country, are many of them, insatiable in their desires after lands, and rather waste and impoverish, than improve them. Many have acquired a roving unsettled temper, and are grown impatient of labor and frugal industry; and having abused their farms, sell them, and move back to purchase new lands, on the borders of the Indian nations."

—*The American Magazine and Monthly Chronicle* on the expansive practices of the colonial farmer (1758)

The struggle created serious problems for the British government during the French and Indian War. This conflict began as a small skirmish between colonial troops and French forces in western Pennsylvania but evolved into a true global conflict that raged from 1756 to 1763. After years of abuse at the hands of corrupt government officials and land speculators, few native people were prepared to build and maintain crucial diplomatic and military alliances with the British. In an effort to restore some degree of credibility, British government officials issued a series of instructions to colonial governors demanding that they take action to contain their land-hungry European populations and punish corrupt land speculators. In the end, such orders had little meaningful impact. But the conciliatory spirit in which they were drafted is evident in the document below, produced in 1761 by authorities in London, and intended for the governors of Nova Scotia, New Hampshire, New York, New Jersey, Virginia, North Carolina, South Carolina, and Georgia.

Whereas the peace and security of our colonies and plantations upon the continent of North America does greatly depend upon the amity and alliance of the several nations or tribes of Indians bordering upon the said colonies and upon a just and faithful observance of those treaties and compacts which have been heretofore solemnly entered into with the said Indians by our royal predecessors, kings and queens of this realm. And whereas notwithstanding the repeated instructions which have been from time to time given by our late royal grandfather to the governors of our several colonies upon this head, the said Indians have made and do still continue to make great complaints that settlements have been made and possession taken of lands, the property of which they have by treaties reserved to themselves, by persons claiming the said lands under pretense of deeds of sale and conveyance illegally, fraudulently, and surreptitiously obtained of the said Indians. And whereas it has likewise been represented unto us that some of our governors or other chief officers of our said colonies, have countenanced said unjust claims and pretensions by passing grants of the lands so pretended to have been purchased of the Indians. We, therefore, taking this matter into our royal consideration, as also the fatal effects which would attend a discontent amongst the Indians in the present situation of affairs, and being determined upon all occasions to support and protect the said Indians in their just rights and possessions and to keep inviolable the treaties and compacts which have been entered into with them, do hereby strictly enjoin and command that neither yourself nor any lieutenant-governor . . . do, upon any pretense whatsoever, upon pain of our highest displeasure and of being forthwith removed from your or his office, pass any grant or grants to any persons whatever of any land within or adjacent to the territories possessed or occupied by the said Indians or the property or possession of which has at any time been reserved to or claimed by them. And it is our further will and pleasure that you do publish a proclamation in our name strictly enjoining and requiring all persons whatever who may either willfully or inadvertently have seated themselves upon any lands so reserved to or lawfully claimed by the said Indians, without any lawful authority for so doing, forthwith to remove therefrom. And in case you shall find, upon strict inquiry to be made for that purpose, that any person or persons do claim to hold or possess any lands . . . upon pretense of purchase made of the said Indians, without a proper license first had and obtained either from us or any of our royal predecessors or any persons acting under our or their authority, you are forthwith to cause a prosecution to be carried on against such person or persons who shall have made such fraudulent purchases, to the end that the land may be recovered by a due course of law. And whereas the wholesome laws which have at different times been passed in several of our said colonies and the instructions which have been given by our royal predecessors for restraining persons from purchasing lands of the Indians without a license for that purpose and for regulating the proceedings upon such purchases, have not been duly observed. It is, therefore, our express will and pleasure that when any application shall be made to you for license to purchase lands of the Indians, you do forbear to grant such license until you shall have first transmitted to us by our Commissioners for Trade and Plantation the particulars of such application, as well in respect to the situation as the extent of the lands so proposed to be purchased, and shall have received our further directions therein. And it is our further will and pleasure that you do forthwith cause these our instructions to you to be made public . . . , to the end that our royal will and pleasure in the premises may be known and that the Indians may be apprised of our determined resolution to support them in their just rights and inviolably to observe our engagements with them.

European officials gave silver ornaments to Indians as a way of securing loyalty, which perhaps indicates that Native peoples had embraced the European idea that silver had special, intrinsic value. Sir William Johnson, a British superintendent of Northern Indian affairs in the Northeast issued these "Happy While United" metals in 1764.

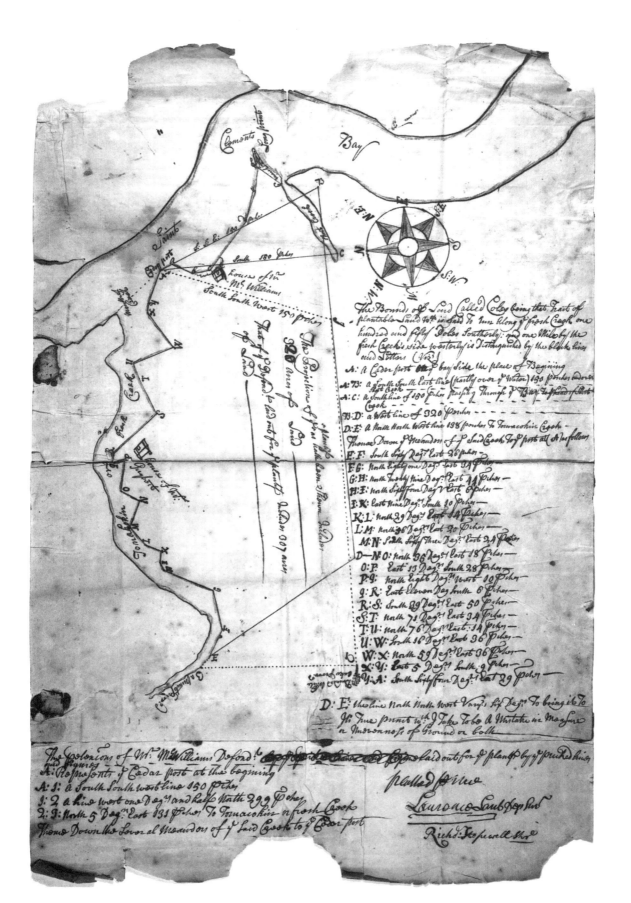

Bay

Clements

Clements Bay

The Bounds of Land Called Coles being that tract of
plantable Land which is said to run along the fresh Creek one
hundred and fifty poles Southerly: and one mile by the
fresh Creek's side westerly is Distinguished by the black lines
and Letters (Viz)

A: A Cedar post on the bayside the place of Begining
A: B: a East South East line (partly over the water) 130 poles to a
B: C: A South line of 150 poles passing through the Bay to the head of the said Creek
C: D: a West line of 320 poles
D: E: a North North West line 138 poles To Tomacohin Creek
Thence Down the meadows of the said Creek to the post at A as follows
E: F: South forty Degrees East 28 poles
F: G: North Eighty one Degrees East 24 poles
G: H: North Twenty nine Degrees East 44 poles
H: E: North Sixty four Degrees West 6 poles
I: K: East nine Degrees South 20 poles
K: L: North 29 Degrees East 14 poles
L: M: North 26 Degrees East 20 poles
M: N: South forty three Degrees East 24 poles
D: N: O: North 36 Degrees East 18 poles
O: P: East 13 Degrees South 28 poles
P: Q: North Eight Degrees West 10 poles
Q: R: East Eleven Degrees South 6 poles
R: S: South 29 Degrees East 50 poles
S: T: North 71 Degrees East 14 poles
T: U: North 76 Degrees West 14 poles
U: W: South 16 Degrees East 36 poles
W: X: North 59 Degrees East 36 poles
X: Y: East 5 Degrees South 9 poles
Y: A: South Sixty four Degrees East 29 poles

D: E: this line North North West Varys sig Degrees To bring it To
His true point which I take to be A Mistake in Measure
or Unevenness of Ground or both

The Projection of this Habitation Thence Shown
920 Acres of Land

The Locations of Mr. McWilliams Defendt. Laid out for the plantr by the
said figures
A: 1: a South South west line 150 poles
1: 2: a line West one Degree and half North 299 poles
2: 3: North 5 Degrees East 831 poles To Tomacohin in fresh Creek
Thence Down the Lower meadows of the said Creek to the Cedar post

Scaled for use

Laurence Saub Depy Survr

Richd Hopewell Clar

Chapter Four

Who Built the Colonies?

L and in the Old World had an almost mystical aura. It seemed to provide its owners not just with personal wealth and security, but also with power; power over the peasants and laborers who worked the land; power over family members who lived off income from the land; and power over local townsfolk who made the tools, barrels and other goods that facilitated use of the land. It also provided more formal kinds of power. In rural England, land ownership was usually a prerequisite for any kind of political privilege, whether that be the right to vote in local elections, to sit on juries, to be members of church vestries (governing bodies of church parishes), or to hold any kind of public office, from sheriff to tax collector.

The prospect of somehow replicating this privileged landowning existence drew many colonists to America. And much as in England, land ownership in the colonies carried with it certain privileges. But, very much in contrast to England, land ownership in the colonies did not necessarily bring wealth. The sheer abundance of land in America meant that its monetary value was quite low, especially when compared to that of English land. Moreover, colonists faced one problem English landowners rarely faced. Although there was plenty of land in America, there was a dire shortage of the poor women and men large-scale English property owners employed to work their land. This problem did not just affect colonists with lofty social and economic ambitions. During planting and harvest time, ordinary English farmers often hired laborers to assist them, but their counterparts in the colonies could not be sure of the availability of such help.

This scarcity of farm labor is perhaps the most crucial single point for understanding the social and economic character of British North America. Virtually every aspect of colonial life was shaped to some degree by this problem—from race relations to provincial politics; from the distribution of wealth to the organization of families; from immigration to trade.

These surveyor's notes from around 1724 describe the property boundaries of land once owned by the Maryland planter Robert Cole. Such surveys were common as colonists endlessly struggled, often in the courts, to determine exactly who owned what land.

Colonists confronted this labor shortage in a wide variety of ways. In early New England, extended families provided the chief labor source. In 18th-century New York, New Jersey, and Pennsylvania much of the labor came from indentured servants, men and women who had willingly agreed to serve a master for a period of up to seven years. In exchange, the master paid their way to the New World and usually provided them with land, livestock, or other resources at the end of their term of servitude. In the southern colonies, particularly coastal South Carolina and tidewater Virginia, African slaves came to be the primary labor force in the 18th century. In other regions, including inland Virginia and the inland Carolinas, colonists turned to a combination of family labor, indentured servitude, and slavery.

All these systems existed in the Old World as well. Family labor was especially important, but slavery and indentured servitude were also present. Nonetheless, it is crucial to recognize that "bound labor," or servitude and slavery, was much more prevalent in the colonies than in England or the British Isles. Consider the following simple fact: as many as half of all Europeans who came to British North America came as indentured servants. The need for labor, that is, accounts for almost half of all European immigration to the colonies. Similarly, by the third quarter of the 18th century, virtually the entire African population of the colonies—more than 325,000 people, or a full one-fifth of the entire population of the mainland British colonies, were enslaved.

The main point here is simple: virtually everyone in the colonies either served a master, employed servants, or owned slaves. Virtually everyone, that is, participated in bound or unfree labor systems—systems designed, above all, to transform worthless land into valued property.

Little of what historians know about the colonial labor problem comes from the laborers themselves. Few indentured servants, and even fewer African slaves, left any record of their experiences. But, using court records, material artifacts and a wide variety of other sources, historians have begun to assemble a picture of the lives of these people. And that picture at once confirms and challenges many of our longstanding assumptions. African slaves, for instance, suffered the horrors of the infamous middle passage, the voyage from Africa to America; the degrading experience of the slave auction; and the brutal labor regimes of southern plantations. But not all slaves had all of these experiences. We now know that many slaves lived and worked in cities, in both the North and the South; some slaves learned trades; slaves worked as sailors,

"Lands, tho' in their nature excellently good, without Hands [of laborers] proportionable, will not enrich any kingdom."
—English economic theorist Sir Josiah Child, from a 1692 pamphlet

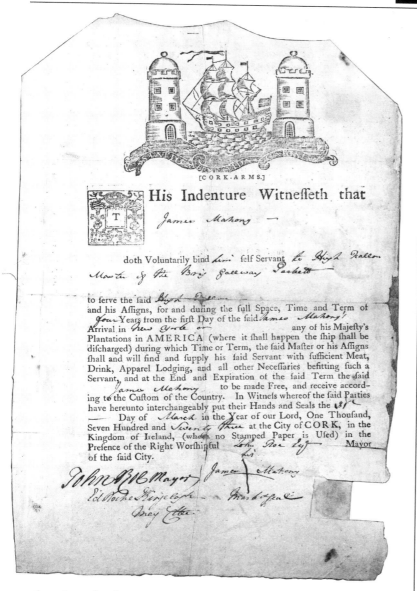

[CORK·ARMS.]

His Indenture Witneffeth that

James Mahony

doth Voluntarily bind ~~him~~ felf Servant *to High Gallon*
Master of the Brig Galleway Sackett
to ferve the faid ~~Hugh Gallon~~
and his Affigns, for and during the full Space, Time and Term of
Four Years from the firft Day of the faid *James Mahony*
Arrival in *New York or* any of his Majefty's
Plantations in AMERICA (where it fhall happen the fhip fhall be
difcharged) during which Time or Term, the faid Mafter or his Affigns
fhall and will find and fupply his faid Servant with fufficient Meat,
Drink, Apparel Lodging, and all other Neceffaries befitting fuch a
Servant, and at the End and Expiration of the faid Term the faid
James Mahony to be made Free, and receive accord-
ing to the Cuftom of the Country. In Witnefs whereof the faid Parties
have hereunto interchangeably put their Hands and Seals the *1ft*
—— Day of *March* in the Year of our Lord, One Thoufand,
Seven Hundred and *Twenty three* at the City of CORK, in the
Kingdom of Ireland, (where no Stamped Paper is Ufed) in the
Prefence of the Right Worfhipful *John Roe Efq* Mayor
of the faid City.

John Roe Mayor   James Mahony
Ed Roche Burgelofs   Mark & Seal
Mey Etter

James Mahoney, who indentured himself at Cork, Ireland, was one of more
than 55,000 Irish to migrate to the
American colonies between 1760 and
1775. So massive was this surge in
migration from the British Isles that
alarmed government officials began to
fear that the mother country would
develop a labor shortage of its own.

tailors, barrelmakers, and at other crafts. And a very small number
were even able to buy their own freedom. Slaves were also not
simply passive victims of the slave regime. They developed strate-
gies to resist the hardships of slavery, created novel and distinct
African-American folk traditions, and devised their own forms of
religious worship.

Similarly, we have long known that many colonists began life
in the colonies as indentured servants. But we now also know that
indentured servitude was not a simple and easy avenue to a comfortable, prosperous life in the colonies. Masters were sometimes
abusive; they sometimes arbitrarily extended terms of servitude; or
they simply went broke, leaving servants with nothing at the end
of their terms. These factors provide a partial explanation for the

"Like one of the patriarchs, I have my
flocks and my herds, my bond-men
[slaves], and bond-women, and every soart
of trade amongst my own servants, so that I
live in a kind of in[ter]dependance on every
one, but Providence. However tho' this soart
of life is without expence yet it is attended
with a great deal of trouble. I must take care
to keep all my people to their duty, to set
all the springs in motion, and to make every
one draw his equal share to carry the
machine forward."

—Virginian William Byrd II writing to his
English friend, Charles Boyle, Earl of Orrey,
about the burdens of plantation life (1726)

Advertisements selling indentured servants appear along with advertisements for houses in the 1734 Pennsylvania Gazette. The second of the four advertisements appears to be for two orphans being sold into servitude.

JOHN FROST, Staymaker, late Servant to *Even Morgan,* now liveth in Secondſtreet, over againſt Doctor Hooper's, in Copartnerſhip with Thomas Carter, where all ſorts of Stays and Coats are made after the beſt manner.

A **BOY** about four Years of Age to be bound out till he is Twenty one; and a likely young *Woman's* Time to be diſpoſed of, for between two and three years, by Thomas Parry, and Iſaac Williams, *Overſeers of the Poor for the City of* Philadelphia.

A **SERVANT** Lad's Time for near Five years to be diſpoſed of, on Reaſonable Terms. He is by Trade a *Taylor,* and can work very well. Enquire of the Printer hereof.

To be Sold

B Y *John Parſons,* a very good new brick Houſe well finiſh'd, thirty foot Front, two Story high, beſides a very large Cellar, and Garret; a good new Brick Kitchen, Stable, and a large Garden. Whoever inclines to purchaſe the ſame, may apply themſelves the aforeſaid *John Parſons* and know further.

N. B. The aforeſaid Houſe ſtands very commodiouſly in the Market-ſtreet in the Town of *Burlington* in New-Jerſey very convenient for any Publick Buſineſs.

growth of a colonial underclass—a class of poor whites, most of whom barely eked out livings as hired laborers or as tenants farming other people's land. We also now know that servants varied widely in their backgrounds. Most were young men, but many others were women; some were from the British Isles, but many also came from various countries in continental Europe. Some were from respected middle-class families, others were vagrants or criminals; some worked as skilled craftsmen, others amongst African slaves in the fields of southern plantations.

Whether African slaves or white servants, the men and women who built colonial America were by no means a uniform group. But their work did have a uniform effect. It transformed the colonies from scanty outposts to vital components of a larger economic system, a system that reached back and forth across the Atlantic Ocean, and that helped to transform England from a tiny island nation into a huge imperial power.

Bound for America

Although tobacco cultivation seemed a more promising endeavor for the Virginia colonists than the quest for gold and silver, it was still no easy road to riches. Tobacco was a

very labor-intensive crop. In addition to growing and harvesting the tobacco leaves, planters had to dry them and carefully pack them in barrels for safe shipment back to England. To do this hard work, colonists initially relied on indentured servants, sometimes called apprentices. So important were these men—and they were mostly men—that by 1625, they constituted more than 40 percent of the entire population of the Virginia colony. One of them was Wessell Webling, who in 1622 indentured himself to a prosperous London merchant and landowner named Edward Bennett. At the end of his three years of labor on Bennett's Virginia property, Webling would be entitled to rent 50 acres of land—a drop in the bucket by colonial standards, but a vast tract by English standards. What follows is Webling's "indenture," or the contract he entered into with Bennett.

To All to Whom these Presents Shall Come Greeting in our Lord God Everlasting.

Know you that I, Wessell Webling, son of Nicholas Webling of London, brewer, for and in consideration that I have been furnished and set out and am to be transported unto Virginia at the costs and charges of Edward Bennett of London, merchant, and his associates, and for and in consideration that they have promised and covenanted to maintain me with sufficient meat, drink, and apparel, do, by these presents, bind myself an apprentice unto the said Edward Bennett for the full term of three years to begin the feast of St. Michael the Archangel next after the date of these presents. And I do promise and bind myself to do and to perform all the said term of my apprenticeship true and faithful service in all such labors and business as the said Edward Bennett or his assigns shall employ me in and to be tractable and obedient as a good servant ought to be in all such things as shall be commanded me by the said Edward Bennett or his assigns in Virginia. And at the end of the said term of three years the said Edward Bennett do promise to give unto the said apprentice a house and 50 acres of land in Virginia to hold to me, my heirs, and assigns forever, according to the custom of land there holden and also shall give to the said apprentice necessary and good apparel and the said apprentice shall inhabit and dwell upon the said land and shall pay yearly for the said fifty acres of land from and after that he shall thereof be possessed unto the said Edward Bennett the yearly rent of 50 shillings sterling forever and two days work yearly and to all and singular the covenants aforesaid on behalf of the

Tobacco production involved much more than growing and cultivating the plant. As this image of African slaves on a West Indian plantation indicates, the preparation of the plant for market was a labor-intensive and elaborate process.

Mad About Tobacco

Tobacco was present in England from as early as 1565, when sailors brought seeds back from Florida. But it was difficult to grow there and costly to import. Tobacco was also a familiar substance around the Jamestown colony. The various Chesapeake tribes—much like most North American Indians—smoked a local variety, nicotiana rustica, but this harsh weed could hardly compete with the smoother Spanish varieties with which Englishmen were familiar. By 1611, colonists had discovered that they could grow a variety of West Indian tobacco—not as smooth as the best Spanish tobacco, but much more palatable than the local variety. And by 1615, the tobacco boom in Virginia was on: In that year, the Jamestown colony exported 2,000 pounds of tobacco; by 1620, the number was 40,000 pounds; 60,000 in 1622; 500,000 in 1626, and by 1629, 1,200,000. Virginia had gone tobacco mad.

said apprentice to be performed and kept in manner and form as aforesaid. The said apprentice binds himself to his said master by these presents. In witness whereof the parties aforesaid to these present indentures have set their hands and seals the 25th of September 1622.

Signet. *Ed. Bennett*

The relations between masters and servants could be very complex, especially when servants worked within the master's household. Such "domestic" servants were usually girls or young women whose parents signed them into servitude as a way to prepare them for lives as mothers and wives. And while many of them came from England, many were also born in the colonies, usually to relatives or friends of their masters.

The work regimes of these young women could be grueling. Not only were they often responsible for child care and other domestic chores, but they also assisted with farm work, and what was often referred to as "domestic manufactures," or the making of things in the home. Female servants, daughters, and house-mistresses—or the lady of the house—manufactured cloth, clothing, candles, soap, and other goods. And these women made these goods not only for their own use, but also for trade with other families. Indeed, domestic manufactures were an essential source of income for many colonial families, making the labor of a domestic servant all the more crucial.

The psychological demands of adolescence combined with the physical demands of domestic labor were, not surprisingly, overwhelming for some young servants. And much like young people in any era, servants were often tempted to rebel. When they did, masters found themselves facing a difficult dilemma. They had to decide if the servant should be punished and how, if so, much punishment was enough. These were the questions raised by the case of Priscilla, an apparently rebellious servant working for a Puritan family in early 17th-century Maine. In the letter below, her master, John Winter, tries to justify his wife's harsh treatment of Priscilla. Implied in his discussion is deep uncertainty about how to cope with this young woman who has, for all intents and purposes, become a part of Winter's family.

"Fruitfull Sisters"

In his pamphlet, Leah and Rachel, *or,* The Two Fruitfull Sisters Virginia and Mary-Land *(1656), the former colonist John Hammond describes the pleasing experience of well-behaved female servants, no doubt in an effort to encourage young women to indenture themselves for a trip to the colonies. But Hammond warned that women not inclined to behave in a suitably subservient fashion would suffer accordingly.*

The Women are not (as is reported) put into the ground to worke, but occupie such domestique imployments and houswifery as in England, that is dressing victuals, righting up the house, milking, imployed about dayries, washing, sowing, etc. and both men and women have times of recreations, as much or more than in any part of the world besides, yet som wenches that are nasty, beastly and not fit to be so imployed are put into the ground, for reason tells us, they must not at charge be transported and then mantained for nothing, but those that prove so aukward are rather burthensome then servants desirable or usefull.

You write me of some yll reports is given of my Wyfe for beatinge the maid; yf a faire waye will not do yt, beatinge must, sometimes, uppon such Idle girrells as she is. Yf you think yt fitte for my wyfe to do all the worke & maide sitt still, she must forbeare her hands to strike, for then the worke will ly undonn. She hath bin now 2 yeares 1/2 in the house, & I do not thinke she hath risen 20 times before my Wyfe hath bin up to Call her, & many tymes light the fire before she Comes out of her bed. She hath twize gon a mechinge [marching] in the woodes, which we have bin faine to send all our Company to seeke. We Cann hardly keep her within doores after we ar gonn to beed, except we Carry the kay of the doore to beed with us. She never Could melke Cow nor goat since she Came hither. Our men do not desire to have her boyle the kit- tle for them she is so sluttish. She Cannot be trusted to serve a few piggs, but my wyfe most Commonly must be with her. She hath written home, I heare, that she was faine to ly uppon goates skins. She might take som goates skins to ly in her bedd, but not given to her for her lodginge. For a yeare & quarter or more she lay with my daughter uppon a good feather bed before my daughter being lacke [gone] 3 or 4 daies to Sacco [Saco, Maine], the maid goes into beed with her Cloth & stockins, & would not take the paines to plucke of[f] her Cloths: . . . Her beating that she hath had hath never hurt her body nor limes [limbs]. She is so fatt & soggy she Cann hardly do any worke. This I write all the Company will Justify. Yf this maid at her lasy tymes, when she hath bin found in her ill accyons [actions] do not deserve 2 or 3 blowes, I pray Judge You who hath most reason to Complaine, my wyfe or the maid . . . . She hath an unthankeful office to do this she doth, for I thinke their was never that steward yet amonge such people as we have Could give them all Content. It does not pleas me well being she hath taken so much paines & Care to order things as well as she Could, & ryse in the morning rath, go to bed soe latte, & to have hard speches for yt.

Much like the more familiar trade in African slaves, the transportation of indentured servants was big business. Upon signing an indenture agreement—usually with recruiters trolling European cities in search of likely candidates for servitude—servants were bought and sold like ordinary merchandise. And the various recruiters, merchants, and sea captains who took charge of them during their journey to America were more concerned with making a profit than with servants' welfare. The trans-Atlantic crossing thus took a heavy toll, particularly on the young and infirm—though nowhere near as heavy as it did on African slaves.

Upon reaching America, the situation improved only marginally. Seeking to recoup the cost of transportation, agents traded and sold indentured servants with little regard for their personal situation. For single men arriving in Virginia, this was bad enough, but for the many families—mostly from Germany—who emigrated to Pennsylvania and other middle colonies during the middle decades of the 18th century, the consequences could be horrible. In an exposé first published in Germany in 1756, Gottlieb Mittelberger, a German tutor and choirmaster who spent several years in the colonies, described some of the perils awaiting his brethren, many of whom came to the colonies as redemptioners, a status similar to indentured servants. Instead of signing indentures before coming to America, these immigrants borrowed the cost of transport to the colonies from professional recruiters. If, after arriving in America, they were unable to repay these loans, they agreed to indenture themselves and their family members. As Mittelberger indicates, such arrangements could have very sad consequences.

When the ships finally arrive in Philadelphia after the long voyage only those are let off who can pay their sea freight or can give good security. The others, who lack the money to pay, have to remain on board until they are purchased and until their purchasers can thus pry them loose from the ship. In this whole process, the sick are the worst off, for the healthy are preferred and are more readily paid for. The miserable people who are ill must often still remain at sea and in sight of the city for another two or three weeks—which in many cases means death. . . .

This is how the commerce in human beings on board ship takes place. Every day Englishmen, Dutchmen, and High Germans come from Philadelphia and other places, some of them very far away, sometime twenty or thirty or forty hours' journey, and go on board the newly arrived vessel that has brought people from Europe and offers them for sale. From among the healthy they pick out those suitable for the purposes for which they require them. Then they negotiate with them as to the length of the period for which they will go into service in order to pay off their passage, the whole amount of which they generally still owe. When an agreement has been reached, adult persons by written contract bind themselves to serve for three, four, five, or six years, according to their health and age. The very young, between the ages of ten and fifteen, have to serve until they are twenty-one, however.

Many parents in order to pay their fares in this way and get off the ship must barter and sell their children as if they were cattle. Since the fathers and mothers often do not know where or to what masters their children are to be sent, it frequently happens that after leaving the vessel, parents and children do not see each other for years on end, or even for the rest of their lives.

People who arrive without the funds to pay their way and who have children under the age of five, cannot settle their debts by selling them. They must give away these children for nothing to be brought up by strangers; and in return these children must stay in service until they are twenty-one years old. Children between five and ten who owe half-fare, . . . must also go into service in return until they are twenty-one years old, and can neither set free their parents nor take their debts upon themselves. On the other hand, the sale of children older than ten can help to settle a part of their parents' passage charges. . . .

It often happens that whole families—husband, wife, and children—being sold to different purchasers, become separated, especially when they cannot pay any part of the passage money. When either the husband or the wife has died at sea, having come more than halfway, then the surviving spouse must pay not only his or her fare, but must also pay for or serve out the fare of the deceased.

When both parents have died at sea, having come more than halfway, then their children, especially when they are still young

Ships, such as this 17th-century sailing vessel, in the servant trade usually did double duty, carrying servants and redemptioners to the colonies and returning to Britain and Europe with tobacco, timber, or other goods. Ship owners made few alterations to accommodate their human cargo, and servants and redemptioners could expect to spend weeks in the same cold, dank, cramped cargo holds that on other voyages held more inert commodities.

and have nothing to pawn or cannot pay, must be responsible for their own fares as well as those of their parents, and must serve until they are twenty-one years old. Once free of service, they receive a suit of clothing as a parting gift, and if it has been so stipulated the men get a horse and the women a cow.

For most of the colonial era, the English saw overseas colonies as potential solutions to serious domestic problems. Perhaps the most acute of these was "idleness," or the condition of being without work. To 17th and 18th-century English social commentators, this was the root of most social ills, including crime, poverty, vagrancy (homelessness), and popular disorder or rioting. With so much land and so little labor, British policy makers reasoned, the colonies could absorb an endless stream of idle English people and transform them into industrious and productive subjects of the crown. To this end, during the 18th century, more than 50,000 convicted felons were brought to the colonies. Unfortunately, the fate of these men (the vast majority of them were male) was usually rather bleak.

Many were purchased by Chesapeake plantation owners for terms of 7 to 14 years, and they spent their working days cultivating tobacco, often alongside African slaves. Unlike indentured servants (who had voluntarily come to America), they did not receive so-called "freedom dues"—land, cattle, money, or other goods— at the end of their service. This meant that for the rest of their lives most simply worked as farm laborers, never owning land of their own, and scarcely eking out a living.

Furthermore, not all convicts were purchased by masters to work as servants. Some were simply too rebellious or too weak or too old to endure the rigors of plantation work. These social outcasts often found themselves forced to join colonial militias. In this capacity, they were sent off to guard frontier regions or fight enemies of the colony, a fate that meant at best a miserable existence amidst hostile forces on the colonial frontier; and at worst untimely death.

Much like slaves or ordinary servants, few convicts left any personal records. One who did was James Revel, a convict brought to Virginia sometime in the middle of the 17th century. In the verses below, this unlikely poet uses his harsh experience as a convict laborer in America to dissuade England's youth from criminal behavior. Among the noteworthy

aspects of his story is the degree to which southern planta-tion owners appear to treat white convict laborers and African slaves as equals.

This detail from an 18th-century handkerchief depicts a white servant working alongside an African slave, a common occurrence in the tobacco-growing Chesapeake.

My loving Countrymen pray lend an Ear,
   To this Relation which I bring you here,
My sufferings at large I will unfold,
Which tho' 'tis strange, 'tis true as e'er was told,
. . . Then to a Tin-man I was Prentice bound,
My master and mistress good I found,
They lik'd me well, my business I did mind,
From me my parents comfort hop'd to find.
   My master near unto Moorfields did dwell,
Where into wicked company I fell;
To wickedness I quickly was inclin'd
Thus soon is tainted any youthful mind.
   I from my master then did run away,
And rov'd about the streets both night and day:
Did with a gang of rogues a thieving go,
Which filled my parents heart with grief and woe.
   At length my master got me home again, . . .
   But to my vile companions went again: . . .
One night was taken up one of our gang,
Who five impeach'd and three of these were hang'd.
   I was one of the five was try'd and cast,
Yet transportation I did get at last; . . .
   In vain I griev'd, in vain my parents weep,
For I was quickly sent on board the Ship:
With melting kisses and a heavy heart,
I from my dearest parents then did part. . . .
   Five of our number in our passage died,
Which were thrown into the Ocean wide:
And after sailing seven Weeks and more,

"Persons convicted of felony and in consequence transported to this continent, if they are able to pay the expense of passage, are free to pursue their fortune agreeably to their inclinations or abilities. Few, however, have means to avail themselves of this advantage. These unhappy beings are, generally, consigned to an agent, who classes them suitably to their real or supposed qualifications; advertises them for sale, and disposes of them, for seven years, to planters, to mechanics, and to such as choose to retain them for domestic service. Those who survive the term of servitude seldom establish their residence in this country: the stamp of infamy is too strong upon them to be easily erased; they either return to Europe and renew their former practices; or, if they have fortunately imbibed habits of honesty and industry, they remove to a distant situation, where they may hope to remain unknown, and be enabled to pursue with credit every possible method of becoming useful members of society."

—The British government official William Eddis writing from Maryland to a friend in England on the fate of convicts brought to the colonies (1770)

We at Virginia all were put on shore. . . .
    At last to my new master's house I cam,
At the town of Wicocc[o]moco call'd by name,
Where my Europian clothes were took from me,
Which never after I again could see.
    A canvas shirt and trowsers then they gave,
With a hop-sack frock in which I was to slave:
No shoes nor stockings had I for to wear,
Nor hat, nor cap, both head and feet were bare.
    Thus dress'd into the Field I nex[t] must go,
Amongst tobacco plants all day to hoe,
At day break in the morn our work began,
And so held to the setting of the Sun.
    My fellow slaves were just five Transports
    [white convicts] more,
With eighteen Negroes, which is twenty four:
Besides four transport women in the house,
To wait upon his daughter and his Spouse,
    We and the Negroes both alike did fare,
Of work and food we had an equal share;
But in a piece of ground we call our own,
The food we eat first by ourselves were sown,
    No other time to us they would allow,
But on a Sunday we the same must do:
Six days we slave for our master's good,
The seventh day is to produce our food.
    Sometimes when that a hard days work we've done,
Away unto the mill we must be gone;
Till twelve or one o'clock a grinding corn,
And must be up by daylight in the morn. . . .
    And if we offer for to run away,
For every hour we must serve a day;
For every day a Week, They're so severe,
For every week a month, for every month a year
But if they murder, rob or steal when there,
Then straightaway hang'd, the Laws are so severe;
For by the Rigour of that very law
They're much kept under and to stand in awe. . . .
    Thus twelve long tedious years did pass away,
And but two more by law I had to stay:
When Death did for my cruel Master call,
But that was no relief to us at all.

The Widow would not the Plantation hold,
So we and that were both for to be sold,
A lawyer rich who at James-Town did dwell,
Came down to view it and lik'd it very well.

He bought the Negroes who for life were slaves,
But no transported Fellons would he have,
So we were put like Sheep into a fold,
There unto the best bidder to be sold,
A Gentleman who seemed something grave,
Unto me said, how long are you to slave;
Not two years quite, I unto him reply'd,
That is but very short indeed he cry'd. . . .

He straightway came to me again,
And said no longer here you must remain,
For I have bought you of that Man said he,
Therefore prepare yourself to come with me. . . .

My kind new master did at James Town dwell;
By trade a Cooper, and liv'd very well:
I was his servant on him to attend.
Thus God, unlook'd for rais'd me up a friend. . . .

Now young men with speed your lives amend,
Take my advice as one that is your friend:
For tho' so slight you make of it while here,
Hard is your lot when once the[y] get you there.

When People Became Property

Of all the solutions to the colonial labor shortage, none is more complex and troubling than African slavery. Part of the reason for this is a fundamental paradox. The English were notoriously sensitive to any intrusion on their rights and freedoms—perhaps more so than any other people of Europe. And yet, they employed a labor system that fundamentally denied such rights to a distinct segment of the population. Exactly why this was so continues to be the source of scholarly debate. What is clear, however, is that slavery emerged in the colonies only gradually. As late as 1670, it was barely present even in the tobacco-growing regions of the Chesapeake, and where it was present, it existed largely as an abstraction in the minds of the English. Very little of the legal, social, and economic apparatus that was to define plantation slavery was in place. Of the small number of

Africans brought to the colonies before 1670, most simply lived as other servants, some eventually achieving full freedom. By 1700, all this had changed. From a highly ambiguous, barely evident institution, African slavery had become prevalent in the southern colonies. And if earlier the social status of a slave was unclear, it was now sharply etched in law and custom.

Perhaps nowhere is this development more evident than in the law books of Virginia. Beginning in the middle of the 17th century, the law was slowly transformed from an instrument that protected African slaves and white servants alike, to one that established the permanent servile and inferior status of African slaves, and, most importantly, established the hereditary nature of slavery. That is, if formerly the status of slaves' children had been unclear, now it was clear: they would automatically become slaves.

The following are statutes enacted in the Virginia colony between 1662 and 1669. They illustrate the slow hardening of a racial divide in Virginia and the growing social distinction between African slaves and white servants. Perhaps the most striking of these is the first, which establishes that regardless of the father's status, a child whose mother is a slave would be born a slave.

Children of Negro Women to Serve According to the Condition of the Mother
December 1662

Whereas some doubts have arisen whether children got by any Englishman upon a Negro woman should be slave or free. Be it therefore enacted and declared by this present Grand Assembly that all children born in this country shall be held in bond or free only according to the condition of the mother and that if any Christian shall commit fornication with a Negro man or woman, he or she so offending shall pay double the fines imposed by the former act.

Europeans had long reasoned that, as heathens lacking the Christian religion, it was morally permissible to enslave Africans and natives. Such thinking raised a serious problem, though: what would be the fate of slaves or their children who accepted and embraced Christianity? The Virginia colonial assembly solved this problem by implementing the following statute, which stipulated that baptism provided no release from bondage.

"*These two words, Negro and Slave, [have] by custom grown Homogenous and Convertible; even as Negro and Christian, Englishman and Heathen, are by the like corrupt nature and Partiality made opposites.*"
—From *The Negro and Indian's Advocate,* a pamphlet published in London in 1680

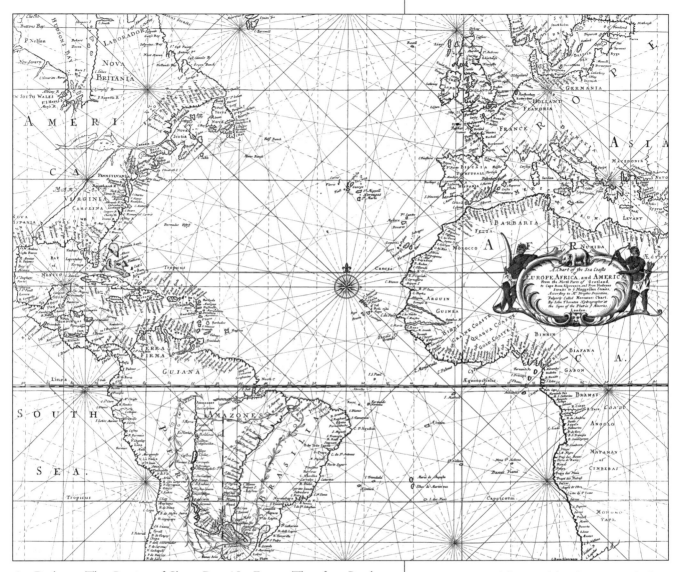

Act Declaring That Baptism of Slaves Does Not Exempt Them from Bondage September 1668

Whereas some doubts have risen whether children that are slaves by birth and by the charity and piety of their owners made partakers of the Blessed Sacrament of Baptism should by virtue of their baptism be made free. It is enacted and declared by the Grand Assembly and the authority thereof that the conferring of baptism does not alter the conditions of the person as to his bondage or freedom; that diverse masters freed from this doubt may more carefully endeavour the propagation of Christianity by permitting children, though slaves, or those of greater growth if capable, to be admitted to that Sacrament.

This map of the Atlantic coasts of Africa, Europe, and the Americas indicates the broad economic effects of the trans-Atlantic slave trade. It transformed the continents abutting the Atlantic Ocean into an integrated economic system. This system carried African slaves to the New World, raw materials produced by those slaves to Europe, and manufactured goods made from those materials to Africa and the New World.

The next statute highlights the growing distinctions between African slaves and white servants. Since the former served for life, masters could not resort to the highest sanction for insubordination; namely, an extension of the term of servitude. The statute below recognized that lacking this sanction, slave owners turned to physical punishment, and absolved them of any criminal responsibility should a slave die from such punishment. In essence, this made it legally permissible for a white person to kill an African.

Act About the Casual Killing of Slaves
October 1669

Whereas the only law in force for the punishment of refractory servants resisting their master or mistress or overseer cannot be inflicted upon Negroes nor the obstinancy of many of them by other than violent means suppressed. Be it enacted and declared by this Grand Assembly if any slave resist his master, or other by his master's order correcting him, and by the extremity of the correction should chance to die that his death shall not be acounted felony, but the master, or that other person appointed by the master to punish him, be acquit from molestation since it cannot be presumed that prepensed malice, which alone makes murder felony, should induce any man to destroy his own estate.

Several factors explain the shift to African slave labor in the colonies. One of the most important of these was simply the declining supply of indentured servants in the Chesapeake. By the mid-1660s, a falling birth rate and improving economy in England resulted in more jobs for men and women who might otherwise have come to the colonies. Similarly, a devastating fire that burned much of London in 1666 created a massive surge in demand for manual labor to rebuild the city. And finally, the rising cost of fertile land in Virginia and Maryland meant diminished opportunities for former servants. Those people still inclined to come to the colonies were now beginning to emigrate to the middle colonies—Pennsylvania, New York, and New Jersey—where land was cheaper.

In addition to the shortage of indentured servants, other less tangible factors account for the rise of slavery, among them the growing sense among colonists that African slaves were more economical and better suited to work in the

sub-tropical south than were whites. Such beliefs are apparent in the following tract justifying the introduction of slavery into the colony of Georgia. Founded as a refuge for debtors and vagrants, the colony initially excluded slaves lest they undermine its purpose: namely to provide employment for idle and indebted English. But within a very short time, the Georgia colonists began emulating their brethren to the north, looking for ways to extract the maximum wealth from their land. And this meant, of course, the introduction of some kind of additional labor force.

The Use and Labour of Negroes has been found indispensably requisite for the Climate and Cultivation of Lands in America; and if in a Point of publick Utility so much contested, it may be allowed to produce in its Favour an Authority, which it is presumed none will object to, General Oglethorpe, a Gentleman of the Trust, (and one, who to all Appearances was as obstinately prejudiced against Negroes as any Man could be) is offer'd; who, 'tis plain, is now become reconciled to their Usefulness, as he keeps a Number of them on his Plantation, bordering on Georgia.

James Oglethorpe

Founder of the Georgia colony

And indeed the extraordinary Heats here, the extraordinary Expences in maintaining, hiring and procuring White Servants, the extraordinary Difficulty and Danger there is in clearing the Lands, attending and Manufacturing the Crops, working in the Fields in Summer, and the poor Returns of Indian Corn, Pease and Potatoes, which are as yet the only chief Produces of the Land there, make it indisputably impossible for White Men alone to carry on Planting to any good Purpose. Besides, our Neighbours having such an Advantage, as the Privilege of Negroes, can always under-sell us in any Manufacture or Produce, which they are as well qualified for as we, should we be ever able to raise more than is necessary for home Consumption without them. The poor People of Georgia, may as well think of becoming Negroes themselves (from whose Condition at present they seem not to be far removed) as of hoping to be ever able to live without them; and they ought best to know, and most to be believed, who have made the Experiment.

'Tis objected, indeed, that the Introduction of Negroes might destroy the Colony; this, as it has never been tried, is but an idle Insinuation. That the Colony is already ruined is certain and evident; and it can't be said, that the Introduction of Negroes has brought this about. Besides, they were never intended to be

Shortly after establishing Georgia, the colony's founder James Oglethorpe escorted a delegation of Native American leaders to London, where they met with a variety of prominent figures including the trustees of the Georgia Colony. The purpose of the trip was to build diplomatic alliances and avert the sort of bloodshed and conflict that had plagued other colonies.

admitted, but under such Limitations, as the Safety, as well as the Improvement of the Colony, would be equally consulted and provided for. . . .

It is also presumed, that the admitting and substituting Negroes to the laborious Parts of [agri]Culture, & c. would make the white Men grow idle and lazy. It has been already shewn, that white Men are unequal to the Task, and yet it must be done. If, therefore, others may be found much fitter and abler for this Work, and who besides doing it better, shall save a Man all the Trouble, and put Money into his Pocket, is this a criminal or unreasonable Piece of Luxury? And as the Labours of the Field here supply but a small Share of that Variety and Stock, which goes to answer the common necessary Demands, may not white Men be still industrious, and to better Purpose, each Man furnishing that Part for which he is best qualified? Moreover, as the principal Springs to that Industry (which the Trustees so much contend for) besides Necessity, seem to be the Possibility of raising those Commodities which are necessary for Life, much cheaper and better at home; the Labour and Money therein employed, being thus turned to better Account, and the Assurance of Men enjoying themselves what they get, or of leaving it to their Children; has not this Government, in the very Foundation of it, entirely relaxed or broke off those Springs in every Motion? The only Difference between an industrious Man in their Sense, and an idle Man hitherto, has been that the former has taken the shortest Way to be ruined, and the latter may possibly hold out till he is put in a better.

Law books and pamphlets reveal much about white attitudes toward slaves. However, because so few slaves were literate, we have very little of their own testimony about what it was actually like to be a slave in colonial America. For such information, historians have had to look elsewhere. Among the more useful sources have been newspaper advertisements offering rewards for runaway servants and slaves. These often contain descriptions of slaves' appearances and personalities, and occasionally say something about a slave's presumed reason for running away. Common among the latter was the desire to rejoin family, an important confirmation that the cruelties of the slave regime did not destroy slaves' emotional attachments. The following ads are from Virginia and South Carolina newspapers. Significantly, their authors give careful attention to the appearance of slaves, particularly skin color, perhaps an indication of widely felt anxiety among slave owners that light-skinned runaways (the lightest of whom are often referred to as "mulatto.") would masquerade as whites and, as a result, be difficult to apprehend.

Virginia Gazette, July 14–July 21, 1783.

Ran away from Coggan's Point on James River, opposite to Col. Byrd's, 3 Negro Men, viz. Basil, a lusty, well-made, black Negro, Virginia born, about 25 years of Age. Glocester, a tall, slim, black Negro, about 30 Years of Age. Sam, a Tawny, well made, Madagascar Negro, about 30 years of Age: They went away in a Canoe on Sunday the 25th of June last; they were seen to go down the River: They had each of them on old Cotton Wastecoats and Breches, and old Oznabriggs Shirts; and 'tis supposed carried with them several Sorts of old Cloaths they had got of their Neighbours, either bought or stole, besides a small Cask of salt

The day-to-day reality of the slave trade involved much more than the transportation of Africans from Africa to America. It also involved the buying and selling of human beings residing in the colonies. As this advertisement from Benjamin Franklin's Pennsylvania Gazette *indicates, mothers and very young children were often sold as a unit. But older children—in this case a slave woman's six-year-old son—were frequently separated from their parents, and that separation was very often permanent.*

THESE are to defire all Perfons, who are poffefs'd of any of the faid Bills, to bring them to the General Loan-Office, where they may have them exchanged for New Ones.

N. B. *The* Currency of the faid Bills being expired, they will not be received in Payment; but all Perfons bringing them to the faid Office, may have them exchanged as above.

THERE is to be fold a very likely Negro Woman aged about Thirty Years who has lived in this City, from her Childhood, and can wafh and iron very well, cook Victuals, few, fpin on the Linen Wheel, milk Cows, and do all Sorts of Houfe-work very well. She has a Boy of about Two Years old, which is to go with her. The Price as reafonable as you can agree.

And alfo another very likely Boy aged about Six Years, who is Son of the abovefaid Woman. He will be fold with his Mother, or by himfelf, as the Buyer pleafes. Enquire of the Printer.

Fish, and some Corn. Whoever secures them so as their Master may get them, shall have Twenty Shillings for each, besides what the Law allows, and all reasonable Charges, paid by me.

Nathaniel Harrison.

Virginia Gazette, June 15—June 22, 1739.

RAN away, from the Subscriber, of James-City County, on Sunday the 17th Instant, a pale Complexion'd Mulatto Fellow, nam'd Natt, with strait Hair, about 2 or 3 Inches long. He is a thick, well-set Fellow, about 26 Years old; has several Black Moles on his Face, a full Mouth, Black Teeth, small Forehead, and broad Feet. He has lately had the foul [venereal] Disease, the Ulcers on his Scrotum and Penis are not yet perfectly heal'd. He had on an old Hat, Cotton Wastecoat, & patch'd Breeches, and an Osnabrig Shirt. He likewise made his Escape on Monday Night last, from Col. Burwell's, who took him from on board the Flamborough Man of War, Capt. Pierse, Commander, where he had conceal'd himself, with Intent to escape to New-York. His Back, I believe, for some time will discover the Stripes [from a beating] he receiv'd on board the Man of War. Whoever shall bring the said Mulatto Slave to me the Subscriber, near Williamsburg, shall receive a Pistole Reward, besides what the Law allows.

William Drummond.

Virginia Gazette, May 9 to May 16, 1745.
North-Carolina, April 24, 1745.

RAN away, on the 18th Instant, from the Plantation of the late Col. William Wilson, deceas'd, Two Slaves belonging to the Subscriber, the one a tall yellow Fellow, named Emanuel, about 6 Feet high, six or seven and Twenty Years of Age; hath a Scar on the outside of his left Thigh, which was cut with an Ax; he had on when he went away, a blue Jacket, an Ozenbrig Shirt and Trousers, and a Worsted Cap; he speaks pretty good English, and calls himself a Portugueze; is by Trade a Cooper, and took with him some Cooper's Tools. The other is a short, thick, well-set Fellow, stoops forward pretty much as he walks; does not speak so plain as the other; had on when he went away an Ozenbrig Pair of Trousers and Shirt, a white Negro Cotton Jacket, and took with him an Axe: They went away in a small Cannoe, and were seen at Capt. Pearson's, on Nuse River, the 18th Inst. and 'tis believ'd are gone towards Virginia. Whoever takes up the said Negros, and brings them to my House on Trent River, North-Carolina, or secures them so that I may have them again, shall have Four Pistoles Reward for each, paid by

Mary Wilson

The following ads from the *South Carolina Gazette* differ from those above in two ways. First, they are for runaway female slaves; and second, they indicate slaveowners' fears that freed slaves or other slaves might conspire to shelter runaways. The latter was a constant concern among elite whites in 18th-century South Carolina, where peoples of African descent constituted a larger proportion of the population than anywhere else in the mainland colonies.

South-Carolina Gazette, May 11—May 18, 1734.

RUN away from Mr. Culcheth Golightly on John's Island, a young Molatto House-Wench, named Franke, not long since sold at Vendure by the execut[or] of Mr. French['s estate], she is known by most People in Charlestown, where she has been seen lately by several, and without doubt harbour'd by some free Negroes or Slaves. Whoever can apprehend the said Wench, and will deliver her to Collon. Fenwicke in Charlestown, shall have Three Pounds reward; as also a farther reward to any one that can prove where & by whom she has been harbour'd since her Elopement.

South-Carolina Gazette, January 18–January 25, 1734-5.

RUn away from his Excellency the Governor about 14 Days ago, a young Negro Wench about 14 or 15 Years of Age, very black of Colour, a flattish Face, had on a Negro cloth Gown dyed yellowish, & a white handkerchief about her head, her name Phillis: Whoever brings her to the Governor's House, shall be rewarded as the Law directs, and whoever harbours or conceals her shall be prosecuted.

Although much information can be gleaned from runaway slave ads, they still offer only a paltry glimpse of the daily lives of slaves. Perhaps a more detailed understanding of the day-to-day experience of African slaves can be obtained from diaries kept by slaveowners. Among the most valuable of these is that of Landon Carter, son of one of Virginia's wealthiest families, and the inheritor of no fewer than eight fully operational plantations. Few documents offer so vivid and detailed a depiction of life on a colonial plantation, and fewer still describe in comparable detail the daily trials of the African slaves who worked those plantations.

None of this suggests that Carter's diary offers as authentic a glimpse of slave experiences as the writings of slaves themselves, but given the scarcity of such writings, these sorts of documents can be useful. Of course, they have to be approached with great care, which means, among other things, being aware of authors' interests and biases. In the case of Carter's diary, for instance, one finds an almost obsessive interest in the physical health of individual slaves. The reason was probably a combination of practical and theoretical concerns. On the one hand, Carter—like most planters—regarded slaves as a vital asset, and hence was concerned with their health. A sick slave was worth little to him. On the other, Carter devoted much time to the study of medicine, and in his diaries detailed the symptoms and medical treatment of slaves and family members. Such behavior was fully consistent with that of other well-to-do colonists, many of whom engaged in philosophical and scientific pursuits.

For historians, Carter's interest in health and medicine has allowed a rare glimpse into one of the little studied aspects of slavery: the physical toll it took on slaves. In the following extracts from Carter's diary, he carefully details the illness of a house slave named Winney. Exactly what

In this portrait of the Virginia planter Landon Carter, his upright posture, his stern gaze, the fine fabrics of his clothes, and the gentle hand upon his dog's head were all intended to send a clear message. Carter is presented as a supremely self-confident, strong man, who was in control of himself and his dependents, whether his wife, his children, his slaves, or his pets.

Winney suffered from is unclear. Indeed, there is even reason to wonder whether or not she was actually ill at all. Some historians have suggested that slaves feigned illness as a way of limiting their workloads. In either case, Winney surely suffered. In the 18th century, medical care often produced as much pain and misery as disease itself. In the first passage below, Carter lists his sick slaves, Winney among them. The list ends with reference to Carter's immediate family, most of whom were apparently also sick.

August 22, 1757

There have been sick: . . . Lame George, Juba, Rose . . . Martha, Billy, Willoughby, Sarah, Mimah. . . . Peg and Mooter . . . . Sukey. . . . Nat, Tom, Sawney, Sam, Nassau, Winney, Bettsey besides my whole family except Johnny Carter.

Carter next mentions Winney on April 10, 1758, when he describes the medications he gave her for a new bout of sickness. He also mentions medications he and a local physician gave Winney, some of which were probably folk remedies originally used by Africans and Native Americans and incorporated into colonists' medical practices. What Carter refers to as "rattlesnake decoction," for instance, was a liquid derived from boiling rattlesnake weed. This flowering plant grew widely in eastern North America and was used by Native Americans to treat snakebites.

Winney continued all yesterday in her fever. Her pain in the head abated a little at night but not the fever. I gave her Rhubarb 5 grains, Conutuptheus . . . 5 grains, Rad Valerian 5 grains, Salt tartar 4 grains in a Cup of Marsh Mallow tead with Salt Prunella in it and 40 drop Spiritus-Minderius. Four of these doses this day but no amendments. Therefore I sent to Dr. Flood as she was usefull (though careless) among my Children. At 2 I gave a spoonfull of Rattle snake decoction finding her cough hard and her pulse prodigeous quick, and as she had one stool the rattle snake I repeated hourly for 3 doses, and at 5 she fell into a plentiful sweat . . .

April 12, 1758

Dr. Flood came last night past 5 to Winney. He ordered her to be blooded [bled] this morning which was done quantity 6 ounces very morbid and almost in a state of Corruption. He then ordered

"[African slaves] are a people by whose labour the other inhabitants [of the colonies] are in a great measure supported, . . . These are a people who have made no agreement to serve us and who have not forfeited their liberty that we know of. These are souls for whom Christ died, and for our conduct toward them we must answer before that Almighty Being who is no respecter of persons."

—Quaker opponent of slavery John Woolman in his journal (1757)

This 1759 illustration reveals the persistent appeal of astrological explanations for natural phenomena during the colonial era. It appeared in an almanac printed in Philadelphia and was intended to help diagnose illnesses by showing the parts of the body and their governing celestial constellations.

great Plenty of Mallow and ground Ivy tea with Spiritus Salis Oleo and Lavender aa 20 drops every two hours and one spoonfull rattlesnake decoction every two hours to break the viscid state of her blood and help on Expectoration with plenty of gruel for food. Her pulse still very quick but the uneasyness in her head abated.

The following entry suggests that Carter and Winney had some disagreement about the latter's condition. It also indicates that in medical care, as in much else on the plantation, the master's will prevailed. Apparently against Winney's wishes, Carter had her bled, a widely used treatment in European medicine.

April 13, 1758

Winney blooded [bled] last night according to order though not such a quantity taken away as was ordered through her fears and difficulty in bleeding. . . . Her cough breaking and she spits a tough matter by means of the rattle snake though no sweating and the pulse not much lower and near as quick as usual. She thinks herself better. This is her 11th day. Her pulse growing so much fuller than it has hitherto been and very quick withall and as yet very little expectoration although a plentiful use of rattlesnake decoction. At 6 this evening I ordered 6 ounces of blood more to be taken away as being the only means to save her. She thinks her self she is better because her cough is not so troublesome and frequent but I observe she is under a great difficulty in breathing and as yet no proper sweat though her flesh is grown much softer.

In the next entry, Carter claims Winney was concealing her symptoms and refusing to take her medicine. Whether or not this was the case is impossible to know. What does seem certain, however, is that Carter had little interest in his slaves' sense of their own well-being. His and his physician's studies, he no doubt assumed, made their diagnoses valid, even when they appeared to contradict the visible symptoms.

April 22, 1758

Winney . . . whose case is fully described before makes very little shew of recovery. She gained a little strength but I believe through aversion to medicin she concealed her want of appetite and eat frequently without any inclination. She had also a purging but it stopped too soon of its own accord. Dr. Flood who was called into her had directed upon any Symptom of sickness at Stomach or want of appetite to exhibit a dose of Ipecacuana but these She concealed and grew very nervously affected. Being with child there was danger in using warm nervines. The Dr. Therefore ordered her warm bitters 3 times a day and Spirit Lavender with 1/5 Sal Volfrigty. She complained this day of sickness at her stomach and being affected in her sences and deaf I gave her 25 grains Ipecacuana which brought off Abundance of filthy Phlegm and bile. She seems a little feverish which She has not been these 5 days, but I think she both hears and speaks better. I shall begin her bitters tomorrow if not obstructed by Circumstances.

Winney recovered from her sickness, but her experience with colonial medicine was by no means over. In a diary entry made 12 years after the above entries, Carter reports that she fell into a ditch of water and again became violently ill. In his usual fashion, Carter responded to the situation by prescribing bleedings, purges, and rattlesnake root. In subsequent years, Carter mentioned Winney from time to time, usually referring to her medical condition. But he tells us little about what ultimately became of her.

Bleeding was a common treatment in colonial-era medicine. Physicians prescribed it for virtually every conceivable malady, including mental illness.

Breathing a vein.

Chapter Five

Ties That Bind

For colonial Americans, family was everything. Of course, we modern Americans also consider family to be important, but the reality is, it is a much less significant part of most of our lives than it was of the colonists'. To grasp the contrast, we might simply consider the following aspects of most modern Americans' lives: For education, we go to schools. For work, we go to places of business. Our sick and infirm are cared for in hospitals; the poor and destitute are cared for by the government or private charitable organizations. In the colonial era, virtually none of this was true. Work, medical care, primary education, charity—nearly all took place in the home. There were few schools or hospitals, and even fewer charitable institutions to care for the indigent or the orphaned, leaving most families with no choice but to educate and care for their own members. Similarly, there were no large factories or businesses. Most household goods and other manufactured items were made by families in their homes. And much business in the colonies, particularly outside of the cities, was transacted in the home.

Colonial families differed from most modern American families in other ways as well. For the most part, when we think of family today, we think of nuclear families—mother, father, and siblings. To be sure, we also have extended families consisting of cousins, grandparents, aunts, uncles, and in-laws. But our relationships with these people are likely to be not much more intimate than those we have with friends and neighbors. In the colonies, this was often not the case. When colonists spoke of their families, they meant whoever lived in the family home, very often including members of the extended family, apprentices, domestic servants, and slaves. And colonists were likely to be as attached to these people as they were to members of their nuclear family. In a colonial home, masters and servants were as likely as parents and children to find themselves sleeping in the same room, eating at the same table, and living in the same house.

Family was also the foundation for colonists' understanding of the ordering of their society. Whether considered the relationship between a servant and his master, a sea captain and his sailors, or even

In this 1741 portrait, the wealthy Massachusetts gentleman Isaac Royall presides proudly over his seated female relatives. Young Isaac, the painting suggests, had become the family patriarch.

"If we compare the natural duties of a father with those of a king, we find them to be all one, without any difference at all but only in the latitude or extent of them."

—The 17th-century English political theorist Sir Robert Filmer defending the fatherly authority of the English king in his treatise *Patriarcha* (1680)

the king and his subjects, one essential truth was clear. Each of these relationships was to one degree or another comparable to that first familial relationship depicted in the Bible—that between Adam and Eve. They all entailed a certain amount of hierarchy—one party was socially superior to the other—but they also entailed certain mutual obligations. Just as a husband was obliged to care for his wife, so the master had to care for his servant; the sea captain was obliged to watch over his sailors; and the king was obliged to protect his subjects.

More than simply a group of people living under the same roof, the colonial family was also a group of people living by the same rules. Those rules varied from family to family, and region to region. But the person who made those rules was usually the same in all families: the father. Colonial families, historians have found, were intensely patriarchal; that is, they were bound to adhere to the wishes and values of the male head of the household. This fact was as true of that father's children as it was of other family members, including those not related by blood. To be a member of a colonial family was, quite literally, to be a member of a little kingdom, presided over by one man.

What this meant was that members of the household subscribed to the father's religious beliefs, endured the father's disciplinary measures and, above all, depended on the father for the basics of life—food, clothing, and other necessities. The reason for this is simple: Husbands or fathers controlled virtually all the wealth and property in colonial America. The significance of this is especially clear in the relationships between husbands and wives.

When a woman married, any property her family might have set aside for her would immediately come under her husband's control. And if that husband died, in all likelihood the widow would receive only a small portion of his estate, and that almost never included land. Married women were thus expected to live their lives much as children or even servants and slaves did: they owned virtually no property, controlled very little wealth, had virtually no formal political power, depended on their husbands for many basic necessities, and were subject to a wide variety of legally sanctioned physical punishments administered by their husbands. Indeed, the very nature of the marriage vows was akin to the terms of a servant's contract: A woman vowed to serve and obey her husband for life, in exchange for his protection and financial support.

Along with the profound legal and social constraints placed upon them, colonial wives bore a host of domestic responsibilities.

They often directed all the work that took place in the home, including both ordinary domestic chores and the manufacturing of household goods. They also oversaw the work of servants and slaves in the house, managed trade with other households, and often collaborated with their husbands in business dealings. Colonial women also took care of the sick and infirm, often functioning as the closest thing to a doctor many ordinary colonists would ever see. They applied various folk remedies and occasionally even performed surgery. Beyond this, when women were not themselves having children, they were often assisting their daughters or neighbors with childbirth.

Although the marriage contract gave the husband legal superiority, when it came time to marry, women often exercised some discretion over the choice of their spouse. Rarely did women marry without the approval of their parents, but marriages were usually not arranged; that is, parents generally did not choose their daughters' husbands. In the case of female indentured servants who had completed their terms of service and sought husbands, parents were even less of a factor because these women often lived an ocean away from their families. Also, in areas where there were more men than women—the 17th-century Chesapeake was particularly striking in this regard—potential brides usually had multiple suitors to choose among.

The point here is simple: Married or unmarried, free colonial women, as well as children, male and female servants, and slaves, lived in a society dominated by free white men.

The Struggle for Family

Although the family came to be the central social institution in colonial life, in the very first phases of settlement, families scarcely existed at all. The majority of colonists who came to Virginia were young, unmarried men—hardly the building blocks of a family-centered society. But Virginia Company officials quickly recognized that a single-sex colony was undesirable. Unmarried men were likely to leave the colony, and with few married couples, a crucial labor source—namely, the family—was unlikely to evolve. To alleviate these problems, the Virginia Company began to send women to the colony in the early 1620s. Given the risks involved, it is perhaps not surprising to find that the Company was unable to recruit an adequate supply of prospective

Controlling Women for Their Own Good

Among the many English legal and political ideas colonists embraced was the notion of coverture, or the idea that a married woman should be identified first and foremost through her husband. That is, the moment a woman was married, her very person was "covered" or replaced by that of her husband. It was this idea that gave husbands total control of wives' property, and in turn left colonial women with few political rights. Voting in early America was almost without exception a right given only to property owners. Few legal and political theorists saw anything at all inappropriate about coverture. Indeed, most justified it as necessary for the protection of women. As the influential English jurist William Blackstone wrote in his *Commentaries on the Common Law*, published in 1771, "Even the disabilities, which the wife lies under, are for the most part intended for her protection and benefit. So great a favourite is the female sex of the laws of England."

brides. And of the several hundred such women it did bring to the colony, only a very small handful survived the Powhatan attack of 1622.

In the letter below, Virginia Company officials provide authorities in Virginia with instructions on how to dispose of brides sent to the colony. The document suggests that the officials were worried that the women would be turned into servants, either by marrying male servants or by being sold into servitude. But it clearly wanted to prevent this, lest the goal of building stable, landowning families be thwarted.

We send you in this ship one widow and eleven maids for wives for the people in Virginia. There hath been especial care had in the choice of them; for there hath not any one of them been received but upon good commendations, as by a note herewith sent you may perceive. We pray you all therefore in general to take them into your care; and more especially we recommend them to you . . . that at their first landing they may be housed, lodged and provided for of diet till they be married, for such was the haste of sending them away, as that straitened with time we had no means to put provisions aboard, . . . And in case they cannot be presently married, we desire they may be put to several householders that have wives till they can be provided of husbands. There are near fifty more which are shortly to come, are sent by our most honorable Lord and Treasurer the Earl of Southampton and certain worthy gentlemen, who taking into their consideration that the Plantation can never flourish till families be planted and the respect of wives and children fix the people on the soil, therefore have given this fair beginning, for the reimbursing of whose charges it is ordered that every man that marries them give 120 lbs. weight of the best leaf tobacco for each of them, and in case any of them die, that proportion must be advanced to make it up upon those that survive . . . And though we are desirous that marriage be free according to the law of nature, yet would we not have these maids deceived

This late-17th-century English song, which tells of a man sending his wife to Virginia for ten pounds sterling, only slightly exaggerates the control husbands had over their wives.

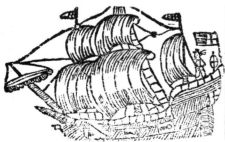

THE
Woman Outwitted :
OR, THE
Weaver's Wife cunningly catch'd in a Trap, by her Husband, who sold her for ten Pounds, and sent her to *Virginny*.

To an excellent new Tune.

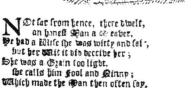

and married to servants, but only to freemen or tenants as have means to maintain them. We pray you therefore to be fathers to them in this business, not enforcing them to marry against their wills; neither send we them to be servants, save in case of extremity, for we would have their condition so much bettered as multitudes may be allured thereby to come unto you. And you may assure such men as marry those women that the first servants sent over by the Company shall be consigned to them, it being our intent to preserve families and to prefer married men before single persons.

As the central relationship of the central social institution in colonial life, the bond between husband and wife was, understandably, the subject of endless discussion. Many colonists believed that if this bond were weak, families might disintegrate. And if families disintegrated, then perhaps the whole society would come apart. Few colonists better expressed these sentiments than Puritan minister Samuel Willard. In his sermon, Willard explains the biblical origins of the relationship between husband and wife. In doing so, he sought to persuade his congregation of the seriousness and gravity of the vows of marriage.

The natural Necessity of [the relationship between husband and wife] was founded in the Order and End of Man's Creation. Humane Nature was at first confined to one Man, and one Woman [Adam and Eve], by whom it was to be Propagated and Multiplyed in its Individuals, which was the reason why God made a distinction of Sex between them: And to prevent Confusion, God from the First appointed Marriage . . . And in this He laid a foundation for distinct Families, to set up each by themselves. . . . So that if this Order be not upheld, either Mankind must cease, or Mankind must degenerate into the State and Order of Brutes, which is altogether disagreeable.

. . . In the further Prosecution of the Duties between these, we are to take Notice, that of all the Orders which are unequals, these do come nearest to an Equality, and in several respects they stand upon even ground. These do make a Pair, which infers so far a *Parity*: They are in the Word of God called *Yoke-Fellows*, and so are to draw together in the Yoke. Nevertheless, God hath also made an imparity between them, in the Order prescribed in his Word, and for that reason there is a Subordination, and they are

Love, Not Money

In his short poem, Caleb Raper, a Quaker, wrote of the need for marriage to be founded on love, not money. Raper was perhaps writing this as a reminder to himself, since it appeared in his Commonplace Book *(1711), a collection of quotes and miscellaneous thoughts about morality and individual conduct. Colonists often produced these collections for themselves as guides to proper behavior and repositories of important bits of human wisdom.*

If thou resolute to change a single life
And hast a purpose to become a wife,
Then chuse thy husband not for worldly gain,
Nor for his comely shape or beauty vain.
If money make the match or Lust impure
Both bride and bridegroom too shall
  weep be sure.

A suitor of Elizabeth Sandwith made this intricate valentine for her in 1753, probably in Philadelphia. Despite all his trouble, the man failed to gain Elizabeth's hand. She married someone else.

ranked among unequals. And from this we may observe some Duties that are *mutual* or common between them, and others that are *proper* to each.

In the following passage, Willard explains that the bonds of marriage are not simply utilitarian bonds, but rather are bonds of conjugal love. Willard distinguishes this form of love from "Special Love," something more akin to obligation or duty. Conjugal love, as Willard describes it, is much more than this. It is a bond of two hearts; it is, quite simply, romantic love.

That therefore which belongs to Married Persons is *Conjugal Love;* which is therein distinguished from that which is due to any other Relation whatsoever. There is also a *Special Love,* which comprehends the whole Duty of the Husband to his Wife, in all the parts of it; and is put in contradistinction to the Submission, which expresseth the whole Duty of the Wife. . . . But this Conjugal Love is *Mutual,* and is the proper Cement of this Relation: And it is enforced from that Conjugal Union, by which they become One Flesh: And tho' this Oneness be not *Natural,* but *Voluntary,* yet it is the nearest relative Conjunction in the World, and on that account it requires the intimatest Affection; and if it be rightly made, it follows from a Preference that these have each of the other in their hearts, above all the World, on account of this Relation: For which reason it is compared to Love between Christ & his Church. . . . And the true Comfort which is to be hoped for from this Relation, must derive from this Love, without which it will prove to be, of all the most unhappy.

Women's Trials

Although colonial law generally denied married women the right to own property or control their financial affairs, some women were nevertheless able to do these things. In the following marital contract, Maryland widow Margaret Preston asserts continued control over a portion of her deceased husband's estate as she prepares to marry William Berry. (Included among the assets Margaret retains is a young slave named Sarah.) It is probably not coincidental that this contract was written in the 17th-century Chesapeake, a place with fewer women than men and, as a result, a place where prospective brides often had more legal leverage than elsewhere in the colonies.

Articles of agreement, made and agreed upon between William Berry of the one part and Margaret Preston, both of Patuxent River in the County of Calvert, of the other part, witnesseth that the abovesaid Margaret Preston and William Berry have fully and perfectly concluded and agreed, that the said Margaret doth reserve for her own proper use and behoof, before she doth engage herself in marriage to the said William Berry, the value of one hundred pounds sterling, to be at her the said Margaret's own disposal, in such goods as shall be hereafter mentioned: viz.

Plate, to the value and worth of forty pounds sterling.

The little Negro girl called Sarah, born in Richard Preston's [Margaret's deceased first husband] house, valued to ten pounds sterling. If the said girl should die, the said William Berry [agreed] to make the same good to the said Margaret by another Negro or the value.

A good mare to ride on, value seven pounds sterling.

A chamber or room to be well furnished with bedding and furniture, with other household [items] to the value of forty-three pounds sterling.

With almost no government support for the very poorest colonists, more prominent colonists occasionally organized fund-raising events such as these plays to raise money for their aid.

Jane Eustis, a Boston merchant who dealt in fine imported goods, was one of the very few colonial women to own her own business. Along with newspaper advertisements and word of mouth, merchants used "shopkeeper's bills" such as this to generate business. A shop-keeper's bill was similar to a business card.

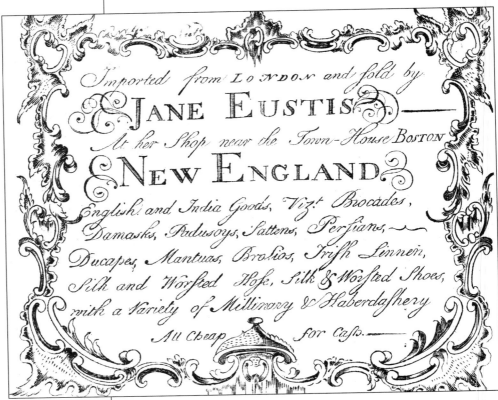

Imported from LONDON and sold by
JANE EUSTIS
At her Shop near the Town-House BOSTON
NEW ENGLAND

English and India Goods, Viz.t Brocades, Damasks, Padusoys, Sattens, Persians, Ducapes, Mantuas, Brolios, Irish Linnen, Silk and Worsted Hose, Silk & Worsted Shoes, with a Variety of Millinary & Haberdashery

All Cheap for Cash.

And for a further testimony that the abovementioned articles are fully and perfectly concluded and agreed upon by the parties aforesaid, the said William Berry both binds himself, his heirs, executors, and administrators to the true performance of all and every [one] of the abovementioned articles, to the full value as is aforementioned, whensoever the said Margaret Preston shall make demand of the same for her own proper use. But if it shall be so ordered after the aforementioned William Berry and Margaret Preston be married that the said William shall die first, that then the abovesaid goods (or the value) do remain firm to and for the said Margaret's own proper use, as she shall think fit to bestow, over and above her proportion of the estate which by the said William Berry shall be left her. For the true performance of this agreement the abovesaid William Berry hath hereunto set his hand and seal this ninth day of the tenth month, called December, in the year one thousand, six hundred, sixty, and nine.

Although premarital contracts may have given some colonial women a certain amount of financial independence, such agreements were rare, especially in the northern

colonies, where the numbers of men and women were more equal than in the South. The absence of such agreements made the choice of a husband all the more important. Colonial women were well aware that once that decision had been made, it was usually for life. Divorce was possible, but whether it was a viable option for married women depended on the colony in which they resided. Some colonial courts were more sympathetic to aggrieved wives than others. Even in the best of circumstances, however, divorce often left colonial women with little.

In the following letters, Esther Edwards Burr advises her friend Sarah Prince to conclude a lengthy courtship and to marry her struggling suitor. Burr, the daughter of the great Connecticut preacher and theologian Jonathan Edwards, writes from a position of experience, having four years earlier married the second president of Princeton University, Aaron Burr. The letters reveal that colonial women often had a good deal of control over this very important decision. The letters also suggest that the 27-year-old Sarah came from a family of means. Women from less well-to-do families often did not have the luxury of taking so long to choose the right spouse.

The expected roles of elite husbands and wives are displayed in this portrait of the Mifflins of Philadelphia, painted by the most renowned of all colonial portrait painters, John Singleton Copley. Mr. Mifflin, taking a break from his studies, gazes admiringly at his wife, who is engaged in the feminine activity of weaving a decorative fringe on a tape loom.

[April 14, 1756]
Wednsday Eve

—If you dont come this spring I shall dispare of ever seeing you in these parts, for if you M-a-r-r-y as I think you will before a nother spring I suppose we shall see no more of you in our world—Well tis a might strang piece of conduct of that sertain Gentleman [Sarah's suitor]—I wonder what ails him—I surspect he is bashfull. You must e'ne do the business for him—Tackle up your Chair and go a Courting, and bring the matter to an issue, [so] that a body may know what to depend on—Its vastly uncomfortable to be hung up between the Heavens and Earth as it were Gibbeted—if Mr Burr goes to Boston he will do something in the affair you may be sertain, for you know he loves to be poking about matches.

[April 16,1756]
Fryday Morn

. . . I never was so near being angry at you in my life. If you was her[e] I should sertainly Cuff you—Indeed my dear I think you are a little Proud—I have incouraged you in it two under a notion of *nobleness of mind, and greatness of soul* but to be plain you have carried matter of this sort two far. *You have stood upon points two much, and two long,* and I should have told you so before if I knew as much as I do now. . . . Why you would not have the Man act like a fool would you? Well why will you oblige him to either become a fool or give up the affair, and without desighn in you two for you don't chuse nither—I am almost two vext to write—I wonder in the name of honesty what business you had to run a way time after time when you knew he was coming—You may repent it when it is two late—for I dont know of such another match on all accounts not on all our shore.

You should consider my dear that he does not, nor cant know the reasons of your conduct—tis most likly that he thinks that you dislike him, or elce that you are a Mortal proud creture, which must sink you in his opinnion, and may lay a foundation for unhapyness all your days after Marriage for my dear no man likes a woman the better for being shy when she means the very thing she pretends to be shy off. . . .

[October 17, 1756]
Sabbath P.M. Oct. 17

. . . I am so distressed for you in your perplexed situation that I cant tarry till the Sabbath is over before I tell you I Pity you from the Bottom of my soul, and have after my poor cold manner many times this day prayed for you, that you may be Directed, that you may be inclined to do what shall be most for the glory of God and your own good and comfort boath for time and Eternity—Once I was the subject of much such perplexities. One case in petecular was very similar to yours. Then I have reason to think God was my director and trust he will be yours—dont sink. All is Wisely Ordered and best—I doubt not but duty will be made plain—When did you ever commit any case to the Lord but he directed your paths. . . .

[October 21, 1756]
Thursday P.M.

3d Objection in my opinnion has more weight in it than all the rest—that you dont think you can esteem him enough—if you cant, tis sufficient objection—for *Let the Wife see that she Reverence her Husband*—if you cant esteem you cant reverence—so there it must end—but I immagine you are mistaken. You cant help esteeming a person of so many good quallifycations as are under the head of Inducements. . . . Objection 4th—that you cant expect relegious

This wax doll was made by Sarah Gardner, prior to her marriage in 1739 to the prominent Boston minister, Joshua Gee. Because they had more leisure time than women and girls from less wealthy families, girls such as Sarah could devote much time to perfecting various crafts.

conversation from him—*How knowest thou O Woman but thou mayest gain thy Husband.* I think there is a good deal of reason to hope it as he has such a desire to have a relegious Wife.

I know it to be the opinnion of my Honored Parents that a person aught not to make concience of this matter. They said that some other things were more necessary to happyness in a Married state, . . . but when Relegion meets those other things it Crowns all—tis proporly the Crown, but my dear this alone will not do—look around, you will soon see that tis not every good Man that you could live happily with in that state. . . .

[October 23, 1756]
Saturday

Upon the Whole—The important point must turn here. If upon mature deliberation and serious consideration you find you cant think of spending your days with that Gentleman with Complaciency and delight, *say No*—but if on the contarary, I think you may venture to answer in the affermative—This must turn the point so you only can determine for your self.

Precisely because the formal institutions of colonial life—the laws, the churches, the governments—did so much to maintain the superior status of free white males, one might conclude that women had a good deal more power and independence in regions where these institutions were weak and fragmentary. Thus, in frontier regions, including northern New England, western Pennsylvania, western Virginia, the western Carolinas, and most of Georgia, one might expect to find women enjoying a level of autonomy unfamiliar in more populated areas.

Though this often was the case, whatever personal independence frontier women enjoyed was generally countered by the incredible hardships of daily life—hardships that in many ways resembled those faced by the first colonists in North America. Aside from their nearly constant clashing with native peoples, colonists in these areas struggled with a host of difficulties, including food shortages and severe weather. Beyond these burdens, the very absence of legal and political institutions freed husbands from even the minimal constraints the law placed on them with regard to their treatment of wives. Among the very few firsthand depictions of women's life on the colonial frontier is that of John Lawson, a young English immigrant and trader who traveled

"For a Single Fornication, whipping or a Fine. And yet for all this Law, the Chastity of some of 'em, for I do not Condemn all the People, may be guess'd at by the Number of Delinquents in this kind: For there hardly passes a Court Day, but some are convened for Fornication; and Convictions of this Nature are very frequent."

—From John Dunton, writing about the prevalence of premarital sex in 17th-century Boston in his book, *Letters Written from New England* (1686)

For most families, life on the colonial frontier was more complex and difficult than what is suggested by this bucolic 1763 engraving. Nonetheless, many Europeans did prosper in America, and for these colonists the rise from modest log-cabin dwellings to large and more permanent homes like the one depicted at the right would have been a familiar reality.

through the Carolina backcountry at the beginning of the 18th century. While Lawson tried to depict women's lives in favorable terms, the overall picture he paints suggests there was little to be gained from living on the far fringes of European settlement.

The Women are the most industrious Sex in that Place, and, by their good Houswifry, make a great deal of Cloath of their own Cotton, Wool and Flax; some of them keeping their Families (though large) very decently apparel'd, both with Linnens and Woollens, so that they have no occasion to run into the Merchant's Debt, or lay their Money out on Stores for Cloathing.

. . . [The women] marry very young; some at Thirteen or Fourteen; and She that stays till Twenty, is reckon'd a stale Maid; which is a very indifferent Character in that warm Country. The Women are very fruitful; most Houses being full of Little Ones. It has been observ'd, that Women long marry'd, and without Children, in the other Places, have remov'd to *Carolina*, and become joyful Mothers. They have very easy Travail in their Child-bearing, in which they are so happy, as seldom to miscarry.

. . . Many of the women are very handy in Canoes, and will manage them with great Dexterity and Skill, which they become accustomed to in this watry Country. They are ready to help their Husbands in any servile Work, as Planting, when the Season of the Weather requires Expedition; Pride seldom banishing good Houswifry. The Girls are not bred up to the Wheel, and Sewing only; but the Dairy and Affairs of the House they are very well acquainted withal; so that you shall see them, whilst very young, manage their Business with a great deal of Conduct and Alacrity. The Children of both Sexes are very docile, and learn any thing with a great deal of Ease and Method; and those that have the Advantages of Education, write good Hands, and prove good Accountants, which is most coveted, and indeed most necessary in these Parts.

Parents and Children

If the bond between husbands and wives was the most important in colonial society, that between parents and children was a very close second. The values of duty, obedience, and obligation that shaped this relationship were also integral to other relations in colonial society, including those between masters and servants. Although these values remained in place throughout the colonial period, the precise nature of parents' obligation to children changed in subtle but important ways. At the beginning of the colonial era, particularly in New England, colonists widely assumed that children had to be forced to obey their parents. Physical punishment was thus an accepted part of a child's upbringing. During the 18th century, however, new European ideas about child rearing began to change colonists' assumptions. These ideas suggested that children were naturally inclined to obey their parents and that gentle persuasion, rather than capricious and harsh physical punishment, would elicit this obedience.

In his book *The Well-Ordered Family* (1712), Boston clergyman Benjamin Wadsworth offers advice to colonial parents. What is interesting about Wadsworth's remarks is the way they combine old and new approaches to child rearing. At once, Wadsworth urges parents to "restrain" and "correct" children, but he urges them to do so in a cautious, sensitive manner.

The Locke Approach: Character Development through Reward and Punishment

The English philosopher John Locke was probably the most widely read educational theorist in the colonies who was not a Christian minister. Unlike many theorists before him, Locke believed children were born with a capacity to be rational, self-interested beings. The duty of education was to exercise that capacity, much as one might exercise a muscle, and this was to be done by rewarding rational behavior while punishing irrational or self-destructive behavior. This was a significant departure from earlier theories, which relied heavily on physical punishment and coercion while leaving little place for any kind of positive reinforcement. As Locke explained in his book Some Thoughts Concerning Education *(1693):*

Good and Evil, *Reward* and *Punishment*, are the only Motives to a rational Creature; these are the Spur and Reins, whereby all Mankind are set on work, and guided, and therefore they are to be made use of to Children too. For I advise their Parents and Governors always to carry this in their Minds, that Children are to be treated as rational Creatures.

SOME THOUGHTS CONCERNING EDUCATION.

§. 1. A Sound Mind in a sound Body, is a short, but full description of a Happy State in this World : He that has these Two, has little more to wish for; and he that wants either of them, is but little the better for any thing else. Mens Happiness or Misery is most part of their own making. He, whose Mind directs not wisely, will never take the right Way; and he, whose Body is crazy and feeble, will never be able to advance in it. I confess, there are some Mens Constitutions of Body and Mind so vigorous and well framed by Nature, that they need not much Assistance from others, but

B   by

The first page of the English philosopher John Locke's highly influential essay on education.

This colorfully illustrated baptismal certificate was produced by Pennsylvania Germans. Written in German, it features characteristic Pennsylvania German costumes.

Parents should govern their children well, restrain, reprove, correct them, as there is occasion. A Christian householder should rule well his own house . . . Children should not be left to themselves, to a loose end, to do as they please; but should be under tutors and governors, *not being fit to govern* themselves . . . Children being bid to obey their parents in all things . . . plainly implies that parents should give suitable precepts to, and maintain a wise government over their children; so carry it, as their children may both fear and love them. You should restrain your children from sin as much as possible . . . You should reprove them for their faults; yea, if need be, correct them too . . . Divine precepts plainly show that, as there is occasion, you should chasten and correct your children; you dishonor God and hurt them if you neglect it. Yet, on the other hand, a father should pity his children . . . You should by no means carry it ill to them; you should not frown, be harsh, morose, faulting and blaming them when they don't deserve it, but do behave themselves well. If you fault and blame your children, show yourself displeased and discontent when they do their best to please you, this is the way to provoke them to wrath and anger, and to discourage them; therefore you should carefully avoid such ill carriage to them. Nor should you ever correct them upon uncertainties, without sufficient evidence of their fault. Neither should you correct them in a rage or passion, but should deliberately endeavor to convince them of their fault, their sin; and that 'tis out of love to God's honor and their good . . . that you correct them. Again, you should never be cruel nor barbarous in your corrections, and if milder ones will reform them, more severe ones should never be used. Under this head of government I might further say, you should refrain your children from bad company as far as possibly you can . . . You should not suffer your children needlessly to frequent taverns, nor to be abroad unseasonably on nights, lest they're drawn into numberless hazards and mischiefs thereby. You can't be too careful in these matters.

Although disease had nowhere near the same devastating effects upon the white population of the colonies as it did upon the natives, it could still create turmoil. This was especially true given the combination of physical intimacy and mutual dependence that characterized family life in the colonies. With so many people, so dependent on each other for the basics of life and living together under the same roof, disease could very quickly ravage a family. In the following journal entries, the great New England theologian and minister Cotton Mather describes the effects of a measles outbreak on his congregation and his family—an outbreak that killed Mather's wife, his servant, and several of his children. Mather blamed his family's suffering not on the random spread of illness, but rather on his and his family's moral shortcomings. God, it appeared, was punishing him and his family for their inadequate devotion. To repent, Mather prays and fasts.

October 18, 1713. The Measles coming into the Town, it is likely to be a Time of Sickness, and much Trouble in the Families of the Neighbourhood. I would by my public Sermons and Prayers, endeavour to prepare the Neighbours for the Trouble which their Families are likely to meet withal.

The Apprehension of a very deep Share, that my Family may expect in the common Calamity of the spreading Measles, will oblige me to be much in pleading the Great Family-Sacrifice, that so the Wrath of Heaven may inflict no sad Thing on my Family; and to quicken and augment the Expressions of Piety, in the daily Sacrifices of my Family; and to lay hold on the Occasion to awaken Piety, and Preparation for Death, in the Souls of the children.

November 4, 1713. In my poor Family, now, first, my Wife has the *Measles* appearing on her; we know not yett how she will be handled.

This 1721 pamphlet advised Bostonians on how to cope with a smallpox epidemic that was ravaging the city. The same epidemic prompted the prominent minister Cotton Mather and the physician Zabdiel Boylston to begin experimenting with inoculation. The experiments were as revolutionary as they were controversial, sparking decades of debate about their medical value.

A Brief Rule to guide the Common People of New-England how to Order themselves and theirs in the Small-Pox and Measels.

THE *Small Pox* (whose nature and cure the *Measels* follow) is a disease in the blood, endeavouring to recover a new form and state.

2. THIS nature attempts — 1. By Separation of the impure from the pure, thrusting it out from the Veins to the Flesh.— 2. By driving out the impure from the Flesh to the Skin.

3. THE first Separation is done in the first four Days by a Feverish boiling(Ebullition) of the Blood, laying down the impurities in the Fleshy parts which kindly effected the Feverish tumult is calmed.

4. THE second Separation from the Flesh to the Skin, or *Superficies* is done through the rest of the time of the disease.

5. THERE are several Errors in ordering these sick ones in both these Opera-

‌

The Lore—and Lure—of Folk Remedies

Illness and injury were, of course, facts of life for colonists, but few physical ailments were ever treated by trained physicians. To the extent that colonists were able to take any action to cope with such problems, it usually took the form of "folk remedies," or concoctions of various sorts handed down through the generations or obtained from popular almanacs—books that contained all sorts of useful information, ranging from medical advice to astrological calendars and weather predictions. The compilers of these books assembled lengthy lists of medicinal remedies, sometimes drawing on the practices of Native American medicine men. For instance, the 1765 South-Carolina and Georgia Almanack explained that to treat leg ulcers, an Indian doctor made "a strong decoction of the root of sassafras, in which he bathed the ulcerated leg, then took some grains of rotten Indian corn, well dried, beaten to a powder, and the soft down that grows upon the turkeys rump, with this he quickly dried up the filthy ulcer, and made a perfect cure."

My Daughter *Nancy* is also full of them; not in such uneasy Circumstances as her prædecessors.

My Daughter *Lizzy*, is likewise full of them; yett somewhat easily circumstanced.

My Daughter *Jerusha*, droops and seems to have them appearing.

My Servant-maid, lies very full and ill of them.

Help Lord; and look mercifully on my poor, sad, sinful Family, for the Sake of the Great Sacrifice!

November 7, 1713. I sett apart this Day, as I had much Cause, and it was high Time, to do, for Prayer with Fasting before the Lord. Not only are my Children, with a Servant, lying sick, but also my Consort [wife] is in a dangerous Condition, and can gett no Rest; Either Death, or Distraction, is much feared for her. It is also an Hour of much Distress in my Neighbourhood. So, I humbled myself before the Lord, for my own Sins, and the Sins of my Family; and I presented before Him the great Sacrifice of my Saviour, that His wrath may be turned away from me, and from my Family; and that the Destroyer might not have a Commission to inflict any deadly Stroke upon us.

November 8, 9, 1713. . . . For these many Months, and ever since I heard of the venemous Measles invading the Countrey sixty Miles to the Southward of us, I have had a strong Distress on my Mind, that it will bring on my poor Family, a Calamity, which is now going to be inflicted. I have often, often express'd my Fear unto my Friends concerning it. And now, *the Thing that I greatly feared is coming upon me!*

When I saw my Consort safely delivered, and very easy, and the Measles appearing with favourable Symptomes upon her, and the Physician apprehending all to look very comfortably, I flattered myself, that my Fear was all over.

But this Day we are astonished, at the surprising Symptomes of Death upon her; after an extreme Want of Rest by Sleep, for diverse whole Dayes and Nights together.

To part with so desireable, so agreeable a Companion, a Dove from such a Nest of young ones too! Oh! the sad Cup, which my Father has appointed me! I now see the Meaning and the Reason of it, that I have never yett been able to make any Work of it, in Prayers and Cries to God, that such a Cup as this might pass from me. . . .

On Munday [November 9, 1713] between three and four in the Afternoon, my dear, dear, dear Friend expired.

Whereupon, with another Prayer in the melancholy Chamber, I endeavoured the Resignation to which I am now called, and cried to Heaven for the Grace that might be suitable to the calamitous Occasion, and carried my poor Orphans unto the Lord.

It comforts me to see how extremely Beloved, and lamented a Gentlewoman, I now find her to be in the Neighbourhood.

Much weakness continues on some of my other Children. Especially the Eldest. And the poor Maid in the Family is very like to dy.

In the following entries, Mather describes the death of his servant and several of his children. The passages not only show the obvious emotional torment these events inflicted on Mather, but also Mather's fatherly feelings toward his maid-servant.

November 14, 1713. This Morning, the first Thing that entertains me, after my rising, is the Death of my Maid-servant, whose Measles passed into a malignant Feaver, which has proved mortal to her.

Tis a Satisfaction to me, that tho' she had been a wild, vain, airy Girl, yett since her coming into my Family, she became disposed unto serious Religion; was awakened unto secret and fervent Supplications; gave herself to God . . . and my poor Instructions, were the means that God blessed for such happy Purposes.

November 15, 1713. Tis a Time of much Calamity in my Neighbourhood, and a Time of much Mortality seems coming on. My Public Prayers and Sermons must be exceedingly adapted for such a Time.

November 21. 1713. This Day, I attended the Funeral, of my two [children]: *Eleazar* and *Martha*.

Betwixt 9 h. and 10 h. at Night, my lovely *Jerusha* Expired. She was two years, and about seven Months, old. Just before she died, she asked me to pray with her; which I did, with a distressed, but resigning Soul; and I gave her up unto the Lord. The Minute that she died, she said, *That she would go to Jesus Christ.* . . . Lord, I am oppressed; undertake for me!

Children's Clothing in the Colonies

In this portrait of his son and grandson, the Boston painter Joseph Badger depicts the boys in the typical clothing of elite New Englanders' sons. The older boy wears a long version of the type of frock or jacket that was worn by adult men, but the younger boy wears a gown identical to what a girl of the same age would have worn. Young colonial boys and girls both wore feminine dresses, petticoats, and aprons. Very young children, women, and servants were all considered dependents, a condition that was associated with feminity. As elite boys grew out of infancy, though, their parents began to prepare them for lives as independent masters, husbands, and fathers. This meant imposing distinctions between boys and girls, who colonists generally expected to remain like dependent children even after they became wives.

November 22, 1713. It will be a great Service unto my Flock for me to exemplify, a patient Submission to the Will of God, under many and heavy Trials, . . .

My poor Family is now left without any Infant in it, or any under seven Years of Age. I must now apply myself with most exquisite Contrivance, and all the Assiduity imaginable, to cultivate my Children, with a most excellent Education. I have now singular Opportunities for it. Wherefore I must in the first Place, earnestly look up to the glorious Lord, who gives Wisdome, for Direction.

One could hardly imagine a sharper contrast than that between Cotton Mather and the Philadelphia printer and statesman Benjamin Franklin. If Mather devoted himself to preaching God's word, Franklin devoted himself to preaching a new gospel of worldly success. If Mather understood the goal of his life to be eternal salvation in the afterlife, Franklin understood it to be the achievement of success in this life. With such profoundly different ways of looking at the world, one might think these men were products of wholly different civilizations. In fact, they were not. They were both products of a colonial world in which the bonds of family—the bonds of love and affection—pervaded every aspect of life. In the following letter to his daughter Sarah (called Sally here), Franklin advises her on how to contend with the burden of being the daughter of the most famous man in the colonies. Most important, in Franklin's view, was

**that she learn to be a moral and ethical person, and one way
to do that was to attend church. There she would learn the
Christian moral code, a code that would keep Sarah from giving fodder to her father's detractors.**

Nov. 8, 1764
My dear Sally,
   . . . My dear Child, the natural Prudence and goodness of heart
that God has blessed you with, make it less necessary for me to be
particular in giving you Advice; I shall therefore only say, that the
more attentively dutiful and tender you are towards your good
Mama, the more you will recommend your self to me; But why
shou'd I mention *me*, when you have so much higher a Promise in
the Commandment, that such a conduct will recommend you to
the favour of God. You know I have many Enemies (all indeed on
the Public Account, for I cannot recollect that I have in a private
Capacity given just cause of offence to any one whatever) yet they
are Enemies and very bitter ones, and you must expect their
Enmity will extend in some degree to you, so that your slightest
Indiscretions will be magnified into crimes, in order the more sen-
sibly to wound and afflict me. It is therefore the more necessary
for you to be extreamly circumspect in all your Behaviour that no
Advantage may be given to their Malevolence. Go constantly to
Church whoever preaches. The Acts of Devotion in the common
Prayer Book, are your principal Business there; and if properly
attended to, will do more towards mending the Heart than
Sermons generally can do. For they were composed by Men of
much greater Piety and Wisdom, than our common Composers of
Sermons can pretend to be. And therefore I wish you wou'd never
miss the Prayer Days. Yet I do not mean that you shou'd despise
Sermons even of the Preachers you dislike, for the Discourse is
often much better than the Man, as sweet and clear Waters come
to us thro' very dirty Earth. I am the more particular on this Head,
as you seem'd to express a little before I came away some
Inclination to leave our Church, which I wou'd not have you do.
   For the rest I would only recommend to you in my Absence to
acquire those useful Accomplishments Arithmetick, and Book-
keeping. This you might do with Ease, if you wou'd resolve not to
see Company on the Hours you set apart for those Studies. . . .
Give my Love to your Brother and Sister, as I cannot now write to
them; and remember me affectionately to the young Ladies your
Friends, and to our good Neighbours. I am, my dear Sally, Your
ever Affectionate Father.

The Singing Choir, 1. Ludwig Miller, 2. John Barnitz, 3. George Snyder
4. Christopher Stochr, 5. Daniel Lauman, 6. Lewis Shive, 7. William Hornschild
8. George Barnitz, 9. Steffe Horn, 10. George Miller, 11. Michael Eurich,
12. mis. Herman, 13. mis. Laub, mis Stochr, 14. mis Cramer, 15. Mis. hay, 16. the Organist
Pastor, Rev. Jacob Goering, John Morris. Charles Fisher.

Matthew. Mark. Luke. John. Paul. Peter. Joshua. Samuel. David. Solomon. Luther.

Goering, Vou gott will ich nicht lassen den er lastnii von mir.

Chapter Six

A Spiritual People

Among the currents of thought swirling through colonial minds in the mid-18th century, one centered on the organizations and institutions through which individuals worshipped the Christian God—organizations and institutions generally referred to as churches. Embraced by a small number of progressive intellectuals, this line of thinking held that churches and their representatives had infiltrated and corrupted governments, forcing them to act not in the interests of ordinary people, but rather in the interests of the small coterie of ministers, priests, bishops, and others who controlled the churches. Out of this thinking emerged the revolutionary idea—promoted most famously by the primary author of the Declaration of Independence, Thomas Jefferson—that sharp, formal barriers should be erected between the institutions that govern people's secular lives (governments) and those that govern their spiritual lives (churches). It was this thinking, Americans often assume, that gave rise to the separation of church and state as established by the 1st Amendment to the U.S. Constitution. But this is really only part of the story—and some historians would argue, a relatively insignificant part at that.

To grasp the full story, we must turn to the colonial religious landscape and its extraordinary variety of churches and belief systems—a variety virtually unique in the Western world. Nowhere else were there so many people, with so many different religious beliefs, practicing those beliefs more or less as they wished. In New York City, as early as 1680, there were members of the Dutch Reformed Church, French Protestants, Anglicans, Presbyterians, Quakers, Roman Catholics, and Jews, as well as Africans and Native Americans, many of whom retained non-Western religious practices. In some colonies, of course, such diversity would have been less pronounced. In Massachusetts, for instance, a single Puritan church organization—the Congregational Church—dominated. But by the early decades of the

Colonial churches—such as this York, Pennsylvania, Lutheran church painted in 1800—were far more than places of worship. They were also an essential part of the colonists' social world. Churches reinforced social disctinctions between elite and ordinary colonists, women and men, and masters and servants. In this church, for example, women are seated separately from the men.

18th century, even the staid and uniform religious environment of Massachusetts had begun to grow more complex and diverse.

The sources of this colonial religious mosaic are many. One of the more important is theological: as we know, many of the first English colonists came to America to escape religious persecution in the Old World. A few of them thus perceived grave hypocrisy when patterns of religious persecution surfaced in the colonies themselves. One such figure was Roger Williams, the outspoken critic of the intolerant leaders of the Massachusetts Bay Colony. So frustrated was Williams with the Massachusetts Bay government that he founded a new settlement along Narragansett Bay that eventually became part of the Rhode Island colony. Instead of demanding—as the leaders of the Massachusetts Bay Colony did—that all colonists embrace the creed of a single church, Williams allowed colonists in his colony to worship more or less as they saw fit. Williams was not the only colonist to take such bold steps. The Quaker founder of Pennsylvania, William Penn, did so as well, creating a huge new colony in which Christians of widely differing orientations could come and live in relative peace.

If Williams and Penn deliberately permitted the coexistence of diverse religious views (albeit views limited to the Judeo-Christian tradition), officials in other colonies did so inadvertently. This was particularly true of large colonies with official, or "established" churches, formally supported by colonial governments. In New York, Virginia, and the Carolinas, colonists were obliged to attend

Perhaps nothing better illustrates the importance of churches in colonial life than the skyline of colonial cities. As this image of New York City in the early 1770s shows, church steeples were almost as common then as skyscrapers are now. The buildings, including a Jewish synagogue, also represent the great variety of religions present in the colonial era.

Prospect of the City of NEW-YORK

1 Fort George	6 The Prison.	11 Old Dutch Church	16 Quaker's Meeting
2 Trinity Church	7 New Brick Meeting	12 Jew's Synagogue	17 Calvinist Church
3 Presbyter. Meeting	8 King's College	13 Lutherian Church	18 Anabaptist Meeting
4 North D. Church	9 St. Paul's Church	14 The French Church	19 Moravian Meeting
5 St. George's Chapel	10 N. Dutch Cal. Church	15 New Scot's Meeting	20 N. Lutheran Church
			21 Methodist Meeting

and support—through a system of taxation—the Church of England. But in these sprawling colonies, such regulations were almost impossible to enforce. Colonists were simply too widely scattered for officials to be able to keep track of their religious activities. And the resources of the established church were simply inadequate to provide churches and ministers to service such far-flung populations. The collective result was that even though, in theory, a close connection between church and state existed in these colonies, the connection had little real impact on colonists. Unlike European governments, colonial governments lacked the capacity to compel colonists to adhere to any single religious persuasion or denomination.

Yet a third factor that contributed to the diversity of colonial religious life was the power of a new kind of evangelical minister. In the late 1730s and 1740s, itinerant ministers, bound to no single congregation, began traversing British North America, particularly those regions where church organization was weakest—especially northeastern Connecticut and western Massachusetts, but also parts of New York, New Jersey, and eventually Virginia and the Carolinas. What these ministers found was not what one might expect: an absence of religious feeling. Rather, they found just the opposite. They found people hungry for spiritual guidance and a connection with a Christian God. And it was precisely this that these ministers provided. So effective were they that they actually created a remarkable revival of piety and religious sentiment in the colonies.

But again, far from bringing uniformity to the colonial religious landscape, this "Great Awakening," as historians refer to it, merely furthered the trend toward diversity and variation. New Christian sects, embodying the spirit of itinerant ministers, began growing at an astonishing pace. Baptists, Methodists, and Presbyterians had scarcely existed in the colonies before the 1740s. By the 1770s, they were by far the fastest growing Christian denominations in colonial America. So inviting were these new denominations, and so energetic were they in their quest for members that some of them even began recruiting African slaves into their ranks. These efforts, in turn, laid the foundation for distinctly African-American forms of Christianity, forms that combined both European and African religious traditions.

The bewildering religious atmosphere of the colonies lies at the heart of later developments in American religious history, particularly the idea that government has no business meddling in people's religious affairs. This belief became enshrined in American

Curbing the Powerful "Popish Church"

Although Roman Catholics lived in the colonies, fears of Roman Catholic conspiracies prompted some colonial officials to take special actions meant to weaken the Catholic or "Popish" Church. In 1700, the New York colonial government passed a law declaring "that all and every Jesuit and seminary priest, missionary, or other spiritual or ecclesiastical person made or ordained by any authority, power, or jurisdiction derived, challenged, or pretended from the Pope or See of Rome, now residing within this province or any part thereof, shall depart from and out of the same at or before November 1 next in this present year 1700."

law and politics not so much because it was consistent with the progressive thinking of Thomas Jefferson and other founding fathers, but rather because it was consistent with the pluralistic religious environment that had begun to evolve in colonial times. As more colonists—and later Americans—embraced an ever-wider variety of Christian religious beliefs, the idea that just one group of Christians should receive the support of the government began to seem unfair.

What makes colonial religious history so important, then, is not a single story. Rather, it is the convergence of a whole host of different stories, stories involving Christians with widely divergent views on the proper way to worship and live, but also stories involving Jews, African slaves, and native peoples, all engaged in the common struggle to satisfy their spiritual needs.

Building a Church

Given their intense commitment to Christian ideals, one might expect that the Puritans had little trouble translating their beliefs into practice in the New World. The reality, however, was somewhat different. The founders of the Massachusetts Bay Colony expected each community or town within the colony to have its own self-contained church and minister. And, similarly, they expected each town to have a collection of "saints" or leaders who claimed a special connection to God. These men—and they were mostly men—were to govern the affairs of both the church and the town. In the following account from his *A History of New England*, published in London in 1654, Edward Johnson, a militia captain and founder of the town of Woburn, Massachusetts, describes the initial steps for forming a Puritan church. The most important of these described in the final paragraph, was the saints' demonstration of their special connection to God before a group of colonial officials.

Now to declare how this people [of the town of Woburn] proceeded in religious matters, and so consequently all the Churches of Christ planted in New England: when they came once to hopes of being such a competent number of people as might be able to maintain a minister, they then surely seated themselves, and not before, it being as unnatural for a right New England man to live without an able ministry as for a smith to work his iron without a fire. Therefore this people that went about placing down a town

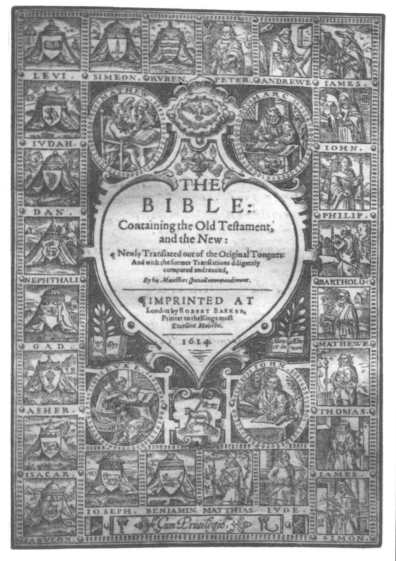

began the foundation stone with earnest seeking of the Lord's assistance, by humbling of their souls before Him in days of prayer, and imploring His aid in so weighty a work. Then they address themselves to attend counsel of the most orthodox and ablest Christians, and more especially of such as the Lord had already placed in the ministry, not rashly running together themselves into a church before they had hopes of attaining an officer to preach the Word and administer the seals unto them, choosing rather to continue in fellowship with some other church for their Christian watch over them till the Lord would be pleased to provide.

They after some search meet with a young man named Mr. Thomas Carter, then belonging to the Church of Christ at

A Covenant with God

Few ideas were as important to the Puritans as the notion that any Christian nation was obliged to form a contract or "covenant" with God. The terms of this covenant stipulated that in return for their work in upholding the moral and social ideals of the Bible, a nation received God's favor. The moment that that agreement was in any way violated—as the Puritans believed it to have been by the majority of the English—God's wrath would fall upon the violators. Every aspect of Puritan life, from personal behavior to church and colony-wide governance, was influenced by this idea. The personal dimension was especially important since every member of a truly Godly society—so the Puritans believed—was obliged to form his or her own covenant with God, forming links in the larger chain that bound God to His children. This was, to be certain, a most heavy burden to bear.

Watertown, a reverend, godly man, apt to teach the sound and wholesome truths of Christ. Having attained their desires, in hopes of his coming unto them were they once joined in Church estate, he exercis[ed] his gifts of preaching and prayer among them in the meantime, and more especially in a day of fasting and prayer. Thus these godly people interest their affections one with the other, both minister and people. After this they make ready for the work, and the 24th of the 6th month, 1642, they assemble together in the morning about eight of the clock. After the reverend Mr. Syms had continued in preaching and prayer about the space of four or five hours, the persons that were to join in covenant, openly and professedly before the congregation and messengers of divers neighbor churches . . .

The persons stood forth and first confessed with the Lord had done for their poor souls, by the work of His Spirit in the preaching of His Word, and providences, one by one. And that all might know their faith in Christ was bottomed upon Him, as He is revealed in His Word, and that from their own knowledge, they also declare the same, according to that measure of understanding the Lord had given them. The elders, or any other messengers there present, question with them, for the better understanding of them in any points they doubt of, which being done, and all satisfied, they in the name of the churches to which they do belong hold out the right hand of fellowship unto them, they declaring their covenant in words expressed in writing to this purpose.

The elaborate process of establishing a church in Puritan Massachusetts reflected more than simply the theological concerns of the colony's founders. It also reflected related political and social concerns. Such a carefully controlled and closely monitored process ensured that only men with certain views—views acceptable to the leaders of the colony—governed the various towns. This, in turn, ensured, or so was the idea, peaceful coexistence between town officials and the authorities who governed the colony. Given the Puritans' goal of creating a model Christian community for all England to emulate, such harmonious relations were essential. But the ground upon which the founders of the Bay Colony built this orderly and placid political order was unstable.

Few events more vividly revealed this instability than the trial and condemnation of one of the most powerful critics of the Massachusetts social order, Anne Hutchinson. After

emigrating to Massachusetts in 1634, Hutchinson quickly clashed with colonial authorities. She believed that they were permitting an inappropriately permissive Christian doctrine to be preached, and therefore she began convening a group of mostly female disciples at her home. The authorities saw in this action a profound threat to the colony's stability, and elected to bring Hutchinson to trial, eventually banishing her and her family to Rhode Island. At the trial, Governor John Winthrop explains to the General Court or colonial assembly, (which acted as judge and jury in this case), why this woman had been brought to trial, and struggles to elicit from her some sort of acknowledgment that in convening meetings of her followers, she was violating the law. But Hutchinson gives no ground to the powerful Winthrop.

Mr. Winthrop, Governor. Mrs. Hutchinson, you are called here as one of those that have troubled the peace of the commonwealth and the churches here; you are known to be a woman that hath had a great share in the promoting and divulging of those opinions that are causes of this trouble, and to be nearly joined not only in affinity and affection with some of those the court had taken notice of and passed censure upon, but you have spoken divers things as we have been informed very prejudicial to the honour of the churches and ministers thereof, and you have maintained a meeting and an assembly in your house that hath been condemned by the general assembly as a thing not tolerable nor comely in the sight of God nor fitting for your sex, and notwithstanding that was cried down you have continued the same, therefore we have thought good to send for you to understand how things are, that if you be in an erroneous way we may reduce you that so you may become a profitable member here among us, otherwise if you be obstinate in your course that then the court may take such course that you may trouble us no further, . . .

Mrs. Hutchinson. I am called here to answer before you but I hear no things laid to my charge.

Gov. I have told you some already and more I can tell you.

Mrs. H. Name one Sir.

Gov. Have I not named some already?

Mrs. H. What have I said or done?

Gov. Why for your doings, this you did harbour and countenance those that are parties in [your] faction . . .

ILL NEWES FROM NEW-ENGLAND: OR A Narative of *New-Englands* PERSECUTION. WHEREIN IS DECLARED That while old *England* is becoming new, *New-England* is become Old.

Also four Proposals to the Honoured Parliament and Council of State, touching the way to *Propagate the Gospel of Christ* (with small charge and great safety) both in Old *England* and New.

Also four conclusions touching the faith and order of the Gospel of Christ out of his last Will and Testament, confirmed and justified

By JOHN CLARK Physician of Rode Island in *America*.

Revel. 2. 25. *Hold fast till I come.*
3. 11. *Behod I come quickly.*
22. 20. *Amen, even so come Lord Jesu.*

LONDON,
Printed by *Henry Hills* living in *Fleet-Yard* next door to the *Rose* and *Crown*, in the year 1652.

The Baptists, a sect which emerged in the early 1640s, dissented from the Puritan mainstream. They held that because Puritan baptisms were performed under the auspices of the Church of England they were not legitimate and true Christians had to be re-baptized as adults. This challenge to the standing order compelled the authorities of the Massachusetts Bay Colony to banish Baptists to Rhode Island along with other dissenters. In this pamphlet, intended to elicit financial and political support from prominent Baptists in England, the Rhode Island Baptist John Clark assailed the intolerant Massachusetts Bay Colony.

Mrs. H. That's matter of conscience, sir.

Gov. Your conscience you must keep or it must be kept for you.

Mrs. H. Must not I then entertain the saints because I must keep my conscience.

Gov. Say that one brother should commit felony or treason and come to his brother's house, if he knows him guilty and conceals him he is guilty of the same. It is his conscience to entertain him, but if his conscience comes into act in giving countenance and entertainment to him that hath broken the law he is guilty too. So if you do countenance those that are transgressors of the law you are in the same fact.

Mrs. H. What law do they transgress?

Gov. The law of God and of the state.

Mrs. H. In what particular?

Gov. Why in this among the rest, whereas the Lord doth say honour thy father and thy mother.

Mrs. H. Ey Sir in the Lord [Hutchinson agrees].

Gov. This honour you have broke in giving countenance to them [who convened at Hutchinson's house].

. . .

Gov. We do not mean to discourse with those of your sex but only this; you do adhere unto them and do endeavor to set forward this faction [of Hutchinson's female disciples] and so you do dishonour us.

Mrs. H. I do acknowledge no such thing neither do I think that I ever put any dishonour upon you.

Gov. Why do you keep such a meeting at your house as you do every week upon a set day?

Mrs. H. It is lawful for me so to do, as it is all your practices and can you find a warrant for yourself and condemn me for the same thing? The ground of my taking it up was, when I first came to this land because I did not go to such meetings as those were, it was presently reported that I did not allow of such meetings but held them unlawful and therefore in that regard they said I was proud and did despise all ordinances, upon that a friend came unto me and told me of it and I to prevent such aspersions took it up, but it was in practice before I came therefore I was not the first.

Gov. For this, that you appeal to our practice you need no confutation. If your meeting had answered to the former it had not been offensive, but I will say that there was no meeting of women alone, but your meeting is of another sort for there are sometimes men among you.

Mrs. H. There was never any man with us. . . . the elder women should instruct the younger . . . Do you think it not lawful for me to teach women and why do you call me to teach the court?

Gov. We do not call you to teach the court but to lay open yourself.

Mrs. H. I desire you that you would then set me down a rule by which I may put them away that come unto me and so have peace in so doing.

Gov. You must shew your rule to receive them.

Mrs. H. I have done it.

Gov. I deny it because I have brought more arguments than you have.

Mrs. H. I say, to me it is a rule.

A Diversity of Beliefs

Although the Puritans went to great lengths to remove themselves from the mainstream of English society and culture, their efforts were only partially successful. Much like Englishmen elsewhere, ordinary people in New England regularly turned to the supernatural to help them understand their world. The popular belief in witchcraft is only the best-known expression of this. Other, more mundane examples abounded. For instance, colonists widely accepted the idea that the movement of celestial bodies—stars, moons, and planets—could help to predict weather, crop yields, and assorted other natural events.

The science of interpreting the signs of the heavens, called astrology, was mastered by few colonists. But many were able to benefit from the guidance of astrological almanacs, the most widely owned books in the colonies next to the Bible. Still, much interest in the supernatural stemmed from the ever-present quest to temper evil spirits, often attributed to malevolent witchcraft. In *An Essay for the Recording of Illustrious Providences* (1684), Puritan minister Increase Mather quotes from another author's description of one New England woman's experience with evil spirits. At the end of the passage, the author inserts a brief suggestion for eliminating such spiritual irritants.

In June 1682. (the day forgotten) at Evening, the said *Mary* heard a voice at the door of her Dwelling, saying, *What do you here?* about an hour after, standing at the Door of her House, she had a blow

Accusations of Witchcraft

Colonial witchcraft is generally associated with New England and the strange outburst of accusations that swept through Salem, Massachusetts, in 1692. In fact, however, accusations of witchcraft were much more widespread, and they occurred throughout the colonies during the 17th century. The following account, from the 1654 annual report that English Jesuit priests were required to make to their superiors in the Catholic Church, describes the shocking punishment of an accused witch aboard a storm-tossed ship sailing to the Catholic colony of Maryland.

The tempest lasted two months in all, whence the opinion arose, that it was not raised by the violence of the sea or atmosphere, but was occasioned by the malevolence of witches. Forthwith they seize a little old woman suspected of sorcery; and after examining her with the strictest scrutiny, guilty or not guilty, they slay her, suspected of this very heinous sin. The corpse, and whatever belonged to her, they cast into the sea.

on her Eye that settled her head near to the Doorpost, and two or three dayes after, a Stone, as she judged about half a pound or a pound weight was thrown along the house within into the Chimney, and going to take it up it was gone; all the Family was in the house, and no hand appearing which might be instrumental in throwing the stone. About two hours after, a Frying-pan then hanging in the Chimney was heard to ring so loud, that not only those in the house heard it, but others also that lived on the other side of the River near an hundred Rods distant or more. Whereupon the said *Mary* and her Husband going in a *Cannoo* over the River, they saw like the head of a man new-shorn, and the tail of a white Cat about two or three foot distance from each other, swimming over before the *Cannoo*, but nobody appeared to joyn head and tail together; and they returning over the River in less than an hours time, the said *Apparition* followed their *Cannoo* back again, but disappeared at Landing. A day or two after, the said *Mary* was stricken on her head . . . with a stone, which caused a Swelling and much soreness on her head, being then in the yard by her house, and she presently entring into her house was bitten

Identifying the evil work of witches was no simple matter. Cotton Mather and other leading ministers charged with this vexing task consulted a wide range of treatises for guidance. Among them was Saducismus Triumphatus, *written by Joseph Glanvil, chaplain to King Charles II of England.*

And Saul perceived that it was Samuel, and he stouped with his face to the ground, and bowed himself. 1ª Samuel. Chap: 28: v. 14.

Saducismus Triumphatus:
Or, full and plain
EVIDENCE
Concerning
Witches and Apparitions.
In Two PARTS.
The First Treating of their
POSSIBILITY.
The Second of their
Real EXISTENCE.
By *Joseph Glanvil*, late Chaplain in Ordinary to his Majesty, and Fellow of the *Royal Society.*
The Third Edition with Additions.
The Advantages whereof, above the former, the Reader may understand out of Dr. *H. More's* Account prefix'd thereunto.
WITH
Two Authentick, but wonderful Stories of certain *Swedish* Witches. Done into *English* by *A. Horneck*, D. D.
LONDON. Printed for *A. L.* and Sold by *Roger Tuckyr*, at the Golden Leg, the corner of *Salisbury-street*, in the *Strand.* MDCC.

on both Arms black and blue, and one of her Breasts scratched; the imressions of the Teeth being like Mans Teeth, were plainly seen by many: Whereupon deserting their House to sojourn at a Neighbours on the other side of the River, there appeared to said *Mary* in the house of her sojourning, a Woman clothed with a green Safeguard, short blue Cloak, and a white Cap, making a profer to strike her with a Fire-brand, but struck her not. The Day following the same shape appeared again to her, but now arrayed with a gray Gown, white Apron, and white Head-clothes, in appearance laughing several times, but no voice heard. Since when said *Mary* has been freed from those Satanical Molestations. . . .

I am further informed, that some . . . advised the poor Woman to stick the House round with Bayes [sprigs from a bay tree or a bay laurel], as an effectual preservative against the power of Evil Spirits. This Counsel was followed. And as long as the Bayes continued green, she had quiet; but when they began to wither, they were all by an unseen hand carried away, and the Woman again tormented.

The Quakers emerged out of wild religious ferment that swept through England in the mid-17th century. Much like Anne Hutchinson and her disciples, they had determined that God's word was being misinterpreted throughout English dominions—even by the righteous Puritans. Central to Quaker doctrine was the idea that God spoke through an inner light that illuminated the soul. A person true to his or her faith was thus the person who followed his or her inner light. Being true to this doctrine meant allowing Christians to practice as they saw fit; that is, in whatever way their personal spirit directed them. Out of this thinking emerged the most liberal, tolerant colony after Roger Williams's Rhode Island: William Penn's Pennsylvania. But even Quaker tolerance only went so far. As the following statute indicates, in Pennsylvania only believers in the Divinity of Christ could vote or hold political office, and slandering of the Christian God would be severely punished.

Whereas the glory of almighty God and the good of mankind is the reason and end of government and, therefore, government in itself is a venerable ordinance of God. And forasmuch as it is principally desired and intended by the Proprietary and Governor and the freemen of the province of Pennsylvania and territories thereunto belonging to make and establish such laws as shall best preserve

The "Society of Friends"

The followers of George Fox, one of numerous spiritual leaders who traveled through England during the 1650s preaching radical new religious ideas, referred to themselves as the Society of Friends. This was in part a reference to their total rejection of all formal practices and institutions associated with the Church of England (indeed, rejection of the very idea of a church itself). For Fox's followers, communion with Christ—or an encounter with "the inner light of Christ"—occurred not through the coming together of a group of Christians to form a church, but rather through every individual's soul. Worship was thus an intensely private affair, and hence often occurred in silent assemblages or meetings. Fox found receptive audiences, many of whom experienced strange physical gyrations as they felt themselves communing with Christ. It was this behavior that earned Fox's followers the name Quakers.

Quakers worshiped in spare and simple meetinghouses. This architectural style reflected their rejection of the sorts of superficial distinctions between ministers and their flock and between churches and secular buildings created by clothing, architectural ornament, clerical credentials, and other trappings of conventional Christianity. For Quakers, the only meaningful distinction was between the soul touched by God's guiding light and the one not so touched.

true christian and civil liberty in opposition to all unchristian, licentious, and unjust practices, whereby God may have his due, Caesar his due, and the people their due, from tyrany and oppression on the one side and insolence and licentiousness on the other, so that the best and firmest foundation may be laid for the present and future happiness of both the Governor and people of the province and territories aforesaid and their posterity.

Be it, therefore, enacted by William Penn, Proprietary and Governor, by and with the advice and consent of the deputies of the freemen [voters] of this province and counties aforesaid in assembly met and by the authority of the same, that these following chapters and paragraphs shall be the laws of Pennsylvania and the territories thereof.

Chap. I. . . . Be it enacted, by the authority aforesaid, that no person now or at any time hereafter living in this province, who shall confess and acknowledge one almighty God to be the creator, upholder, and ruler of the world, and who professes him or herself obliged in conscience to live peaceably and quietly under the civil government, shall in any case be molested or prejudiced for his conscientious persuasion or practice. Nor shall he or she at any time be compelled to frequent or maintain any religious worship, place, or ministry whatever contrary to his or her mind, but shall freely and fully enjoy his, or her, christian liberty in that respect, without any interruption or reflection. And if any person shall abuse or deride any other for his or her different persuasion and practice in matters of religion, such person shall be looked upon as a disturber of the peace and be punished accordingly. . . .

Chap. II. And be it further enacted . . . that all officers and persons commissioned and employed in the service of the government in this province and all members and deputies elected to serve in the Assembly thereof and all that have a right to elect such deputies shall be such as profess and declare they believe in Jesus Christ to be the son of God, the savior of the world, and that are not convicted of ill-fame or unsober and dishonest conversation and that are of twenty-one years of age at least.

Chap. III. And be it further enacted . . . that whosoever shall swear in their common conversation by the name of God or Christ or Jesus, being legally convicted thereof, shall pay, for every such offense, five shillings or suffer five days imprisonment in the house of correction at hard labor to the behoof of the public and be fed with bread and water only during that time.

Chap. V. And be it further enacted . . . for the better prevention of corrupt communication, that whosoever shall speak loosely and profanely of almighty God, Christ Jesus, the Holy Spirit, or the scriptures of truth, and is legally convicted thereof, shall pay, for every such offense, five shillings or suffer five days imprisonment in the house of correction at hard labor to the behoof of the public and be fed with bread and water only during that time.

In some ways, the religious beliefs of Native Americans could not have been more different from European religious beliefs—and yet, at the same time, they had elements that would have been familiar to Christians. Nearly all of them, for example, had an explanation for the creation of the universe. In the northeast, that explanation centered on the idea that the world existed on the back of a giant sea turtle, and hence, northeastern Native Americans often referred to North America as "turtle island." These beliefs—much like analogous Christian ones—persist to the present day, and it is partly for this reason that scholars have some idea of what Native American religious practices involved in the colonial era. Scholars have also learned much from the very few early

Supplanting Native Religious Beliefs

Throughout the colonial period, Christian missionaries struggled to supplant traditional Native American beliefs with Christian ones. But native peoples did not easily abandon those beliefs. The frustrated missionary David Brainerd recalled, "when I have instructed them respecting the miracles wrought by Christ in healing the sick, etc., and mentioned them as evidences of his divine mission and the truth of his doctrines, they have quickly observed the wonders of that kind which [their own native priest] had performed by his magic charms: Whence they had a high opinion of him and his superstitious notions, which seemed to be a fatal obstruction to some of them in regard of their receiving the Gospel [of Jesus Christ]."

accounts written by native peoples, including one by a Mohawk named John Norton. The following selection from Norton's journal describes the first stages of creation, and reveals the close connection between Native American spiritualism and daily life.

The tradition of the Nottowegui or Five Nations [the Iroquois] says, "that in the beginning before the formation of the earth; the country above the sky was inhabited by Superior Beings, over whom the Great Spirit presided. His daughter having become pregnant by an illicit connection, he pulled up a great tree by the roots, and threw her through the cavity thereby formed; but, to prevent her utter destruction, he previously ordered the Great Turtle, to get from the bottom of the waters, some slime on its back, and to wait on the surface of the water to receive her on it. When she had fallen on the back of the Turtle, with the mud she found there, she began to form the earth, and by the time of her delivery had encreased it to the extent of a little island. Her child was a daughter, and as she grew up the earth extended under their hands. When the young woman had arrived at the age of discretion, the Spirits who roved about, in human forms, made proposals of marriage for the young woman: the mother always rejected their offers, until a middle aged man, of a dignified appearance, his bow in his hand, and his quiver on his back, paid his addresses. On being accepted, he entered the house, and seated himself on the birth of his intended spouse; the mother was in a birth on the other side of the fire. She observed that her son-in-law did not lie down all night; but taking two arrows out of his quiver, he put them by the side of his bride: at the dawn of day he took them up, and having replaced them in his quiver, he went out.

"After some time, the old woman perceived her daughter to be pregnant, but could not discover where the father had gone, or who he was. At the time of delivery, the twins disputed which way they should go out of the womb; the wicked one said, let us go out of the side; but the other said, not so, lest we kill our mother; then the wicked one pretending to acquiesce, desired his brother to go out first: but as soon as he was delivered, the wicked one, in attempting to go out at her side, caused the death of his mother.

"The twin brothers were nurtured and raised by their Grandmother; the eldest was named Teharonghyawago, or the Holder of Heaven; the youngest was called Tawiskaron, or Flinty rock, from his body being entirely covered with such a substance. They grew up, and with their bows and arrows, amused themselves

Redemption for "Our Sable Race"

In the following short poem, "On Being Brought from Africa to America" (1773), Phillis Wheatley, a Boston slave who published her first poem by age 13, expressed a sentiment that was not uncommon among African slaves whose masters exposed them to Christian teachings. But like most descriptions of slave religion, this one too contains subtle ambiguities. The last two lines, for instance, seem as much a declaration of Africans' humanity as a warning to slaveholders.

'Twas mercy brought me from my pagan land,
Taught my benighted soul to understand
That there's a God—that there's a Saviour too;
Once I redemption neither sought nor knew.
Some view our sable race with scornful eye—
'Their color is a diabolic dye.'
Remember, Christians, Negroes black as Cain
May be refined, and join the angelic train.

SHEWING THAT

GOD Dealeth with MEN As with

Reasonable Creatures

IN A

SERMON

Preach'd at BOSTON, N. E.
Nov. 23. 1718.

With a brief account of the State of the *Indians*
on *Martha's Vineyard*, & the Small Islands adjacent
in *Dukes* County, from the Year 1694. to 1720.

By the Reverend

Mr. EXPERIENCE MAYHEW,

Preacher of the GOSPEL to the
𝕴𝖓𝖉𝖎𝖆𝖓𝖘 in *Martha's Vineyard*.

Ezek. 34. laft. *And ye the Flock of my Pafture
are MEN, and I am your GOD.*
Hof. 11. 4. *I Drew you with cords of A MAN,
and with Bands of Love.*

BOSTON: Printed by *B. Green*, for
Samuel Gerrifh, at his Shop. 1720.

*The reverend Experience Mayhew,
author of this sermon, devoted much
of his life to converting the native
peoples of Martha's Vineyard,
Massachusetts, to Christianity.*

throughout the island, which encreased in extent, and they were
favoured with various animals of Chace. Tawiskaron was the most
fortunate hunter, and enjoyed the favour of his Grandmother.
Teharonghyawago was not so successful in the Chace, and suffered from their unkindness. When he was a youth, and roaming
alone, in melancholy mood, through the island, a human figure,
of noble aspect, appearing to him, addressed him thus. 'My son,
I have seen your distress, and heard your solitary lamentations;
you are unhappy in the loss of a mother, in the unkindness of
your Grandmother and brother. I now come to comfort you, I am
your father, and will be your Protector; therefore take courage,
and suffer not your spirit to sink. Take this (giving him an ear of
maize) plant it, and attend it in the manner, I shall direct; it will

Festival dances remain an integral part of the spiritual life of many Native Americans.

yield you a certain support, independent of the Chace, at the same time that it will render more palatable the viands, which you may thereby obtain. I am the Great Turtle which supports the earth, on which you move. Your brother's ill treatment will increase with his years; bear it with patience till the time appointed, before which you shall hear further.'"

Of all the religious traditions present in colonial America, the most difficult to study are those of African slaves. These men and women came from a wide variety of cultures and societies, many of which had distinct religious practices. But the cruelties of the slave trade and the vagaries of slave life made the preservation of these traditions extraordinarily difficult. And although Africans were able to preserve elements of those traditions, we have very little evidence about their exact nature. Literate Europeans who might have written about them instead usually dismissed African beliefs as

pagan or heathen rites. And precisely for this reason, slaves were probably inclined to practice traditional religious rituals in secret. There are, however, several valuable accounts of religion as practiced by Africans in Africa, and these help historians understand the fragmentary evidence for African religion in the colonies.

One of these appears in the autobiography of Olaudah Equiano, an African slave who was probably born in South Carolina and who resided in the colonies for a period during the mid-1700s. Although Equiano's autobiography offers much detail about his childhood, recent scholarship has cast doubt on the authenticity of some of his claims, particularly the claim that he was born in Africa. Nonetheless, Equiano's description of the African religion he claims to have practiced as a child is useful, if for no other reason than that it illuminates the ways slaves born in the colonies may have understood their ancestral religions. This matter is of considerable importance to anyone seeking to understand the distinct qualities of African-American Christianity. What Equiano describes is the religion of the Ibo people, a large west African ethnic group. Like most religions, Equiano's discussion suggests, Ibo religion did not simply govern the Ibo's spiritual existence; it also shaped their approach to more mundane matters such as personal cleanliness and medical care.

As to religion, the natives believe that there is one Creator of all things, and that he lives in the sun, and is girted round with a belt; that he may never eat or drink, but, according to some, he smokes a pipe, which is our own favorite luxury. They believe he governs events, especially our deaths or captivity; but, as for the doctrine of eternity, I do not remember to have ever heard of it: some, however, believe in the transmigration of souls [reincarnation] in a certain degree. Those spirits which were not transmigrated, such as their dear friends or relations, they believe always attend them, and guard them from the bad spirits or their foes. For this reason they always, before eating, as I have observed, put some small portion of the meat, and pour some of their drink, on the ground for them; and they often make oblations [offerings] of the blood of beasts or fowls at their graves. I was very fond of my mother, and almost constantly with her. When she went to make these oblations at her mother's tomb, which was a kind of small solitary thatched house, I sometimes attended her. There she made her libations, and spent most of the night in cries and lamentations. . . . and these, concurring with the doleful cries of birds, by which these places were frequented, gave an inexpressible terror to the scene. . . .

I have before remarked, that the natives of this part of Africa are extremely cleanly. This necessary habit of decency was with us a part of religion, and therefore we had many purifications and washings; indeed almost as many, and used on the same occasions, if my recollection does not fail me, as the Jews. Those that touched the dead at any time were obliged to wash and purify themselves before they could enter a dwelling-house. . . .

Though we had no places of public worship, we had priests and magicians, or wise men. I do not remember whether they had different offices, or whether they were united in the same persons, but they were held in great reverence by the people. They calculated our time, and foretold events, as their name imported, for we called them *Ah-affoe-way-cah*, which signifies calculators, or yearly men, our year being called *Ah-affoe*. They wore their beards, and, when they died, they were succeeded by their sons. Most of their implements and things of value were interred along with them. Pipes and tobacco were also put into the grave with the corpse, which was always perfumed and ornamented, and animals were offered in sacrifice to them. None accompanied their funerals, but those of the same profession or tribe. They buried them after sunset, and always returned from the grave by a different way from that which they went.

These magicians were also our doctors or physicians. They practised bleeding by cupping, and were very successful in healing wounds and expelling poisons. They had likewise some extraordinary method of discovering jealousy, theft, poisoning, the success of which, no doubt, they derived from the unbounded influence over the credulity and superstition of the people. I do not remember what those methods were, except that as to poisoning; I recollect an instance or two, which I hope it will not be deemed impertinent here to insert, as it may serve as a kind of specimen of the rest, as is still used by the negroes in the West Indies. A young woman had been poisoned, but it was not known by whom; the doctors ordered the corpse to be taken up by some persons, and carried to the grave. As soon as the bearers had raised it on their shoulders, they seemed seized with some sudden impulse, and ran to and fro, unable to stop themselves. At last, after having passed through a number of thorns and prickly bushes unhurt, the corpse fell from them close to a house, and defaced it in the fall; and the owner being taken up, he immediately confessed the poisoning.

The Awakening Comes

The so-called Great Awakening that swept through the colonies in the mid-18th century did not meet with universal approval. Many colonists were alarmed by what they perceived to be the incredible power and popularity of the itinerant preachers who began crisscrossing the colonies. In the minds of these critics, ordinary colonists everywhere were abandoning themselves to their emotions and throwing themselves at the feet of these 18th-century celebrities.

(137)

THE
Chriſtian Hiſtory;

Containing Accounts of the Propagation and Revival of Religion in *Great Britain, America,* &c.

Saturday JUNE 30. 1744. § Nᵒ· 70.

Account of the Revival of Religion at LYME *Weſt Pariſh in* Connecticut, *continu'd.*

NOW thoſe that could not reſtrain themſelves were generally carried out of the Meeting-Houſe, and a *ſecond* Sermon was preach'd by Mr. *Jewet* to others that were able to attend; aſter which the Aſſembly was diſmiſs'd; and my Houſe ſoon fill'd with wounded Souls: And I took Pains to ſatisfy my ſelf & others, by inquiring into the Reaſons of the trembling, crying, fainting, and other Signs of Fear that were ſo manifeſt in the Aſſembly: And they declar'd, in their own Words, all to this Purpoſe, *viz.* that a deep Senſe of paſt Senſualities, and careleſs Neglects of the Concerns of their Souls; their ſlighting frequent and ſolemn Warnings, and withſtanding the Calls of the Goſpel; together with a deep Senſe of their Liableneſs, every Moment, to be arreſted and caſt into the Priſon of Hell, where thoſe Sinners lay, that refuſed to hearken to the Warnings given by *Noah* the Preacher of Righteouſneſs, was truly the Spring of all theſe various Signs of Diſtreſs. Some run back upon the Sins of riper Years (for there were ſeveral Perſons upwards of 40 and ſome of more than 50 Years old, that diſcover'd great Concern by their pale Countenances and Tears, and trembling too.) Some cried out of the Hardneſs of their Hearts, others of their Unbelief: ſome were crying, *God be merciful to me a Sinner*; and others intreated Chriſtians to pray for them. Thus they continued, at my Houſe, for ſeveral Hours; and after I had taken what Pains with them, I tho't neceſſary for that Evening, and pray'd with them, they were adviſed

S   to

As indicated in the title of this religious periodical, the Great Awakening was a trans-Atlantic phenomenon, affecting both Britain and her American colonies.

Condemning "Idle Cerimonies"

Of course, not all Europeans who came to the New World were Christians; similarly, not all colonists living in the era of religious revival embraced the enthusiastic brand of Christianity propagated by itinerant preachers. For example, Abigail Franks, a member of a prominent New York family, was clearly skeptical about the less rational aspects of Western religion—whether Christianity or Judaism, the latter being her own religion. In a letter she wrote to her eldest son Naphtali in 1739, she criticized Judaism for its embrace of overwrought, superstitious ceremony and praised the leaders of the Protestant Reformation, Martin Luther and John Calvin, both of whom criticized such practices as superfluous to true belief: "I Must Own I cant help Condemning the Many Supersti[ti]ons wee [Jews] are Clog'd with & heartly wish a Calvin or Luther would rise amongst Us I Answer for my Self, I would be the first of there followers for I dont think religeon Consist in Idle Cerimonies & works of Supperoregations Wich if they Send people to heaven wee & the papist [Catholics] have the Greatest title too."

Perhaps no itinerant preacher elicited as much controversy as James Davenport, a figure so extravagant in his beliefs that he once preached for 24 hours straight. In the long run, Davenport's extreme behavior discredited other itinerant preachers and contributed to the decline of the Great Awakening in New England. The following account from a Boston newspaper describes Davenport's exploits in New London, Connecticut, in March 1743 and captures the tumult and bizarre behavior his visits yielded.

Upon his [Davenport's] Arrival, the Christians, or dear Children, gather'd round about him in Crouds, who paid him such profound Respect, Reverence and Homage, that his well-known great Modesty and Humility oblig'd him to check their Devotion, by telling them, he was not a God, but a man. However this did not abate their Veneration for him so much, but that even the Chief of them . . . made auricular Confessions to him; and this being over, . . . they might judge themselves to be in a good Condition to do some memorable Exploits, to the lasting Honour of their Sect, and the Establishment of their Religion; and having by Fasting and Prayer sought for Direction to do something, one of them declar'd, he had a Revelation; which was, that they should root out Heresy and pull down Idolatry: The Motion was well approved by the Assembly, who soon resolv'd to make a bold and vigorous Attempt to effect it; and accordingly on the 6th Instant, it being the Lord's Day, just before the Conclusion of the Publick Worship, and also as the People were returning from the House of GOD [Church], they were surpriz'd with a great Noise and Outcry; Multitudes hasten'd toward the Place of Rendezvous, directing themselves by the Clamor and Shouting, which together, with the ascending Smoak bro't them to one of the most public Places in the Town, and there found these good People encompassing a Fire which they had built up in the Street, into which they were casting Numbers of Books, principally on Divinity, and those that were well-approved by *Protestant* Divines, . . . Nothing can be more astonishing than their insolent Behaviour was during the Time of their Sacrifice, as 'tis said they call'd it; whilst the Books were in the Flames they cry'd out, *Thus the Souls of the Authors of those Books, those of them that are dead, are roasting in the Flames of Hell;* and that *the Fate of those surviving, would be the same, unless speedy Repentance prevented:* On the next Day they had at the same Place a second Bonfire of the like Materials, and manag'd in the same manner. Having given this fatal Stroke to *Heresy,* they made ready to attack *Idolatry,* and sought for Direction, as in the Case before; and then Mr. [Davenport] told them to look at Home first, and that they themselves were guilty of idolizing their Apparel, and should therefore divest themselves of those Things especially which were for Ornament, and let them be burnt: Some of them in the heighth of their Zeal, conferred not with Flesh and Blood, but fell to stripping and cast their Cloaths down at their Apostle's Feet; . . . Next Mr. [Davenport] pray'd himself; and now the Oracle spake clear to the Point, without Ambiguity, and utter'd that *the* [clothing] *must be burnt;* and to confirm the Truth of the Revelation, [Davenport] took his wearing Breeches, and hove them with Violence into the Pile, saying *Go you with the Rest.*

Given the strange scenes that accompanied preachers such as Davenport as they traveled through the colonies, it would be easy to forget that these preachers sometimes did have profound effects on the lives of ordinary people. But a look at the reflections of some of their followers makes their influence impossible to minimize. For instance, Sarah Osborne, who emigrated with her family to the colonies in 1722 and later settled in Newport, Rhode Island, described in a personal memoir a deep feeling of spiritual inadequacy, a feeling that was relieved only after several visits from two great itinerant preachers, George Whitefield and Gilbert Tennent. So affected was Osborne by these preachers that she began spreading their teachings among a circle of receptive female friends.

The instances of the remarkable hand of God in his providence, in ordering my temporal affairs, are innumerable. But, oh vile wretch! after all this I grew slack again, and got into a cold, lifeless frame. As I grew better in bodily health, my soul grew sick. I daily laid up a stock for repentance. But, through rich grace, I was again convinced of my stupidity, and began to be more diligent in attending on the means of grace. But I found I could not profit by the word preached: Nothing reached my heart; all seemed but skin deep: And the more I went to [church], the more I found it so. Then I began to think I must take some other course. . . .

After all this, I began to grow more conformed to the world. Things which, when I was thus lively, appeared insipid, and indeed odious to me, began to grow more tolerable, and by degrees in a measure pleasant. And depraved nature and Satan together pleaded for them thus, "That there was a time for all

George Whitefield and other itinerant preachers defied the constraints of ordinary churches by drawing listeners to large, open-air gatherings.

George Whitefield: "A Perfectly Honest Man"

Although two men could hardly be more different in their religious beliefs than Benjamin Franklin and the great Methodist preacher George Whitefield, they managed to maintain a long friendship. As he explained in his posthumously published autobiography, Franklin admired Whitefield's courage and integrity:

I, who was intimately acquainted with [Whitefield], . . . never had the least Suspicion of his Integrity, but am to this day decidedly of Opinion that he was in all his Conduct, a perfectly *honest* Man. And methinks my Testimony in his Favour ought to have the more Weight, as we had no religious Connection. He us'd indeed sometimes to pray for my Conversion, but never had the Satisfaction of believing that his Prayers were heard. Ours was a mere civil Friendship, sincere on both Sides, and lasted to his Death.

The Boston slave Phillis Wheatley published this eulogy to George Whitefield in
her late teens. The poem was well received
in the colonies and Great Britain, but
Phillis and her owners—the Wheatleys—
were unable to get a collection of her poems
published in the colonies. When a London
publisher eventually agreed to publish
Phillis's Poems on Various Subjects,
Religious and Moral (1773), critics
dismissed the possibility that such refined
poems could have been produced by a
young slave. This prompted a group of
prominent Bostonians including the governor of Massachusetts to publicly testify
to their authenticity.

AN

ELEGIAC

POEM,

On the DEATH of that celebrated Divine, and eminent
Servant of JESUS CHRIST, the Reverend and
learned

George Whitefield,

Chaplain to the Right Honourable the Countess of
HUNTINGDON, &c. &c.

Who made his Exit from this transitory State,
to dwell in the celestial Realms of Bliss, on LORD's-Day,
30th of September, 1770, when he was seiz'd with a Fit of the
Asthma, at Newbury-Port, near BOSTON, NEW-ENGLAND.

In which is a Condolatory Address to His truly noble
Benefactress the worthy and pious Lady HUNTINGDON ;---
and the Orphan-Children in GEORGIA, who, with many
Thousands are left, by the Death of this great Man, to la-
ment the Loss of a Father, Friend, and Benefactor.

By PHILLIS,

A Servant Girl, of 17 Years of Age, belonging to Mr.
J. WHEATLEY, of BOSTON :—She has been but 9
Years in this Country from AFRICA.

BOSTON:

Printed and Sold by EZEKIEL RUSSELL, in Queen-street,
And JOHN BOYLES, in Marlboro'-street.

things; and singing and dancing now and then, with a particular
friend, was an innocent diversion. Who did I see, besides myself,
so precise and strict? Other christians allowed themselves in such
things, who, I had reason to think, were far superior to me in
grace; especially one with whom I was very intimate. Sure, if it
was sin, she would not allow herself in it. It was for extraordinary
christians, such as ministers, and others who were eminent for
piety, to avoid the practice of such things, and not for *me*. Who did
I think I was, that I should pretend to outdo other christians? They
could talk of worldly things. What ailed me?" Thus the devil and
carnal reasoning argued me out of a great part of my resolutions
for strict godliness; . . .

Thus I sunk by degrees lower and lower, till I had at last almost lost all sense of my former experiences. I had only the bare remembrance of them, and they seemed like dreams or delusion; at some times. At others again, I had some revivals. . . . But I knew I was a dreadful backslider, and had dealt treacherously with God. . . .

In Sept. 1740, God in mercy sent his dear servant [George] Whitefield here, which in some measure stirred me up. But when Mr. Tennent came soon after, it pleased God to bless his preaching so to me, that it roused me. But I was all the winter after exercised with dreadful doubts and fears about my state. I questioned the truth of all I had experienced, and feared I had never yet passed through the pangs of the new birth, or ever had one spark of grace.

. . . I continued thus till March, 1741. And then it pleased God to return Mr. Tennent to us again, and he preached twenty one sermons here. But while he was here, I was more than ever distressed. I had lost the sensible manifestations of Christ's love. . . . And [Mr. Tennent] struck directly at those things, for which I had so foolishly and wickedly pleaded christian example, such as singing songs, dancing and foolish jesting, which is not convenient. He said, he would not say there was no such thing as a dancing christian, but he had a very mean opinion of such as could bear to spend their time so, when it is so short, and the work for eternity so great. Then, and not till then, was I fully convinced what prodigal wasters of precious time such things were. And, through grace, I have abhorred them all ever since.

. . . After I was thus revived, my longings to be made useful in the world returned, and I earnestly pleaded with God that he would not suffer me to live any longer an unprofitable servant; but would point out some way, in which I might be useful: And that I might now be as exemplary for piety, as I had been for folly. And it pleased God so to order it, that I had room to hope my petitions were both heard, and in a measure answered. For soon after this a number of young women, who were awakened to a concern for their souls, came to me, and desired my advice and assistance, and proposed to join in a society, provided I would take the care of them. To which, I trust with a sense of my own unworthiness, I joyfully consented.

Chapter Seven

Gentlewomen and Gentlemen

Contrary to what historians once believed, the colonial era does not constitute a long, continuous march toward the egalitarian and democratic world of 19th-century America. In many respects, the degree to which colonists were masters of their own domain—the degree to which they were "free"—actually declined during the nearly two centuries preceding the American Revolution. Colonial political institutions, for instance, in many ways became less inclusive and democratic, so that by the middle of the 18th century, they had more in common with those of monarchical Britain than of the early colonies, let alone the modern United States.

A vivid expression of this trend is revealed in the ways white male colonists related to each other in daily life. As scholars have paid more attention to these patterns, they have found an almost universal tendency in the colonies toward more sharply defined social groupings. If white men interacted with each other on more or less equal terms early in the colonial era, by the middle of the 18th century this was no longer the case. A sharp division of status had emerged. From a place where few could claim special privileges or entitlements, the colonies had evolved into a place divided between ordinary white colonists, native peoples, African slaves, and a distinct privileged class, a class that dominated almost every aspect of colonial life. Much like the aristocrats of the Old World, these individuals exercised a level of power disproportionate to their small numbers. And they were able to do this through a combination of economic good fortune, shrewd political maneuvering, and a burning desire to achieve the security and status of the wealthiest classes of England.

Well-bred children were expected to behave like small adults. Hence the poses and clothing of these children differed little from those of adults in similar portraits.

Gentility: The Mark of the Elite

By "gentry," colonists meant an elite social class, a class composed of "gentlemen" and "gentlewomen." Another related word, "gentility," expressed what it was that made that class so distinctive. More than simply wealth, it was gentility, a cluster of qualities marking a person as uniquely elevated and refined and distinguishing the gentry from ordinary people. Such people, their homes, their occupations, their clothing, their manners were all genteel; that is, they possessed qualities often evoked by other terms commonly used at the time, including polite, polished, tasteful, well-bred, urbane, civil, fashionable, and gay. Indeed, the term genteel came to function in the 18th century like a kind of litmus test for the well-bred. A traveling gentleman would thus rent a room only in a genteel rooming house, and would never think of purchasing clothing from anyone but a genteel shop or tailor.

In terms of the latter goal, no members of this elite class—or "gentry" as it was called—had more success than the great tobacco planters of the Chesapeake Bay. These gentlemen, which is what male members of the gentry class called themselves, built grand homes, purchased art and European fineries, sent their children to Britain to be educated, dressed in the most luxurious fabrics, and, above all, enjoyed the fellowship of other gentlemen. But even the wealthiest members of Virginia's gentry did not approach the level of wealth enjoyed by prominent members of Britain's landowning gentry. William Byrd's Westover, the grandest of all Chesapeake houses, was a mere cottage when compared with such venerable English homes as the Marquess of Rockingham's Wentworth. The latter was more than 600 feet long, while Byrd's home was a comparatively modest 65 feet long.

The Virginia gentry differed from that of Britain in other ways as well. Aside from simply being less wealthy, far less of their wealth existed in the form of land—and far more in the form of labor. It would be no exaggeration to say that the very existence of Virginia's gentry depended on human "chattel", or human property in the form of African slaves. In addition to simply having high monetary value, slaves could provide owners with a degree of financial security similar to that enjoyed by wealthy British landowners. Unlike indentured servants, slaves provided a lifetime of labor. For the many colonists who could afford to own only one or two slaves, this meant only marginal advantages. If a slave died, one had to bear the high cost of purchasing another slave. Furthermore, the prospects for passing one's property on to subsequent generations were limited if a substantial part of that property included one or two slaves. The slaveholder's children still faced the costly prospects of purchasing slaves to replace those who died or ran away.

For the few planters able to afford 10, 20, or even 30 slaves, the situation could be very different. These individuals had a labor supply that was sustainable over not just one lifetime, but over many. As their slaves intermarried and had families of their own, they provided their owner with a fresh, renewable source of labor. In theory, what this meant was that these slave owners did not have to bear the burden of labor costs—costs that far exceeded any other for plantation owners. While smaller planters were struggling to maintain their workforce, larger planters, their children, and their children's children could rest assured that they would never face such a struggle. Thus labor, not land, gave members of the southern gentry the sort of wealth that freed them from the day-to-day concerns of ordinary colonists and allowed them to emulate the wealthiest classes of Europe.

These wealthy gentlemen prided themselves on having an abundance of leisure time, time during which they might bet on horse races or cockfights, engage in lofty philosophical discussions, or undertake practical scientific projects. The latter often included agricultural experiments aimed at improving productivity on the plantation, but they might also have included experimentation with other valuable commodities, including wine grapes and silk.

The wealthy gentry of the Chesapeake were not, however, a remote, distant group. As much of their time as they devoted to gaming, philosophy, and science, they devoted to public service. Indeed, there was an overwhelming sense among the colonial gentry that they had an obligation—much like that of parents to their child—to care for the less prominent members of their communities. In some sense, this was self-serving: it allowed members of the gentry to justify their disproportionate dominance of colonial political life. At the same time, though it was an impulse with a long and celebrated pedigree in Anglo-American political thought, and few colonists questioned the gentry's political dominance.

These factors made for a colonial political world that is very difficult for modern Americans to comprehend. When we think of political office, we hardly think of words like "obligation" or "duty." When our public servants use these words, they are often dismissed as mere window dressing, as an effort to disguise selfish

"We were accustomed to look upon what were called gentle folks as beings of a superior order. . . . A periwig [wig], in those days, was a distinguishing badge of gentle folk; and when I saw a man riding the road, near our house, with a wig on, it would so alarm my fears and give me such a disagreeable feeling that, I daresay, I would run off as for my life. Such ideas of the difference between gentle and simple were, I believe, universal among all my rank and age."

—Virginia planter and minister Devereux Jarratt on growing up an ordinary Virginian in the 1740s

The prominent display of these young men's delicate hands would have demonstrated to any 18th-century viewer of this portrait that these were hands that had never labored in the fields. This was no doubt true. These sons of a wealthy Boston merchant were born into the colonial gentry, and could expect to pass genteel lives free from manual labor.

"Whosoever studieth the lawes of the realme, who studieth in the universities, who professeth liberall sciences, . . . who can live idly and without manuall labour, and will beare the port, charge and countenaunce of a gentleman, he shall be called master, . . . and shall be taken for a gentleman."

—The definition of a gentleman according to Elizabethan statesman and legal scholar Sir Thomas Smith, from his 1583 treatise *De Republica Anglorum* (The Republic of the English)

During the latter 17th and much of the 18th centuries, young gentlemen—especially those receptive to the Church of England—turned to books such as this for guidance in matters of personal and moral conduct. In them, they generally found a simple message: men should be pious without being fanatical, they should be learned without being tedious, and they should be sensitive without being overly emotional. They should, that is, exhibit supreme self-control.

motives. But when the colonial gentry used them, few sensed hypocrisy or corruption. Coupled with this sense of duty, this idea that gentlemen have an obligation to serve the people, was a more alien sense—at least alien to our modern, democratic way of thinking. The colonial gentry generally believed that they were obliged to hold political office, not simply out of a desire to do good works, but also out of an elitist sense that ordinary people were, for all intents and purposes, like naïve children: they did not know what was in their own best interest. Hence, they needed the father-like gentry to govern them and care for them. As much as anything else, it is our general hostility to this way of thinking that separates our world from that of colonial Americans.

How to Be a Gentleman

The founding fathers were, Americans often imagine, modern men: they understood politics, economics, social relations, and other aspects of life in ways familiar to us. How could one think otherwise? After all, they devised so many of the institutions that govern life in the United States. In fact, however, few generations of Americans could be more distinct from our own; few were more obsessed with such issues as status, manners, courtly behavior, the rules of conduct, and liberal education. Few, that is, were more obsessed with the makings of a gentleman. And none of the founding fathers better exemplifies this obsession than the singular George Washington.

As a child and a young man growing up in colonial Virginia, Washington dedicated himself to becoming a gentleman. This pursuit was apparent in some of his earliest known writings—a set of school exercise books 15-year-old Washington wrote in 1747. In these books appears a section entitled "Rules of Civility and Decent Behaviour in Company and Conversation," which consisted of 110 maxims on proper conduct for a young gentleman. Washington probably copied these points of proper conduct, some of which are excerpted below, from one of the dozens of "etiquette books," or gentleman's handbooks, to which he had access. Young Washington's scrupulous attention to these rules reveal the beginnings of his lifelong quest to distinguish himself as a man of uncommon grace and refinement—attributes that would, in the aftermath of the American Revolution, earn him the admiration of much of the Western world.

4 In the Presence of Others Sing not to yourself with a humming Noise, nor Drum with your Fingers or Feet.

5th : If You Cough, Sneeze, Sigh, or Yawn, do it not Loud but Privately; and Speak not in your Yawning, but put Your Handkercheif or Hand before your face and turn aside.

11th : Shift not yourself in the Sight of others nor Gnaw your nails

12th : Shake not the head, Feet, or Legs rowl not the Eys lift not one eyebrow higher than the other wry not the mouth, and bedew no mans face with your Spittle, by appr[oaching too nea]r him [when] you Speak

15th: Keep your Nails clean and Short, also your Hands and Teeth Clean yet without Shewing any great Concern for them

16th : Do not puff up the Cheeks, Loll not out the tongue rub the Hands, or beard, thrust out the lips, or bite them or keep the Lips too open or too Close

37th In Speaking to men of Quality do not lean nor Look them full in the Face, nor approach too near to them at lest Keep a full Pace from them

54th : Play not the Peacock, looking every where about you, to See if you be well Deck't, if your Shoes fit well if your Stokings Sit neatly, and Cloths handsomely.

56th : Associate yourself with Men of good Quality if you Esteem your own Reputation; for 'tis better to be alone than in bad Company

61st Utter not base and frivilous things amongst grave and Learn'd Men nor very Difficult Questians or Subjects, among the Ignorant or things hard to be believed, . . .

70th : Reprehend not the imperfections of others for that belong[s] to Parents Masters and Superiours

71st Gaze not on the marks or blemishes of Others and ask not how they came. What you may Speak in Secret to your Friend deliver not before others

73d Think before you Speak pronounce not imperfectly nor bring ou[t] your Words too hastily but orderly & distinctly

85th: In Company of these of Higher Quality than yourself Speak not ti[ll] you are ask'd a Question then Stand upright put [off] your Hat & Answer in few words

[9]4th If you Soak bread in the Sauce let it be no more than what you [pu]t in your Mouth at a time and blow not your broth at Table [bu]t Stay till Cools of it Self

[95]th Put not your meat to your Mouth with your Knife in your ha[nd ne]ither Spit forth the Stones of any fruit Pye upon a

"To Be a Virtuoso"

To be a gentleman was to possess good judgment, sound taste, and broad learning. It was not to be some sort of one-dimensional "scholar," as the great English social theorist the Earl of Shaftesbury explained in his widely read book, Characteristics of Men, Manners, Opinions, Times, *published in 1714:*

I am persuaded that to be a virtuoso, so far as befits a gentleman, is a higher step towards the becoming a man of virtue and good sense than the being what in this age we call a scholar. For even rude nature itself, in its primitive simplicity, is a better guide to judgment than . . . pedantic learning. The *they are so knowing that they know nothing at all* will ever be applied by men of discernment and free thought to such logic, such principles, such forms and rudiments of knowledge as are established in certain schools of literature and science.

Dish nor Cast [an]ything under the table

[9]6 It's unbecoming to Stoop much to ones Meat Keep your Fingers clean [&] when foul wipe them on a Corner of your Table Napkin

98th Drink not nor talk with your mouth full neither Gaze about you while you are a Drinking

99th Drink not too leisurely nor yet too hastily. Before and after Drinking wipe your Lips breath not then or Ever with too Great a Noise, for its uncivil

100 Cleanse not your teeth with the Table Cloth Napkin Fork or Knife but if Others do it let it be done wt. a Pick Tooth

101st Rince not your Mouth in the Presence of Others

107th : If others talk at Table be attentive but talk not with Meat in your Mouth

108th : When you Speak of God or his Atributes, let it be Seriously & [with] Reverence. Honour & Obey your Natural Parents altho they be Poor

109th Let your Recreations be Manfull not Sinfull.

110th Labour to keep alive in your Breast that Little Spark of Ce[les]tial fire Called Conscience.

In a sense, the best way to understand the gentry is to think of it as a giant, trans-Atlantic social club, a club whose members shared a common level of education, a particular sense of style and taste, and, perhaps above all, a mutual capacity for correct social exchange. The latter took a variety of forms, the most important of which were letter writing and, of course, conversation. Proper conversation functioned as a kind of identity badge that any gentleman could trundle out on social occasions to show himself to be a member of the social elite. Unfortunately, conversation is fleeting, so we have few documents illustrating its power and social importance. But occasionally colonists described scenes of gentlemanly exchange. One who did so was Maryland physician Alexander Hamilton (no relation the first U.S. secretary of the treasury by the same name). In a series of notes he kept while traveling through the northern colonies in 1744, Hamilton described the conversation at one dinner with a group of New York City gentlemen, a conversation that featured a characteristic discussion of agriculture.

I arrived in New York about eleven o clock and put up my horses at Waghorn's. After calling att Mrs. Hog's I went to see my old

"Very little difference is, in reality, observable in the manners of the wealthy colonist and the wealthy Briton. Good and bad habits prevail on both sides of the Atlantic."

—English government official William Eddis writing from Maryland to a friend in England (1771)

friend Todd, expecting there to dine but accidentally I encountered Stephen Bayard who carried me to dine att his brother's. There was there a great company of gentlemen, among the rest Mr. D[elan]cie, the Chief Justice; Mr. H[orsemande]n, the City Recorder; and one Mr. More, a lawer. There was one gentleman there whom they stiled cpatain who squinted the most abominably of any body ever I saw. His eyes were not matched, for one was of a lighter colour than the other. Another gentleman there wore so much of a haughty frown in his countenance, that even when he smiled it did not disappear. There were 13 gentlemen att table but not so much as one lady. We had an elegant, sumptuous dinner with a fine desert of sweetmeats and fruits, among which last there were some of the best white grapes I have seen in America.

The table chat run upon privateering and such discourse as has now become so common that it is tiresome and flat. One there, who set up for a dictator, talked very much of the discredit of Old England, preferring New York to it in every respect whatsoever relating to good living. . . . [but] it seemed as if he did not know much of that fine country England. He said that the grapes there were good for nothing but to set a man's teeth on edge; but to my knowledge I have seen grapes in gentlemen's gardens there far preferable to any ever I saw in these northern parts of America. He asserted also that no good apple could be brought up there without a [magnifying] glass and artificall heat, which assertion was palpably false and glaringly ignorant, for almost every fool knows that apples grow best in northern climates betwixt the latitudes of 35 and 50, and that in the southern hot climes, within the tropics, they don't grow att all, and therefore the best apples in the world grow in England and in the north of France. He went even so far as to say that the beef in New York was preferable to that of England. When he came there I gave him up as a triffler, and giving no more attention to this discourse, he lost himself, the Lord knows how or where, in a thicket of erroneous and ignorant dogmas which any the most exaggerating traveler would have been ashamed of. But he was a great person in the place, and therefor none in the company was imprudent enough to contradict him tho some were there that knew better. I have known in my time some of these great dons take upon them to talk in an extravagant and absurd manner: "What a fine temperate climate this is!" says a certain dictating fop, while every body that hears him is conscious that it is fit for none but the devil to live in. "Don't you think them fine oysters," says another exalted prigg, while every body knows he is eating of eggs. This we cannot conceive proceeds from

Colonial gentlemen congregated in a wide variety of informal and formal clubs. For the Ancient and Honorable Tuesday Club of Annapolis, an anniversary procession—such as the one depicted here—allowed members to at once impress townsfolk with the assemblage of prominent men while mocking the very same public displays the gentry used to secure its social superiority.

ignorance but from a certain odd pleasure they have in talking nonsense without being contradicted. This disposition may arise from the naturall perverseness of human nature, which is always most absurd and unreasonable when free from curb or restraint. This company after dinner set in for bumpers so I left them at three o'clock.

While manners, conversation, and friends were all crucial marks of gentlemanly status, none was more important than a gentleman's relation to work. Gentlemen, simply put, did not work. They engaged in no manual labor—a fact demonstrated endlessly by the prominent depiction of men's graceful and unsullied hands in 18th-century portraits—and they avoided any work that involved handling money. Trade, finances, and small business activities were all regarded as beneath a true gentleman. Such activities, Europe's social elite had long thought, elicited a crass spirit of greed and selfishness and distracted gentlemen from more elevated, selfless pursuits. This attitude is wonderfully captured in a letter from Benjamin Franklin to his friend, the New York physician Cadwallader Colden. Like all ambitious colonists, Franklin aspired to become a gentleman, and as he indicates in this letter, that involved retiring from his business pursuits and

Unlike modern cities where the wealthy live in exclusive neighborhoods or suburbs, in colonial cities, elites and ordinary colonists commonly lived side by side. Nonetheless, it was never difficult to identify the homes of the most wealthy and powerful residents.

devoting all his time to scientific and philosophical activities—activities aimed at bettering all humanity. Franklin also
disclaims any interest in public office, an appropriate state-
ment for a gentleman. He would hold office only out of a
sense of duty, not personal ambition.

Sir

Philada. Sept. 29. 1748

I received your Favour of the 12th Inst. which gave me the greater
Pleasure, as 'twas so long since I had heard from you. I congratu-
late you on your Return to your beloved Retirement: I too am taking the proper Measures for obtaining Leisure to enjoy Life and
my Friends more than heretofore, having put my Printing house
under the Care of my Partner David Hall, absolutely left off
Bookselling, and remov'd to a more quiet Part of the Town, where
I am settling my old Accounts and hope soon to be quite a Master
of my own Time, and no longer (as the Song has it) *at every one's
Call but my own.* If Health continues, I hope to be able in another
Year to visit the most distant Friend I have, without Incon-
venience. With the same Views I have refus'd engaging further in
publick Affairs; The Share I had in the late Association, &c. having given me a little present Run of Popularity, there was a pretty
general Intention of chusing me a Representative for the City at
the next Election of Assemblymen; but I have desired all my
Friends who spoke to me about it, to discourage it, declaring that
I should not serve if chosen. Thus you see I am in a fair Way of
having no other Tasks than such as I shall like to give my self, and
of enjoying what I look upon as a great Happiness, Leisure to read,
study, make Experiments, and converse at large with such inge-
nious and worthy Men as are pleas'd to honour me with their
Friendship or Acquaintance, on such Points as may produce something for the common Benefit of Mankind, uniterrupted by the little Cares and Fatigues of Business. Among other Pleasures I
promise my self, that of Corresponding more frequently and fully
with Dr. Colden is none of the least; I shall only wish that what
must be so agreable to me, may not prove troublesome to you. . . .
I am, with great Esteem and Respect, Dear Sir Your most obliged
humble Servant

B Franklin

**The gentleman's contempt for work could produce a rather
strange lifestyle. Governed by few of the rhythms that
shaped ordinary colonists' lives, gentlemen filled their days**

This is a page from William Byrd's personal diary. The strange writing is a shorthand, no doubt used by Byrd to ease the burden of daily diary keeping.

with leisurely meals, prayer, language study, weather observation, strolls, friendly gaming, dancing, horseback riding, hunting, fine meals, and conversation. Still, as the diary entries excerpted below suggest, a gentleman's life could be quite regimented, indeed even somewhat monotonous. The author of these entries, 66-year-old Virginia planter William Byrd II, was obsessed with recording the small particulars of his daily existence, and kept a personal diary for much of his adult life. The section below, from January 1740, was written fairly late in Byrd's life, during the coldest month of the year, and at a time when Byrd's public obligations were perhaps reduced. But it still conveys a sense of what life could be like for a member of the colonial leisure class.

January, 1740

1. I rose about 6, read Hebrew and Greek. I prayed and had tea. I danced. The weather cleared up and was warm but blowing fiercely at southwest and then northwest. I settled some accounts till dinner when I ate beefsteak. After dinner I put things in order but it was too cold to walk. I talked with my people [his slaves] and played piquet [a card game played with 32 cards] and prayed.

2. I rose about 6, read Hebrew and Greek. I prayed and had tea. I danced. The weather was cold and clear, the wind northwest. My people carted gravel. I settled some accounts and read records till dinner, when I ate venison pasty. In the afternoon we played billiards and then walked a little. In the evening came the sloop for my wheat. I prayed.

3. I rose about 6, read Hebrew and Greek. I prayed and had coffee. I danced. The weather continued very cold, the wind west. We put the wheat on board the sloop. I read English till dinner when I ate roast beef. After dinner we talked and walked, notwithstanding it was very cold. Old Joe [a white servant whom Byrd had brought from England] died and was buried. I talked with my people and prayed. It was exceedingly cold.

4. I rose about 6, read Hebrew and Greek. I prayed and had hominy. I danced. The weather was very cold and clear, the wind northwest. We began to cut wood in the swamp. I read English and played billiards till dinner when I ate fried venison pasty. After dinner we played at billiards again and walked a little. In the evening played piquet and talked with my people, then retired and prayed.

5. I rose about 6, read Hebrew and Greek. I prayed and had sage [or sack] tea. I danced. The weather was still cold and clear,

the wind northwest. I wrote a letter and walked, then read English till dinner when Miss Brun came. I ate broiled beef. After dinner we played billiards and walked a little. At night talked with my people. All well above, thank God. I played piquet and prayed.

6. I rose about 6, [read] Hebrew and Greek. I prayed and had coffee. I danced. The weather continued very cold and clear, the wind north. I went not to church because it was cold, but all the family went besides, and I put my person in order and wrote a letter . . . I ate roast venison and Mrs. Greenhill dined with us and went away. I talked with my people and prayed.

7. I rose about 6, read Hebrew and Greek. I prayed and had tea. I danced. The weather was cold and clear, the wind northwest. My man Bob went to the Falls. I wrote [cheery?] papers for the day and walked till dinner when I ate cold boiled beef. After dinner we played billiards but it was too cold to walk. I talked with my people, drew twelfth cake [a cake for celebrating the twelfth night] and cider, and prayed.

8. I rose about 6, read Hebrew and Greek. I prayed and had hominy. I danced. The weather was cold and clear, the wind still northwest. Mrs. Greenhill came from the Secretary's and told us of their elegant diversions. I read English till dinner and then ate roast beef. After dinner it rained so that I could not walk. At night played cards and talked with my people.

9. I rose about 6, read Hebrew and Greek. I prayed and had coffee. I danced. The weather was cold and cloudy, with little rain, the wind southwest. It rained a little all day so that Mrs.Greenhill

This page from a colonial hunting and fishing manual identifies some of the fish that an angler might catch. Manuals such as this provided instruction in the pursuits available for colonial gentlemen's entertainment.

could not go. I read Latin till dinner when I ate sheldrake [duck]. After dinner we talked and I danced because I could not walk. At night talked with my people, played piquet and prayed. It blew very hard.

10. I rose about 6, read Hebrew and Greek. I prayed and had tea. I danced. The weather was warm and cloudy, but cleared up about 10, the wind west. I played billiards with my son and then read English till one, then Latin till dinner, when I ate roast goose. After dinner we talked and Mrs. Greenhill went over the river and we played billiards and then walked. I talked with my people and prayed.

11. I rose about 6, read Hebrew and Greek. I prayed and had hominy. I danced. The weather was cold and clear, the wind north. I read Latin and played billiards and read records and Latin till dinner, when I ate goose. After dinner we played billiards and then walked about the garden because the ground was damp. I talked with my people, played cards, and prayed.

12. I rose about 6, read Hebrew and Greek. I prayed and had tea. I danced. The weather was cold and cloudy, the wind north, but cleared up about 10. I read Latin and records till dinner when I ate stewed oysters. After dinner played billiards and walked a little. All was well . . . , thank God. At night talked with my people, played piquet, and prayed.

13. I rose about 6, read Hebrew and Greek. I prayed and had coffee. I danced. The weather was overcast and cold, the wind north. . . . I went not to church but sent the children, but nobody beside was there, nor nobody came to dine. I ate roast hare. After dinner we walked. At [night] Robin Mumford came. I talked with my people and prayed.

14. I rose about 6, read Hebrew and Greek. I prayed and had tea. I danced. The weather was cold and clear, the wind southwest. Mr. Mumford went away, the best with a dram of cherry brandy in his belly. I read records and Latin till dinner when I ate boiled beef. After dinner we played billiards and walked. At night talked with my people, played piquet, and prayed. It rained in the night with much wind.

While the Chesapeake gentry bore the closest resemblance to gentry in the British Isles, there were of course gentlemen throughout the colonies. Even in New England, where many of the austere tendencies of the Puritans persisted into the 18th century, a class of social elites had emerged. What distinguished this latter group from ordinary New Englanders was more muted than what one found in the Chesapeake, or even in the great merchant centers of Philadelphia and New York. Houses tended to be less grand, clothes less colorful and luxurious, and manners somewhat more controlled. But beneath this more egalitarian façade was an acute awareness of social status. Where one lived in town and where one sat in church were, elite New Englanders believed, crucial markers of social standing.

Higher education had a similar function. Given that there were only three colleges in colonial New England (Harvard, Yale, and Dartmouth), little status was attached to institutional affiliation. Rather, status came from where one was situated in academic rankings within the colleges—rankings that were usually predetermined according to the social status of students' families. In the following letter to the president of Harvard College, General John Winslow defends his family pedigree as part of a desperate attempt to secure for his son a high rank in his college class.

Reverend and Honored Sir,   Boston, Oct. 20th, 1749
As I am bound to sea, and rank in our way is looked upon as a sacred thing, and it is generally allowed that the sons of the New England Cambridge are placed according to the degrees of their ancestors, I have therefore put in my pretensions for my son, beginning with the country in which we breathe, and [as] for genealogy [I] say:

That Edward Winslow, my great grandfather, was the eldest of the name in England and of five brothers [who were] first settlers

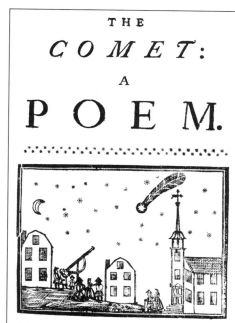

Mather Byles, the author of this poem, was one of Boston's elite ministers. These men distinguished themselves from ordinary Bostonians in a number of ways. Most were Harvard educated, most engaged in literary and philosophical pursuits beyond their minister-ial duties, and most corresponded with prominent figures in the colonies and Britain. Byles himself could count among his correspondents Benjamin Franklin and the great English poet Alexander Pope.

"Dined at Mr. Nick Boylstones, . . . An elegant Dinner indeed! Went over the House to view the Furniture, which alone cost a thousand Pounds sterling. A Seat it is for a noble Man, a Prince. The Turkey Carpets, the painted Hangings, the Marble Tables, the rich Beds with crimson Damask Curtains and Counterpins, the beautiful Chimny Clock, the Spacious Garden, are the most magnificent of any Thing I have ever seen."

—John Adams writing in his diary about the home of a prominent Boston merchant (1766)

This embroidered banner showing the main building at Harvard College was most likely made by an elite Massachusetts woman, perhaps for a husband or son who attended the college.

of what is now this province; and that the said Edward was one of the first planters and in the first ship of what was lately the colony of Plymouth, and [was] some time Governor thereof, and [was] one of the Grand Commissioners of the unhappy expedition against Hispaniola and died at the taking of Jamaica, leaving one son (Josiah), who in his day was [for] many years Governor of said colony and Captain General of the United Forces of New England in the memorable Indian war called King Philip's War, in which he got his death, leaving one son (named Isaac, my father), who had the honor to have the first place in both civil and military affairs in the County of Plymouth for many years, and [who] until he resigned was President of the Council of this province. And [I say further] that in the year 1738 he died, leaving two sons, of which I am the eldest. And [I] have to say for myself that from my early days I have been entrusted in the public affairs of the county and province, until 1740, when I had a company in the unfortunate expedition against Cartagena; and [I] have had since two commissions of the same rank under His Majesty and [have been] entrusted with the command of the second garrison in North America, which is my present station. Pardon my saying thus much; [I] offer these things as facts and leave the events to the honorable and reverend body to and for whom I have the greatest regard. And at all times with the utmost respect [I] shall take leave to subscribe yours and their very humble servant,

J. Winslow

A Gentlewoman's Burden

Although the colonial elite was a largely male social class, it was not exclusively so. Wives and daughters of gentlemen were, in essence, "gentlewomen." They shared a similar sense of privilege, a similar sense of social superiority, and a similar concern for manners and etiquette. Family wealth also, at times, allowed them to obtain educations normally reserved for boys and young men. These women frequently learned to read, write, and do arithmetic; they sometimes even studied classical languages and literature. Despite such advantages, "gentlewomen" probably had more in common with ordinary colonial women than with their male counterparts. They were, much like most colonial women, rarely able to own property, unable to hold political office, and generally dependent on husbands and fathers for the basics of life.

Embedded in etiquette books for young women—books similar to those that gentlemen used to refine their own conduct—were a host of maxims about the proper role for well-bred, refined ladies. One of the most popular of these books was written by English nobleman George Savile, marquess of Halifax, for his daughter. The clear message of the marquess's *Miscellanies* was that while gentlewomen needed to have educated tastes and refined manners, they also needed to be reminded that they were ultimately the subordinates of their husbands. In the following section, Halifax justifies to his daughter women's status with the claim that inequality is beneficial to both sexes.

It is one of the *Disadvantages* belonging to your *Sex*, that young Women are seldom permitted to make their own *Choice*; their Friends' Care and Experience are thought safer Guides to them, than their own *Fancies*; and their *Modesty* often forbiddeth them to refuse when their Parents recommend, though their *inward Consent* may not entirely go along with it. In this case there remaineth nothing for them to do but to endeavour to make that easie which falleth to their *Lot*, and by a wise use of every thing they

The title page of the Marquess of Halifax's The Lady's New Year's Gift *indicates the essential arenas for female gentility and good conduct in a series of brief headings. Such a carefully ordered scheme for good breeding is indicative of the way this and other similar books were intended to be used. Much like schoolbooks, they were to be studied and fully absorbed by young minds.*

THE
Lady's New-years Gift:
OR
ADVICE
TO A
DAUGHTER,

Under these following Heads: *Viz.*

Religion,
Husband,
House and *Fa-*
mily.
Servants,
Behaviour and
Conversation,

Friendships,
Censure,
Vanity and
Affectation,
Pride.
Diversions,
Dancing.

The Third Edition Corrected by the Original.

London, Printed for *Matt. Gillyflower*
in *Westminster-Hall,* and *James*
Partridge at *Charing-Cross.* 1688.

may dislike in a *Husband,* turn that by degrees to be very supportable, which, if neglected, might in time beget an *Aversion.*

You must first lay it down for a Foundation in general, That there is *Inequality* in the *Sexes,* and that for better Œconomy of the World, the *Men,* who were to be the Law givers, had the larger share of *Reason* bestow'd upon them; by which means your Sex is the better prepar'd for the *Compliance* that is necessary for the better performance of those *Duties* which seem to be most properly assign'd to it. This looks a little uncouthly at the first appearance; but upon Examination it will be found, that *Nature* is so far from being unjust to you, that she is partial on your side. She hath made you such large *Amends* by other Advantages, for the seeming *Injustice* of the first Distribution, that the Right of Complaining is come over to our Sex. You have it in your power not only to free your selves, but to Subdue your Masters, and without violence throw both their *Natural* and *Legal Authority* at your Feet. We are made of differing *Tempers,* that our *Defects* may the better be mutually supplied: Your *Sex* wanteth our *Reason* for your *Conduct,* and our *Strength* for your *Protection: Ours* wanteth your *Gentleness* to soften, and to entertain us. The first part of our Life is a good deal subjected to you in the *Nursery*, where you Reign without Competition, and by that means have the advantage of giving the first *Impressions*. Afterwards you have stronger influences, which, well manag'd, have more force in your behalf, than all our *Privileges* and *Jurisdictions* can pretend to have against you. You have more strength in your *Looks*, than we have in our *Laws*, and more power by your *Tears*, than we have by our *Arguments*.

. . . you live in a time which hath rendred some kind of Frailties so habitual, that they lay claim to large *Grains* of *Allowance*. The World in this is somewhat unequal, and our Sex seemeth to play the *Tyrant*, in distinguishing *partially* for our selves, by making that in the utmost degree *Criminal* in the *Woman*, which in a *Man* passeth under a much *gentler Censure*. The Root and Excuse of this Injustice is the *Preservation* of Families from any Mixture that may bring a Blemish to them: And whilst the *Point* of *Honour* continues to be so plac'd, it seems unavoidable to give your Sex the greater share of the Penalty. . . .

With all this, that which you are to pray for, is a *Wise Husband*, one that by knowing how to be a *Master*, for that very reason will not let you feel the weight of it; one whose Authority is so soften'd by his Kindness, that it giveth you ease without abridging your *Liberty*; one that will return so much tenderness for your *Just Esteem* of him, that you will never want *power*, though you will seldom care to use it. Such a *Husband* is as much above all other Kinds of them, as a *rational Subjection* to a Prince, great in himself, is to be preferr'd before the disquiet and uneasiness of *Unlimited Liberty*.

The colonial elite was forever struggling to balance the temptations of daily life with the moral burden brought upon them by their station. Like parents, the gentry regarded themselves as moral educators, people whose behavior would be the model for others to follow. But, also like parents, they often found themselves struggling against hypocrisy, against the temptation to do one thing and say another. To counter this, they often wrote out a set of personal maxims or resolutions describing the qualities of a moral life—qualities that, they believed, it was their duty to uphold. For elite women, the burden was made all the greater by the addition of obedience (to fathers and husbands) to the various other rules for polite and refined behavior. Eliza Pinckney, wife of a wealthy South Carolina planter, wrote a series of resolutions that were discovered

Few colonists could afford sumptuous gowns such as this one, worn by the granddaughter of a governor of the Massachusetts colony.

In addition to the usual rules of obedience, elite women, much like elite men, were obliged to uphold complex rules of etiquette. They were to be calm and stable, yet also capable of feelings; they were to defer to their husbands and other men, and yet serve as instructors and moral guides to children and servants. To capture this balancing act, colonial portrait painters usually depicted women with ambiguous facial expressions. The expression of Mrs. Thomas Newton Jr. of Virginia, in this 1770 portrait, is typically difficult to characterize.

among her private papers. These resolutions are unified by one, overriding concern: that she appear calm, even-tempered, and pious. These qualities were to prevail over emotion and passion in the lady of good breeding, and for Pinckney, who at 36 was widowed and left to manage her husband's plantation, they seem to have had special importance.

I am resolved by the Grace of God asisting me to keep these resolutions which I have frequently made, and do now again renew.

I am resolved to believe in God; that he is, and is a rewarder of all that diligently seek him. To believe firmly and constantly in all his attributes etc. etc. I am resolved to believe in him, to fear him and love him with all the powers and faculties of my soul. To keep a steady eye to his commands, and to govern myself in every circumstance of life by the rules of the Gospel of Christ, whose disciple I profess myself, and as such will live and dye.

I am resolved by the Divine will, not to be anxious or doubtful, not to be fearful of any accident or misfortune that may happen to me or mine, not to regard the frowns of the world, but to keep a steady upright conduct before my God, and before man, doing my duty and contented to leave the event to God's Providence.

I am resolved by the same Grace to govern my passions, to endeavour constantly to subdue every vice and improve in every virtue, and in order to [do] this I will not give way to any the least notions of pride, haughtiness, ambition, ostentation, or contempt of others. I will not give way to Envy, Ill will, Evil speaking, ingratitude, or uncharitableness in word, in thought, or in deed, or to passion or peavishness, nor to Sloath or Idleness, but to endeavour after all the contrary Virtues, humility, charity, etc, etc, and to be always usefully or innocently imploy'd.

I am resolved not to be luxurious or extravagant in the management of my table and family on the one hand, nor niggardly and covetous, or too anxiously concern'd about it on the other, but to endeavour after a due medium; to manage with hospitality and Generosity as much as is in our power, to have always plenty with frugality and good Economy.

To be decent but frugal in my own Expences.

To be charitably disposed to all mankind.

I am resolved by the Divine Assistance to fill the several Stations wherein Providence has placed me to the best advantage.

To make a good wife to my dear Husband in all its several branches; to make all my actions Corrispond with that sincere love and Duty I bear him. To pray for him, to contribute all in my power to the good of his Soul and to the peace and satisfaction of his mind, to be careful of his Health, of his Interests, of his children, and of his Reputation; to do him all the good in my power; and next to my God, to make it my Study to please him.

I am resolved to make a good child to my Mother; to do all I am able to give her comfort and make her happy.

I am resolved to be a good Mother to my children, to pray for them, to set them good examples, to give them good advice, to be careful both of their souls and bodys, to watch over their tender minds, to carefully root out the first appearing and budings of vice, and to instill piety, Virtue and true religion into them; to spair no paines or trouble to do them good; to correct their Errors whatever uneasiness it may give myself; and never omit to encourage every Virtue I may see dawning in them.

I am resolved to make a good Sister both to my own and my Husband's brothers and sisters, to do them all the good I can, to treat them with affection, kindness, and good-manners, to do them all the good I can etc, etc.

In the following passage, Pinckney expresses the commonly professed attitude of large planters toward their slaves. She suggests that her treatment of them will differ little from her treatment of her own children.

I am resolved to make a good Mistress to my Servants, to treat them with humanity and good nature; to give them sufficient and comfortable clothing and Provisions, and all things necessary for them. To be careful and tender of them in their sickness, to reprove them for their faults, to Encourage them when they do well, and pass over small faults; not to be tyrranical peavish or impatient toward them, but to make their lives as comfortable as I can.

I am resolved to be a sincere and faithful friend wherever I profess'd it, and as much as in me lies an agreable and innocent companion, and a universal lover of all mankind.

All these resolutions by God's assistance I will keep to my life's end.

So help me O My God! Amen.

Memdum [Memorandum]

Read over this dayly to assist my memory as to every particular contained in this paper. Mem. Before I leave my Chamber recolect in Genl. the business to be done that day.

Chapter Eight: Photo Essay

A World of Things

By the middle of the 18th century, European colonists, native peoples, and Africans living in eastern North America had much more in common with each other than simply the continent on which they resided. They also shared an overlapping "material culture." That is, nearly all the clothes they wore, the tools they used, and the furnishings in their homes came from the same large web of trade and manufacturing that stretched from the colonies to Great Britain and Europe. Whether in an Iroquois village in upstate New York or a sea captain's home in Charleston, South Carolina, the source of most manufactured goods was likely to have been the same.

Boot buckles, guns, cookware, fabric, men's shirts, knives, hand tools, and pewter drinking cups all were the sorts of goods that found their way into households throughout the colonies. And such goods, more than religion or ethnicity, or custom, gave the disparate peoples and societies of colonial America any unity at all. For in the end, it was things, more than ideas or beliefs, that brought the peoples of colonial America together.

To study some of those things is thus to gain a unique perspective on colonial society. It is to see the materials with which the peoples of colonial America tried to improve their lives, but it is also to see the very same materials that made the colonists' lives much more complex and difficult. These materials brought about new economic relations, changed traditional patterns of food production, and left people in debt—but they also spurred a new acquisitive spirit, a spirit not entirely removed from the consumer society of which we are all now a part.

The portraits, Chinese porcelain, and fine furniture in this Williamsburg, Virginia, parlor would have left visitors with little doubt that they were in the home of a gentleman. And, indeed, this is precisely why prominent colonists often collected their finest possessions in rooms designed to receive visitors. Expensive things were, much like speech and manners, crucial signs of gentility and therefore were meant as much for display as for personal pleasure.

A New World of Trade

Long before the English established permanent settlements in North America, native peoples had begun acquiring European-made goods. Metal goods—knives, axes, pots, and other items—were particularly valued, and they often made their way across the continent as natives traded these prized commodities among themselves. In recent years, archaeologists working in Native American burial grounds or sites of former villages have discovered such items, and with them fashioned a new picture of eastern Native American life. That picture makes the once-popular notion that native peoples existed in isolated wilderness enclaves impossible to sustain. We now know that throughout the 16th century, Native Americans were increasingly involved in a trans-Atlantic network of trade and economic relations.

Archaeologists recovered these iron strike-a-lights (for starting fires) from sites in New England. They probably made their way into native trade networks during the 16th century when northeastern Native Americans began trading with English fishermen.

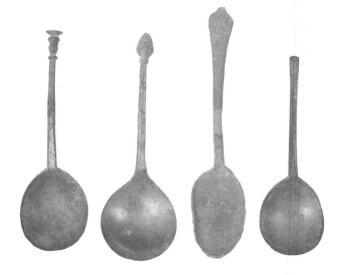

Archaeologists recovered these European-made objects—a ceramic plate and pewter and silver spoons —from a 17th-century Indian burial ground in eastern Rhode Island. Native peoples widely adopted European-style eating utensils, particularly metal spoons, in place of the traditional wooden, clay, or stone implements. As Indians relied more and more on European manufactured products, they lost the skills their ancestors employed to make their own goods.

The Things of War

In addition to many Native American artifacts, archaeologists have unearthed hundreds of objects used by the early English colonists. In Virginia, for instance, they have found assorted instruments of war, including cannonballs, musket shot, and body armor. These items confirm what historians have long assumed about early Virginia: It was a dangerous and often violent place.

Archaeologists recovered these military artifacts from the mid-1620s at a site in Virginia. The coiled object at center-left is a "worm," used for cleaning cannon barrels. The other objects, from top to bottom, are a metal breastplate, cannonballs, a halberd blade, and, at bottom center, a stand on which to rest a musket barrel.

A metal helmet from an archaeological dig near the site of the Jamestown colony, possibly discarded by an English soldier during the 1622 Powhatan attack.

A Colonial Home

Much like other things 17th-century colonists owned, homes bore the marks of a difficult life in an often-hostile environment. Furnishings were simple, lacking in functionless ornamentation, and they were fashioned from easily obtained materials. Seventeenth-century New England houses thus often had a dreary appearance. They lacked most of the embellishment that might have decorated an English home of that same period; similarly, they were almost without exception made from wood, a resource that abounded in New England but that had become relatively scarce in Old England. The interiors of these homes had a similar functional quality. They possessed few of the luxuries and decorations that started to become common late in the colonial era. Instead, they were spare spaces designed to provide essential warmth and shelter during the long New England winters.

This house in Dedham, Massachusetts, was built in the mid-1630s. The additions at the ends of the house were probably built in the 18th century.

This reconstructed interior of a late-17th-century Massachusetts house has several telling features. The most obvious of these is the massive hearth or fireplace on the far wall. This would have been used for cooking and heating. The hearth was also an important social focal point within the New England house, as family members would congregate near it during the cold winter months.

*This sampler was made by
Mary Hollingsworth of Salem,
Massachusetts, in the late 1660s.*

*This elaborate sampler was made in 1737 by
a 15-year-old Philadelphian named Elizabeth
Hudson. In addition to demonstrating Elizabeth's
skills with needle and thread the sampler also suggests that she was learning to be a pious Christian.
The story the sampler tells is based on a passage
from the Book of Genesis and conveys basic principles of Judeo-Christian morality.*

A Girl's Work

Perhaps the most striking material remnants of colonial women's work are some of the many remaining "samplers" produced by young women and girls to display their talent at needlework. These large pieces of fabric, often more than two feet long, reflect the process through which girls learned to sew. A teacher (often a mother or grandmother) would demonstrate a certain stitch, which the child would then emulate on the sampler. Sometimes too, as a means of preparing girls for the burden of repairing a family's clothing, the mother would intentionally tear the fabric from which the sampler was made. The girl would then repair the tear in the proper manner. Like so many of the objects remaining from the colonial era, these samplers have a rich social significance. Most were made by girls from middle and upper-class colonial families—families who could afford servants and slaves to perform domestic work, while daughters perfected their sewing techniques.

The Good Life

Until the late 17th century, little distinguished the houses of ordinary colonists from those of well-to-do planters. But as a distinct colonial gentry began to emerge, that state of affairs changed dramatically. This was particularly the case in the colonial Chesapeake, where wealthy planters began building lavish homes and estates featuring richly decorated interior spaces for leisure and entertainment. Perhaps the greatest of all Chesapeake homes was William Byrd's Westover.

From a Colonial Table

Among the most common manufactured objects in colonial homes were tableware—silverware, pewter plates, mugs, and candlesticks. The nature of these goods, however, changed during the course of the colonial era. If for most of the 17th century they betrayed a utilitarian quality, by the middle of the 18th century more ornate styles had become commonplace. This development signified much more than a change in taste. It was also a product of the new manufacturing techniques that were emerging in an industrializing Britain. Fine china and elaborate silverware that was once affordable for only the wealthiest English gentlemen could now be imported from Great Britain and purchased by prosperous colonists.

Any wealthy colonist interested in adding fine porcelain to the dinner table would have had to import it from England. This changed briefly in the late 1760s when two entrepreneurs began manufacturing porcelain dinner- and tea-ware in Philadelphia. Their business only lasted a few years and its products are thus extremely rare. This sauceboat—exhibiting the characteristic white-and-blue coloring and Asian-inspired design of 18th-century English porcelain—is one of fewer than 20 examples known to exist. It was purchased in a garage sale in the 1940s before finding its way to the Museum of Fine Arts in Houston.

Wealthier colonists could commission the manufacture of fine hand-crafted tableware, such as this silver bowl made in New York City between 1700 and 1710.

Furniture

Few objects from the colonial era are as valuable to antique collectors as furniture. One of the reasons for this is that many of the furnishings made in the colonies reveal an extraordinarily high level of artisanal skill. The carefully carved details, the elaborate decorative inlays, the specially selected woods, and the handmade metal fittings all indicate the immense care and labor that went into fashioning these objects. But there is another, more basic reason for their high value, and that is simply that such furniture is relatively scarce. The number of people in the colonies who could afford fine, handcrafted furniture was very small compared to that number in Great Britain or other European countries. Nevertheless, their numbers grew, and by the middle of the 18th century colonial craftsmen were producing elaborately crafted, finely ornamented furnishings to satisfy wealthy colonists' increasingly opulent tastes.

The hand-carved details on Thomas Hart's valuables cabinet suggest much labor and, hence, high cost. But compared to what colonial craftsmen produced 75 years later, these details were meager indeed. This chest of drawers, made in eastern Massachusetts some time in the mid-18th century, is not only much larger than Hart's cabinet, it also features much more delicate and finely worked decorations. Few colonists could afford such luxuries. But the fact that any could is indicative of the immense purchasing power of the 18th-century colonial gentry.

Hand-crafted wooden chests and cabinets were common fixtures in the homes of prosperous colonists. This small cabinet, made in 1679 for Thomas Hart of Lynn, Massachusetts, may have been purchased by Hart to commemorate an important date, possibly a wedding anniversary. Hart probably used it to store jewelry, coins, important legal documents, and other valuables. These items would have been well concealed in the series of small drawers behind the cabinet's ornamental front, which features Hart's initials and the date the cabinet was made.

Timeline

1492
Christopher Columbus completes his first voyage to America.

1497
John Cabot sails to Newfoundland.

1498
John Cabot dies at sea on his second voyage.

1516
Sir Thomas More writes *Utopia.*

1522
Bartolomé de Las Casas publishes *The Devastation of the Indies* in Seville, Spain.

1566
Sir Humphrey Gilbert writes *A discourse of a discoverie for a new passage to Cataia* (Cathay), promoting the search for a Northwest Passage.

1584
Richard Hakluyt writes *Discourse of Western Planting* to persuade Queen Elizabeth to establish an American colony.

1584
Sir Walter Raleigh sends seven ships, carrying 100 colonists to Roanoke Island, on the outer banks of present-day North Carolina.

1587
Raleigh sends a second group of colonists to Roanoke and colony vanishes, never to be heard from again.

1588
England defeats the Spanish Armada.

1607
The Jamestown colony is established on the James River in Virginia.

1611
First tobacco crop grown in Virginia.

1618
Sir Walter Raleigh is executed in England.

1619
First Africans brought to Virginia.

1620
Pilgrims land at Plymouth.

1622
Powhatan Confederacy revolts; dozens of Virginia colonists are killed.

1624
Virginia Company Charter is revoked. Virginia becomes a royal colony.

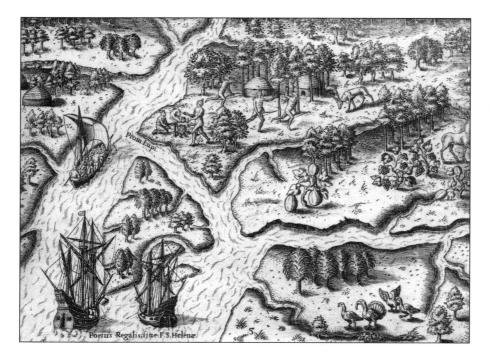

1630

Massachusetts Bay Colony founded.

1633

Smallpox epidemic kills hundreds of native people in eastern Massachusetts.

1634

The Catholic Lord Baltimore establishes the Maryland Colony.

1634

Roger Williams is expelled from Massachusetts Bay and founds a new colony at Providence, Rhode Island.

1634

The colony of Connecticut is founded.

1637

The Pequot War. Anne Hutchinson expelled from Massachusetts Bay Colony.

1663

The Carolina Colony founded.

1664

The colony of New Jersey founded.

1675–76

King Philip's War.

1681

William Penn receives a royal land grant and founds Pennsylvania.

1692

Salem witch trials.

1706

Benjamin Franklin born in Boston.

1712

Carolina Colony divided into North and South Carolina.

1715

War breaks out between the Yamasee Indians and colonists in South Carolina.

1730–34

William Byrd II builds the Byrd family mansion, Westover.

1732

George Washington is born in Virginia. Georgia founded.

1739

Itinerant preacher George Whitefield arrives in the colonies.

1756–63

French and Indian War.

1763

Pontiac, the Ottawa chief, leads rebellion against British forts in the Northeast.

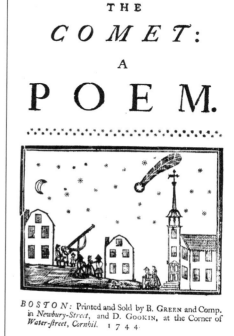

Further Reading

Autobiographies and Journals

Dunn, Richard S., and Laetitia Yeandle, eds. *The Journal of John Winthrop, 1630–1649: Abridged Edition.* Cambridge, Mass.: Harvard University Press, 1996.

Equiano, Olaudah. *The Interesting Narrative and Other Writings.* Vincent Carretta, ed. New York: Penguin, 1995.

Franklin, Benjamin. *Autobiography: An Authoritative Text.* J. A. Leo Lemay and P. M. Zall, eds. New York: W.W. Norton, 1986.

General History

Bailyn, Bernard. *The Peopling of British North America: An Introduction.* New York: Knopf, 1986.

———. *Voyagers to the West: A Passage in the Peopling of America on the Eve of the Revolution.* New York: Knopf, 1986.

Butler, Jon. *Becoming America: The Revolution before 1776.* Cambridge, Mass.: Harvard University Press, 2000.

Deetz, James. *In Small Things Forgotten: An Archaeology of Early American Life.* 1977. Rev. ed., New York: Anchor, 1996.

Demos, John, ed. *Remarkable Providences: Readings on Early American History.* 1972. Rev. ed. Boston: Northeastern University Press, 1991.

Fischer, David Hackett. *Albion's Seed: Four British Folkways in America.* New York: Oxford University Press, 1989.

Greene, Jack P. *Pursuits of Happiness: The Social Development of Early Modern British Colonies and the Formation of American Culture.* Chapel Hill: University of North Carolina Press, 1988.

Greene, Jack P., and J. R. Pole, eds. *Colonial British America: Essays in the New History of the Early Modern Era.* Baltimore: Johns Hopkins University Press, 1984.

Gunn, Giles, ed. *Early American Writing.* New York: Penguin, 1994.

Hawke, David Freeman. *Everyday Life in Early America.* New York: Harper & Row, 1988.

Innes, Stephen, ed. *Work and Labor in Early America.* Chapel Hill: University of North Carolina Press, 1988.

Kulikoff, Allan. *From British Peasants to Colonial American Farmers.* Chapel Hill: University of North Carolina Press, 2000.

Landsmen, Ned C. *From Colonials to Provincials: American Thought and Culture, 1680–1760.* Ithaca, N.Y.: Cornell University Press, 2001.

Nash, Gary. *Red, White, and Black: The Peoples of Early America.* 4th ed. Englewood Cliffs, N.J.: Prentice Hall, 1999.

Taylor, Alan. *American Colonies.* New York: Viking, 2001.

Exploration and the First Colonies

Kupperman, Karen Ordahl. *Roanoke: The Abandoned Colony.* Totowa, N.J.: Rowman and Allanheld, 1984.

———, ed. *Captain John Smith: A Select Edition of His Writings.* Chapel Hill: University of North Carolina Press, 1988.

Quinn, David B. *North America from the Earliest Discovery to First Settlements: The Norse Voyages to 1612.* New York: Harper & Row, 1977.

Quinn, David B., and Alison M. Quinn, eds. *The First Colonists: Documents on the Planting of the First English Settlements in North America 1584–1590.* Raleigh: North Carolina Department of Cultural Resources, 1982.

Vaughan, Alden T. *American Genesis: Captain John Smith and the Founding of Virginia.* Boston: Little, Brown, 1975.

New England

Anderson, Virginia DeJohn. *New England's Generation: The Great Migration and the Formation of Society and Culture in the 17th Century.* New York: Cambridge University Press, 1991.

Demos, John. *A Little Commonwealth: Family Life in Plymouth Colony.* 2nd ed. New York: Oxford University Press, 1999.

———. *The Unredeemed Captive: A Family Story from Early America.* New York: Alfred A. Knopf, 1994.

Kamensky, Jane. *Governing the Tongue: The Politics of Speech in Early New England.* New York: Oxford University Press, 1997.

Lepore, Jill. *The Name of War: King Philip's War and the Origins of American Identity.* New York: Alfred A. Knopf, 1998.

Morgan, Edmund S. *The Puritan Dilemma: The Story of John Winthrop.* Boston: Little, Brown, 1958.

Vaughan, Alden T., ed. *The Puritan Tradition in America, 1620–1730.* 1972. Rev. ed. Hanover, N.H.: University Press of New England, 1997.

Vickers, Daniel. *Farmers and Fishermen: Two Centuries of Work in Essex County, Massachusetts, 1630–1830.* Chapel Hill: University of North Carolina Press, 1994.

The Chesapeake

Breen, T. H. *Tobacco Culture: The Mentality of the Great Tidewater Planters on the Eve of the Revolution.* Princeton, N.J.: Princeton University Press, 1982.

Breen, T. H., and Stephen Innes. *Myne Owne Ground: Race and Freedom on Virginia's Eastern Shore.* New York: Oxford University Press, 1980.

Carr, Lois Green, Russell R. Menard, and Lorena S. Walsh. *Robert Cole's World: Agriculture and Society in Early Maryland.* Chapel Hill: University of North Carolina Press, 1991.

Hume, Ivor Noël. *Martin's Hundred.* New York: Alfred A. Knopf, 1983.

Isaac, Rhys. *The Transformation of Virginia, 1740–1790.* Chapel Hill: University of North Carolina Press, 1982.

Lockridge, Kenneth A. *The Diary, and Life, of William Byrd II of Virginia, 1674–1744.* Chapel Hill: University of North Carolina Press, 1987.

Smith, Daniel Blake. *Inside the Great House: Family Life in 18th-Century Chesapeake Society.* Ithaca, N.Y.: Cornell University Press, 1980.

Native Americans

Axtell, James. *The Invasion Within: The Contest of Cultures in Colonial North America.* New York: Oxford University Press, 1985.

Calloway, Colin G., ed. *The World Turned Upside Down: Indian Voices from Early America.* Boston: Bedford, 1994.

———. *New Worlds for All: Indians, Europeans, and the Remaking of Early America.* Baltimore: Johns Hopkins University Press, 1997.

Demos, John. *The Tried and True: Native American Women Confronting Colonization.* New York: Oxford University Press, 1995.

Gray, Edward G. *New World Babel: Languages and Nations in Early America.* Princeton, N.J.: Princeton University Press, 1999.

Merrell, James H. *The Indians' New World: Catawbas and Their Neighbors from European Contact through the Era of Removal.* Chapel Hill: University of North Carolina Press, 1989.

Richter, Daniel K. *Facing East from Indian Country: A Native History of Early America.* Cambridge, Mass.: Harvard University Press, 2001.

Salisbury, Neal. *Manitou and Providence: Indians, Europeans, and the Making of New England, 1500–1643.* New York: Oxford University Press, 1982.

African Americans

Berlin, Ira. *Many Thousands Gone: The First Two Centuries of Slavery in North America.* Cambridge, Mass.: Harvard University Press, 1998.

Morgan, Edmund S. *American Slavery, American Freedom: The Ordeal of Colonial Virginia.* New York: W.W. Norton, 1975.

Morgan, Philip D. *Slave Counterpoint: Black Culture in the 18th-Century Chesapeake and Lowcountry.* Chapel Hill: University of North Carolina Press, 1998.

Palmer, Colin A. *The First Passage: Blacks in the Americas 1502–1617.* New York: Oxford University Press, 1995

Wheatley, Phillis. *Complete Writings.* Vincent Carretta, ed. New York: Penguin, 2001.

Wood, Peter. *Strange New Land: African Americans 1617–1776.* New York: Oxford University Press, 1996.

Women and Gender

Berkin, Carol. *First Generations: Women in Colonial America.* New York: Hill and Wang, 1997.

Brown, Kathleen M. *Good Wives, Nasty Wenches, and Anxious Patriarchs: Gender, Race, and Power in Colonial Virginia.* Chapel Hill: University of North Carolina Press, 1996.

Cott, Nancy F., et al, eds. *Root of Bitterness: Documents of the Social History of American Women.* 2nd ed. Boston: Northeastern University Press, 1996.

Kamensky, Jane. *The Colonial Mosaic: American Women 1600–1760.* New York: Oxford University Press, 1995.

Moynihan, Ruth Barnes, Cynthia Russett, and Laurie Crumpacker, eds. *Second to None: A Documentary History of American Women: Volume I: From the 16th Century to 1865.* Lincoln: University of Nebraska Press, 1993.

Norton, Mary Beth. *Founding Mothers and Fathers: Gendered Power and the Forming of American Society.* New York: Alfred A. Knopf, 1996.

Treckel, Paula A. *To Comfort the Heart: Women in 17th-Century America.* New York: Twayne, 1996.

Ulrich, Laurel Thatcher. *Good Wives: Image and Reality in the Lives of Women in Northern New England, 1650–1750.* New York: Alfred A. Knopf, 1982.

Religion and Belief

Bonomi, Patricia U. *Under the Cope of Heaven: Religion, Society, and Politics in Colonial America.* New York: Oxford University Press, 1986.

Butler, Jon. *Awash in a Sea of Faith: Christianizing the American People.* Cambridge, Mass.: Harvard University Press, 1990.

Butler, Jon. *Religion in Colonial America.* New York: Oxford University Press, 2000.

Hall, David D. *Worlds of Wonder, Days of Judgment: Popular Religious Belief in Early New England.* New York: Knopf, 1989.

Lambert, Frank. *Inventing the "Great Awakening."* Princeton, N.J.: Princeton University Press, 1999.

Stout, Harry S. *The Divine Dramatist: George Whitefield and the Rise of Modern Evangelicalism.* Grand Rapids, Mich.: William B. Eerdmans, 1991.

Gentility

Bushman, Richard L. *The Refinement of America: Persons, Houses, Cities.* New York: Alfred A. Knopf, 1992.

Carson, Cary, Ronald Hoffman, and Peter J. Albert, eds. *Of Consuming Interests: The Styles of Life in the 18th Century.* Charlottesville: University of Virginia Press, 1994.

Text Credits

Main Text

pp. 20–21: David B. Quinn, ed., *New American World: A Documentary History of North America to 1612* (New York: Arno Press, 1979), vol. 1, 94.

pp. 22–23: Edward Surtz, and J. H. Hexter, eds., *The Complete Works of St. Thomas More, Volume 4* (New Haven: Yale University Press, 1965), 197–99.

pp. 24–26: Bartolomé de Las Casas, *The Devastation of the Indies: A Brief Account*, Herma Briffault, trans. (Baltimore: Johns Hopkins University Press, 1992), 59–60.

pp. 27–28: Quinn, *New American World*, vol. 3, 9–10.

pp. 29–30: Quinn, *New American World*, vol. 3, 82–83.

pp. 31–33: David B. Quinn and Alison M. Quinn, *The First Colonists: Documents on the Planting of the First English Settlements in North America 1584–1590* (Raleigh: North Carolina Department of Cultural Resources, 1982), 124–26.

pp. 34–36: Giles Gunn, *Early American Writing* (New York: Penguin, 1994), 71–73.

p. 37: Colin G. Calloway, ed., *The World Turned Upside Down: Indian Voices from Early America* (Boston: Bedford, 1994), 33–34.

pp. 43–44: *The Complete Works of Captain John Smith (1580–1631) in Three Volumes*, Philip L. Barbour, ed. (Chapel Hill: University of North Carolina Press, 1986), vol. I, 205–7, 209–10.

p. 45: Alden T. Vaughan, ed., *The Puritan Tradition in America, 1620–1730*, rev. ed. (Hanover, N.H.: University Press of New England, 1997), 48–9.

pp. 46–47: William Bradford, *Of Plymouth Plantation, 1620–1647*, Samuel Eliot Morison, ed. (New York: Alfred A. Knopf, 1959), 77–78.

pp. 47–48: Vaughan, *The Puritan Tradition*, 50–51.

pp. 48–50: John C. Miller, ed., *The Colonial Image* (New York: George Braziller, 1962), 79–80.

pp. 50–51: Harrison T. Meserole, ed., *Seventeenth-Century American Poetry* (New York: W.W. Norton, 1968), 397–8.

pp. 52–54: Clayton Colman Hall, ed., *Narratives of Early Maryland, 1633–1684* (New York, Charles Scribner's Sons, 1925), 93–95.

pp. 55–57: John Demos, ed., *Remarkable Providences: Readings on Early American History* (Boston: Northeastern University Press, 1972), 73–75.

pp. 57–59: Demos, *Remarkable Providences*, 37–41.

pp. 64–66: Susan Kingsbury, ed., *Records of the Virginia Company of London* (Washington, D.C.: Government Printing Office, 1906–85), 556–59.

p. 67: Richard S. Dunn and Laetitia Yeandle, eds., *The Journal of John Winthrop, 1630–1649: Abridged Edition* (Cambridge, Mass.: Harvard University Press, 1996), 60, 63.

pp. 69–71: William Bradford, *Of Plymouth Plantation*, 294–96.

pp. 72–74: William L. Andrews, et al., eds. *Journeys in New Worlds: Early American Women's Narratives* (Madison: University of Wisconsin Press, 1990), 33–34, 36, 57–58, 61.

pp. 74–75: James Axtell, ed., *The Indian Peoples of Eastern America: A Documentary History of the Sexes* (New York: Oxford University Press, 1981), 161–62.

pp. 76–78: J. A. Leo Lemay, ed., *Benjamin Franklin: Writings* (New York: The Library of America, 1987), 1421–22.

pp. 78–79: Calloway, *The World Turned Upside Down*, 85–86.

pp. 80–81: W. Keith Kavenagh, ed., *Foundations of Colonial America: A Documentary History* (New York: Chelsea House, 1983), vol. 2, part 2, 1380–81.

pp. 87–88: Kavenagh, *Foundations of Colonial America*, vol. 3, part 1, 2071.

pp. 88–89: Ruth Barnes Moynihan, Cynthia Russett, and Laurie Crumpacker, eds., *Second to None: A Documentary History of American Women. Volume I: From the 16th Century to 1865* (Lincoln: University of Nebraska Press, 1993), 66–67.

pp. 90–92: John C. Miller, ed., *The Colonial Image: The Origins of American Culture as Revealed in the Writings of Men and Women Who Shared the Colonial Experience* (New York: George Braziller, 1962), 88–90.

pp. 93–95: Warren M. Billings, ed., *The Old Dominion in the 17th Century: A Documentary History of Virginia, 1606–1689* (Chapel Hill: University of North Carolina Press, 1975), 137–42.

pp. 96–98: Kavenagh, *Foundations of Colonial America*, vol. 3, part 1, 2076–77.

pp. 99–101: Alan Gallay, ed., *Voices of the Old South: Eyewitness Accounts, 1528–1861* (Athens: University of Georgia Press, 1994), 139–40.

pp. 101–104: Lathan A. Windley, *Runaway Slave Advertisements: A Documentary History from the 1730s to 1790, Volume 1: Virginia and North Carolina* (Westport, Conn.: Greenwood, 1983), 6–7, 9, 12; *Volume 3: South Carolina*, 9, 12–13.

pp. 105–107: Jack P. Greene, ed., *The Diary of Colonel Landon Carter of Sabine Hall, 1752–1778* (Charlottesville: The Virginia Historical Society, 1965), vol. 1, 168, 214–16, 219–20.

pp. 112–13: Robert H. Bremner, ed., *Children and Youth in America: A Documentary History. Volume I: 1600–1865* (Cambridge, Mass.: Harvard University Press, 1970), 31.

pp. 113–15: Moynihan et al, *Second to None*, 58–59.

pp. 115–16: Demos, *Remarkable Providences*, 148–49.

pp. 117–19: Moynihan et al, *Second to None*, 138–40.

pp. 120–21: John Lawson, *A New Voyage to Carolina*, Hugh Talmage Lefler, ed. (Chapel Hill: University of North Carolina Press, 1967), 90–91.

pp. 122–23: Bremner, *Children and Youth in America*, vol. 1, 35–36.

pp. 123–26: Bremner, *Children and Youth in America*, vol. 1, 46–48.

pp. 126–27: Lemay, *Benjamin Franklin: Writings*, 808–9.

pp. 132–34: Vaughan, *The Puritan Tradition*, 74–76.

pp. 135–37: Gunn, *Early American Writing*, 159–62.

pp. 137–39: Increase Mather, *An Essay for the Recording of Illustrious Providences* (1684; facsimile reprint ed., New York: Scholar's Facsimiles, 1977), 164–67.

pp. 139–41: Kavenagh, *Foundations of Colonial America*, vol. 2, 1340–41.

pp. 142–44: Calloway, *The World Turned Upside Down*, 23–25.

pp. 145–47: Olaudah Equiano, *The Interesting Narrative of the Life of Olaudah Equiano Written by Himself*, Robert J. Allison, ed. (Boston: Bedford Books, 1995), 41–43.

pp. 148–49: Richard L. Bushman, *The Great Awakening: Documents on the Revival of Religion, 1740–1745* (Chapel Hill: University of North Carolina Press, 1969), 51–52.

pp. 149–51: Nancy F. Cott et al, eds., *Root of Bitterness: Documents of the Social History of American Women*, 2nd ed. (Boston: Northeastern University Press, 1996), 51–52.

pp. 157–58: Charles Moore, ed., *George Washington's Rules of Civility and Decent Behaviour in Company and Conversation* (Boston: Houghton Mifflin, 1926), 3, 5, 9, 13, 15, 17, 19, 21.

pp. 158–60: Carl Bridenbaugh, ed., *Gentleman's Progress: The Itinerarium of Dr. Alexander Hamilton 1744* (Pittsburgh: University of Pittsburgh Press, 1948), 173–74.

p. 161: *The Papers of Benjamin Franklin*, Leonard W. Labaree, ed. (New Haven: Yale University Press, 1961), vol. 3, 317–18, 320.

pp. 162–64: Maude H. Woodfin, ed., *Another Secret Diary of William Byrd of Westover, 1739–1741, With Letters & Literary Exercises, 1696–1726* (Richmond, Va.: Dietz, 1942), 27–30.

pp. 165–66: Demos, *Remarkable Providences*, 207.

pp. 167–69: Moynihan et al., *Second to None*, 128–131.

pp. 169–71: Harriott Horry Ravenel, *Eliza Pinckney* (New York: Charles Scribner's Sons, 1896), 115–18.

Sidebars

p. 11: Abbé Raynal, *A Philosophical and Political History of the Settlements and Trade of the Europeans in the East and West Indies* (London: T. Cadell, 1777), vol. 1, 1.

p. 12: Adam Smith, *The Wealth of Nations* (Chicago: University of Chicago Press, 1976), vol. 2, 83.

p. 14: *Samuel Johnson: Political Writings*, Donald J. Greene, ed. (New Haven, Conn.: Yale University Press, 1977), 425.

p. 15: Antonello Gerbi, *The Dispute of the New World: The History of a Polemic, 1750–1900*. Jeremy Moyle, trans. (Pittsburgh: University of Pittsburgh Press, 1973), 121.

p. 18: Christy Miller, ed., *The Voyages of Captain Luke Foxe of Hull, . . .* (New York: Burt Franklin, 1966), vol. 1, 10–11.

p. 19: Gunn, *Early American Writing*, 67.

p. 31: William Shakespeare, *The Tempest*, Frank Kermode, ed. (London: Routeledge, 1990), 124.

p. 33: Hugh Talmage Lefler, ed., *A New Voyage to Carolina*, (Chapel Hill: University of North Carolina Press, 1967), 69.

p. 34: Bertrand T. Whitehead, *Brags and Boasts: Propaganda in the Year of the Armada* (Dover, N.H.: Alan Sutton, 1994), 122.

p. 40: Philip L. Barbour, ed., *The Complete Works of Captain John Smith (1580–1631) in Three Volumes* (Chapel Hill: University of North Carolina Press, 1986), vol. 2, 232.

p. 49: James Axtell, ed., *America Perceived: A View from Abroad in the 17th Century* (West Haven, Conn.: Pendulum, 1974), 20.

p. 52: William Wood, *New England's Prospect*, Alden T. Vaughan, ed. (Amherst: University of Massachusetts Press, 1977), 65–66.

p. 57: Jon Butler, *Becoming America: The Revolution before 1776* (Cambridge, Mass.: Harvard University Press, 2000), 20.

p. 63: John Locke, *Two Treatises of Government (1698)*, Peter Laslett, ed.(Cambridge, U.K.: Cambridge University Press, 1963), 313.

p. 64: Karen Ordahl Kupperman, ed., *Captain John Smith: A Select Edition of His Writings* (Chapel Hill: University of North Carolina Press, 1988), 190.

p. 65: Roy Harvey Pearce, *Savagism and Civilization: A Study of the Indian and the American Mind* (Berkeley: University of California Press, 1988), 10.

p. 69: Patrick M. Malone, *The Skulking Way of War: Technology and Tactics Among the New England Indians* (Lanham, Md.: Madison, 1991), 98.

p. 71: Demos, *Remarkable Providences*, 312.

p. 74: *The Papers of Benjamin Franklin*, Leonard W. Labaree, ed. (New Haven: Yale University Press, 1961), vol. 4, 482.

p. 78: Calloway, *The World Turned Upside Down*, 78.

p. 80: Michael G. Kammen, *People of Paradox: An Inquiry Concerning the Origins of American Civilization* (New York: Alfred A. Knopf, 1972), 153.

p. 84: Anon. *Select Tracts Relating to Colonies . . .* (London: J. Roberts, 1732), 32.

p. 85: Marion Tingling, ed., *The Correspondence of the Three William Byrds of Westover, Virginia, 1684–1776* (Charlottesville: University Press of Virginia, 1977), vol. 1, 355.

p. 88: Hall, *Narratives of Early Maryland*, 290–91.

p. 94: William Eddis, *Letters from America*, Aubrey C. Land, ed. (Cambridge, Mass.: Harvard University Press, 1969), 36–37.

p. 96: George M. Fredrickson, *White Supremacy: A Comparative Study in American and South African History* (New York: Oxford University Press, 1981), 79.

p. 105: *The Journal and Major Essays of John Woolman*, Phillips P. Moulton, ed. (New York: Oxford University Press, 1971), 65–66.

p. 110: Sir Robert Filmer, *Patriarcha and Other Writings*, Johann P. Sommerville, ed. (Cambridge, U.K.: Cambridge University Press, 1991), 12.

p. 111: Linda K. Kerber, *Women of the Republic: Intellect and Ideology in Revolutionary America* (Chapel Hill: University of North Carolina Press, 1980), 140.

p. 113: David Hackett Fischer, *Albion's Seed: Four British Folkways in America* (New York: Oxford University Press, 1989), 486.

p. 119: Axtell, *America Perceived*, 118.

p. 121: John Locke, *Some Thoughts Concerning Education*, John W. Yolton and Jean S. Yolton, eds. (Oxford: Clarendon Press, 1989), 115.

p. 124: Kevin J. Hayes, *A Colonial Woman's Bookshelf* (Knoxville, University of Tennessee Press, 1996), 91.

p. 131: Kavenagh, *Foundations of Colonial America*, vol. 2, part 2, 1340–41.

p. 137: Hall, *Narratives of Early Maryland*, 141.

p. 141: Jonathan Edwards, *The Life of David Brainerd*, Norman Pettit, ed. (New Haven, Conn.: Yale University Press, 1985), 392.

p. 142: Gunn, *Early American Writing*, 566.

p. 148: *The Lee Max Friedman Collection of American Jewish Colonial Correspondence: Letters of the Franks Family (1733–1748)*, Leo Hershkowitz and Isidore S. Meyer, eds. (Waltham, Mass.: American Jewish Historical Society, 1968), 66.

p. 149: Lemay, *Benjamin Franklin: Writings*, 1408.

p. 154: Richard L. Bushman, *The Refinement of America: Persons, Houses, Cities* (New York: Knopf, 1992), 61.

p. 155: Kenneth A. Lockridge, *Settlement and Unsettlement in Early America* (Cambridge, U.K.: Cambridge University Press, 1981), 98.

p. 156: Thomas Smith, *De Republica Anglorum* (facsimile reprint, Menston, U.K.: Scolar Press, 1970), 27.

p. 157: Anthony Ashley Cooper, Third Earl of Shaftesbury, *Characteristics of Men, Manners, Opinions, Times*, Lawrence E. Klein, ed. (Cambridge, U.K.: Cambridge University Press, 1999), 148–49.

p. 158: William Eddis, *Letters From America*, Aubrey C. Land, ed. (Cambridge, Mass.: Harvard University Press, 1969), 58.

p. 165: *Diary and Autobiography of John Adams*, L. H. Butterfield, ed. (Cambridge, Mass.: Harvard University Press, 1961), vol. 1, 294.

Picture Credits

Index

Acknowledgments

I would like to thank Carol Karlsen for the invitation to write this book and for her encouragement and advice during its evolution. At Oxford University Press, Nancy Toff and Brigit Dermott have provided expert editorial support. I am also grateful to Jon Butler for his suggestions about chapter 6 and to Matt Childs for advice on chapter 4. And, of course, thanks to Stacey.

About the Author

Edward G. Gray teaches early American history at Florida State University. He was a Mellon post-doctoral fellow at the Huntington Library from 1988 to 1989. He is the author of *New World Babel: Languages and Nations in Early America* and co-editor with Norman Fiering of *The Language Encounter in the Americas, 1492–1800*.